Routledge Revivals

Nickel

First published in 1963, *Nickel* presents a readable account of Nickel's development from early times to the present day. Weapons and implements containing a small proportion of nickel have been found on the 3500-year-old sites of Ur and Kish in Sumeria; while in 1962 the first United States manned space capsule to orbit the earth made use of nickel alloys to withstand the effects of exposure to elevated temperature, dynamic and acoustical stress, and fatigue.

Nickel was identified as an element in the 18th century and the steps leading up to this are vividly described. New information on the origin of Kupfer Nickel, regarded with such disdain by early Saxon miners, is revealed as a result of a visit made by the author to the Freiburg Bergakademie in Eastern Germany. Nickeliferous occurrences in Europe, the South Pacific and North America are described; charts and flowsheets illustrate progress in production and methods of extracting this matter from its complex compounds. There are incidental portraits of the men who built up the industry. A survey of the applications of nickel today includes references to nickel silver, electroplating, the steel field, and it's hundred and one uses in industry, architecture and the home. This account of the development of nickel, combining scientific and economic fact with the quirks of human history makes informative and imaginative reading.

Nickel
An historical review

F.B. Howard - White

First published in 1963
by Methuen and Co Ltd.

This edition first published in 2024 by Routledge
4 Park Square, Milton Park, Abingdon, Oxon, OX14 4RN

and by Routledge
605 Third Avenue, New York, NY 10017

Routledge is an imprint of the Taylor & Francis Group, an informa business

© 1963 F.B. Howard - White

All rights reserved. No part of this book may be reprinted or reproduced or utilised in any form or by any electronic, mechanical, or other means, now known or hereafter invented, including photocopying and recording, or in any information storage or retrieval system, without permission in writing from the publishers.

Publisher's Note
The publisher has gone to great lengths to ensure the quality of this reprint but points out that some imperfections in the original copies may be apparent.

Disclaimer
The publisher has made every effort to trace copyright holders and welcomes correspondence from those they have been unable to contact.

A Library of Congress record exists under LCCN:

ISBN: 978-1-032-63874-4 (hbk)
ISBN: 978-1-032-63883-6 (ebk)
ISBN: 978-1-032-63878-2 (pbk)

Book DOI 10.4324/9781032638836

Nickel

AN HISTORICAL REVIEW

Altarpiece in St. Anne's Church, Annaberg, Saxony, painted by Hans Hesse in 1521, showing mediæval mining in the Erzgebirge, where the *Kupfer Nickel* originated
(For key see Appendix V)

From an art print in the possession of Verlag der Kunst, Dresden

Nickel
AN HISTORICAL REVIEW

by F. B. Howard-White, M.C., M.A.

METHUEN & CO LTD
36 Essex Street, London, W.C.2

First published in London
by Methuen and Co Ltd 1963
Catalogue Number 2/2722/1
Copyright © 1963 F. B. Howard-White

Printed in England
by Eyre and Spottiswoode Limited
at The Thanet Press, Margate, Kent

Contents

	FOREWORD	*page* vii
	AUTHOR'S PREFACE	ix
1	In the Heart of the Earth	1
2	Civilisation Dawns	6
3	'The Thing that fell from the Sky'	15
4	'I have called it Nickel'	23
5	'On Absolutely Pure Nickel'	35
6	'It looks exactly like Silver'	42
7	'Nickel is very much sought after'	50
8	'Men not easily Baffled'	69
9	Here was a Material Second to None	91
10	Nickel Plate denotes Quality	104
11	Foundations of an Industry	121
12	An Unparalleled Demand	144
13	The Bottom falls out of the Nickel Market	157
14	The Metallurgist comes into his own	167
15	A Time for Expansion	178
16	New Growth of the Nickel Industry	186
17	Nickel in Coinage	197
18	The Continuing Search	210
19	Mach I and Beyond	230
	NOTES AND BIBLIOGRAPHY	259
	APPENDICES	
I	Periodic Table of the Elements	303
II	Physical Properties of Nickel	304
III	Published Price of Nickel from 1840 to 1961	308
IV	Some High-Temperature, High-Strength Nickel-containing Alloys for Aero Engines	310
V	Annaberg Altar Piece (Key to frontispiece)	315
	INDEX	317

Foreword

In recent years the broad development of the nickel industry has reached a point where there is need for an historical review of the metal. Frank B. Howard-White, my friend and colleague for many years, qualified both as an engineer and as a barrister, has applied that professional knowledge to the nickel industry. He has always had in addition that breadth of interest in anything having to do with nickel necessary to qualify him as a 'nickel man'. And by a 'nickel man' I mean a man who is so thoroughly immersed in the metal nickel and the nickel industry that he feels anything having to do with nickel is an integral part of his life.

In this book I was delighted to find a treasure of information concerning the industry in which Mr. Howard-White and I have spent our lives. Especially, it brings back to me the atmosphere which surrounds the life and development of a great mining industry in much the same way that the odour of a burning sulphur match brings back to any mining man the days when he worked on the converters or blast furnaces.

JOHN F. THOMPSON

Author's Preface

My gratitude is due to all my associates in the nickel industry who, so unstintingly, have given me the benefit of their specialised knowledge and experience. Space does not permit of my mentioning them by name, but this acknowledgment serves to express my warm appreciation of their courtesy and help; their names should be linked with mine in authorship.

I am also indebted to the following Learned Societies, Institutions and Libraries, for consultation and advice: the Admiralty Library; the American Institute of Aeronautics and Astronautics (Miss Elizabeth B. Brown, Historical Librarian); the American Meteorite Museum (Dr. H. H. Nininger); the American Museum–Hayden Planetarium; the American Museum of Natural History (Dr. Brian Mason, Chairman, Department of Mineralogy); the Trustees of the British Museum; the British Museum, Department of Coins and Medals (Dr. D. W. McDowell and Mr. G. K. Jenkins), and the British Museum (Natural History) Department of Mineralogy (Dr. M. H. Hey and Dr. W. Campbell Smith); Freiberg Bergakademie (Professor Dr. Ing. O. Oelsner, Professor Dr. Ing. A. Lange and Direktor Schellhas); Institut für Lagerstättenforschung und Rohstoffkunde, Berlin (Professor Dr. Ing. M. Donath); the Institute of Metals; the Iron and Steel Institute; Jernkontoret (Stockholm); Librairie Hachette; the Library of Congress (Mr. Marvin

Author's Preface

W. McFarland, Guggenheim Chair of Aeronautics); the Metropolitan Museum of Art, New York; the Mineralogical Society; the National Aeronautic Association (U.S. representative of Fédération Aéronautique Internationale (Mr. H. E. Mahlman, former Secretary, Contest Board); the National Institute of Oceanography (Dr. R. A. Cox); Overseas Geological Surveys (Dr. S. H. Shaw and Mr. T. Deans); the Royal Aeronautical Society; the Royal Canadian Geographical Society; the Royal Geographical Society (Mr. E. E. T. Day and Mr. G. S. Dugdale); the Royal Greenwich Observatory; the Royal Institution, Davy Faraday Research Laboratory (Professor R. King); the Royal Society; the Master and Fellows of Trinity College, Cambridge; the U.S. National Bureau of Standards; the University of Arizona (Dr. Carleton Moore); the University Club, New York (Mr. Mark Kiley, former Librarian); the University of Pennsylvania (Wharton School); the U.S. National Archives (Mr. Forest L. Williams); the Victoria and Albert Museum; the Worshipful Company of Goldsmiths.

Many individuals and firms too have gone out of their way to help. Among those whom I desire especially to thank are Mr. Richard Sanders Allen; Mr. R. A. Annan; Barker and Allen Ltd.; Mr. R. G. Barrett; Mr. V. R. Berris; Mrs. Brackley (daughter of the late Sir Robert Mond); British Broadcasting Corporation (Radio Times Hulton Picture Library); W. Canning & Co. Ltd.; Mr. Terence Cuneo; Curtiss-Wright Corporation; Deutsche Edelstahl Werke A.G.; Monsieur Joseph Dhavernas; Dr. F. Dixey (formerly Director of Colonial Geological Surveys); Dominion Bridge Company (Canada); Dover

Author's Preface

Publications Inc.; Fairchild Aerial Surveys (New York); Herr R. Th. Fleitmann; Mr. Walter Gardner; Mr. F. D. Garrett; Professor Gunnar Hägg (Uppsala University); the Hanna Mining Company; Professor R. S. Hutton (University of Cambridge); Iliffe Books Ltd.; Johnson, Matthey & Co. Ltd. (Mr. D. McDonald); Madame Marbeau; the late Mr. Robert Mathias and Mr. A. R. Mathias; the Rt. Hon. Lord Melchett of Landford; Mr. Edmund C. Monell; Dr. Joseph Needham (Gonville and Caius College, Cambridge); Mr. Raymond P. R. Nielson; North American Aviation (Mr. Jack Green, Space & Information Systems Division; Mr. C. W. Guy, Rocketdyne Division; Mr. W. E. VanDyke, General Offices); Mr. John H. G. Pell (New York); Civilekonom Harald Pihl and Civilingenjor Gunnar Pihl (Stockholm); Martin Secker and Warburg Ltd.; Mr. H. de S. Shortt (Curator of Salisbury, South Wilts and Blackmore Museum, Salisbury); Mrs. Robert C. Stanley and Mr. Robert C. Stanley, Jr. (New York); Sir Edmund Teale; Thiokol Chemical Corporation, Reaction Motors Division; Monsieur C. Thurneyssen (S.A. Le Nickel); Sir Charles Wiggin, Bt.; Lieut.-Col. R. A. Wiggin; Mr. A. Wiggin; Dr. Pearce Williams (Cornell University, Ithaca, N.Y.); the Western Mail, Cardiff.

Finally, I acknowledge with pleasure the care expended on the indexing by Mr. Geoffrey C. Jones, and the unfailing help and consideration accorded to me by Mr. D. J. Mothersill of Messrs. Eyre and Spottiswoode Ltd., in the various stages of production of this book.

F. B. HOWARD-WHITE

A free translation of the above is:—

"This is our dear wish for those engaged in mining and for all who hold mining in high esteem: Praise be to God and to Him our grateful thanks for his bountiful blessings. The everlasting future of all good mining we place in his tender care."

>Extract from
>BERGMANNISCHER BERICHT
>ODER BRENNENDES
>GRUBENLICHT
>('Mining Review or Lighted Pit Candle') published in Schneeberg in 1727, in which reference is made to *Kupfer Nickel*.

(1)

In the Heart of the Earth

METALS have been known and used by man since the dawn of civilisation but it was only as recently as a couple of centuries ago that nickel was recognised as a chemical element. Although never occurring in nature by itself, nickel is a separate element, as is platinum, silver, or lead.

In spite of diverse theories with regard to the formation of the earth, there is little doubt that it has a finite age and, by various methods of calculation, including those involving the radioactive life of certain elements, the upper limit is now placed roughly at 4·6 thousand million years.

It is now possible to track space probes millions of miles away, but no apparatus has been devised by which man can determine the internal structure of the earth. Nevertheless, it is now the generally accepted theory that there is a central core, about 4,300 miles in diameter. That core, part of which may be molten, is believed to be similar in composition to some iron meteorites, consisting of a nickel-iron alloy containing about $8\frac{1}{2}$% nickel. Using the British billion,[1] and multiplying the average nickel content by the estimated mass of the core, the enormous

Nickel: An Historical Review

figure of 160 million billion metric tons[1] is suggested as the probable weight of nickel in the central core of the earth. Inasmuch as no mining shaft has as yet been sunk to more than about 2 miles (11,000 ft.), nor any oil drillhole put down to a depth greater than about $4\tfrac{3}{4}$ miles (25,000 ft.), it is inconceivable that the gigantic volume of nickel in the core of the earth will ever become accessible to man.

The major portion of the earth, in the centre of which the nickel-iron core lies embedded, is about 1,800 miles thick and comprises more than two-thirds of the total mass. It is believed that this mantle contains only a small percentage of nickel, of the same order as that found in *peridotite* rocks and in the silicate phase of stony meteorites. Some authorities have suggested that the deeper parts of the mantle may also contain appreciable amounts of disseminated nickel-iron, whereas others visualise a clean separation of the silicate mantle from the metallic core.

The crust of the earth, which encases the mantle, has a mean thickness of no more than $10\tfrac{1}{2}$ miles and, by weight, is less than a half of 1% of the total mass of the earth. This crust, all-important to man, contains about 0·001% of the total nickel in the earth.[2] Only time can show to what extent the major nickel orebodies in the crust have already been located or to what extent other large deposits have so far evaded search.

Nearly seven-tenths of the surface of the earth is covered by water, and nickel is found wherever the oceans spread, although it is present in trace quantities only. In clean sea water, according to Laevastu and Thompson,[3] the concentration of dissolved nickel averages around 0·034 microgram atom per kilogram,[4] which is equivalent to two parts per thousand million by weight,

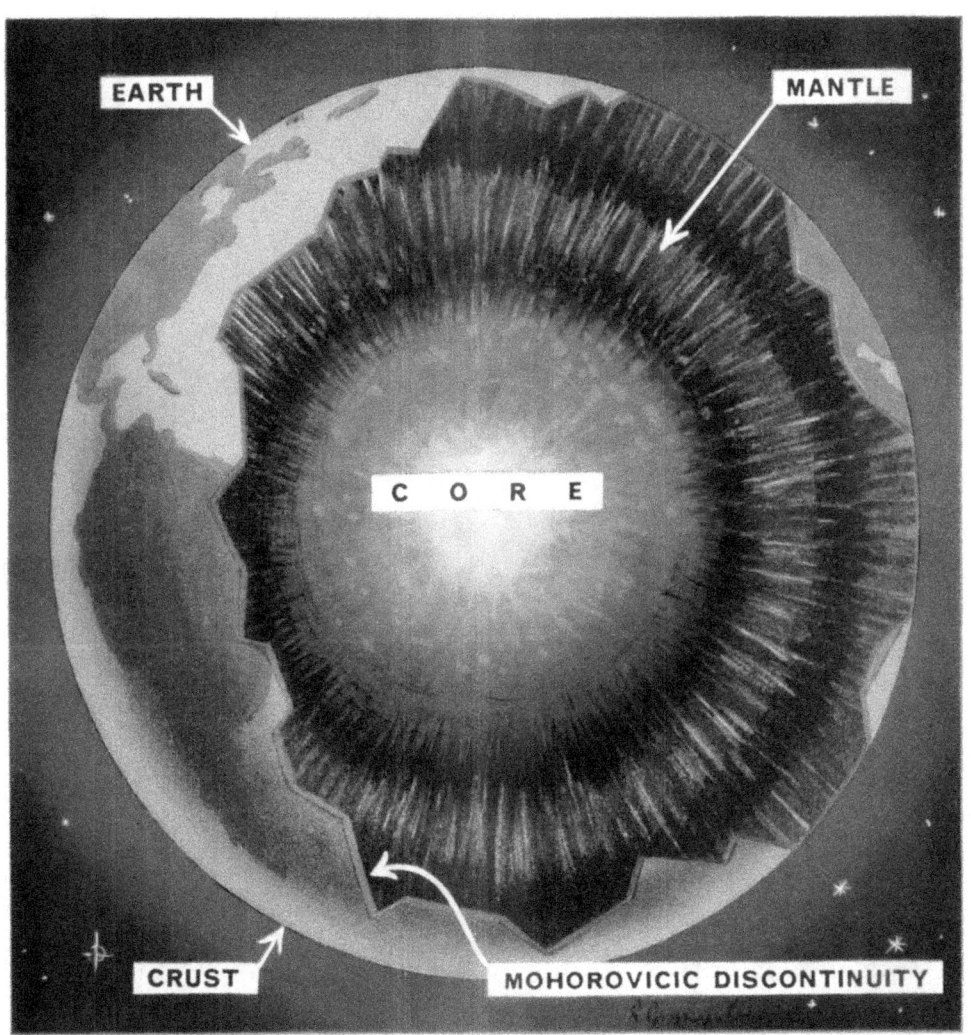

In the Heart of the Earth

or, as computed by the National Institute of Oceanography, about 8 tons per cubic mile. It has been estimated that there are some two thousand five hundred million metric tons of nickel in the oceans.[5]

Cores and dredge hauls obtained from the bottom of the Pacific and Atlantic Oceans show that unexpected quantities of nickel are also present in the materials which make up the floor of the oceanic depressions. Richest in nickel are the basic igneous rocks, the red clays and the organic sediments; less rich in nickel are the acid igneous rocks, the sedimentary rocks, the soils and the shallow-water sediments. A figure of 40 parts per million may be taken as a typical nickel concentration for sea-bed rocks, soils and sediments. Sediments collected across the Continental shelf to the deep sea show an increase in nickel content as the depth of the water and the distance from the shore increase. In the Pacific a quarter to half of the sea floor is littered with concentrations of iron and manganese, called manganese nodules.[6] These nodules were found to contain about 1% of nickel.

By means of a spectrograph[7] the presence of nickel in celestial bodies can be detected and the quantity of each particular element present can be computed. In all stars the constituent elements exist as incandescent gases and it is their light that gives rise to the characteristic lines in the respective spectra. The moon and planets are non-incandescent, and thus give no spectra. While there is as yet no scientific apparatus which can detect metals in the moon or any of the planets, there is no evidence that nickel is not there. Dust certainly exists on the lunar surface, and much has been written on the thickness of the layer and its composition, but there is general agreement that at least part of it consists of cosmic infall

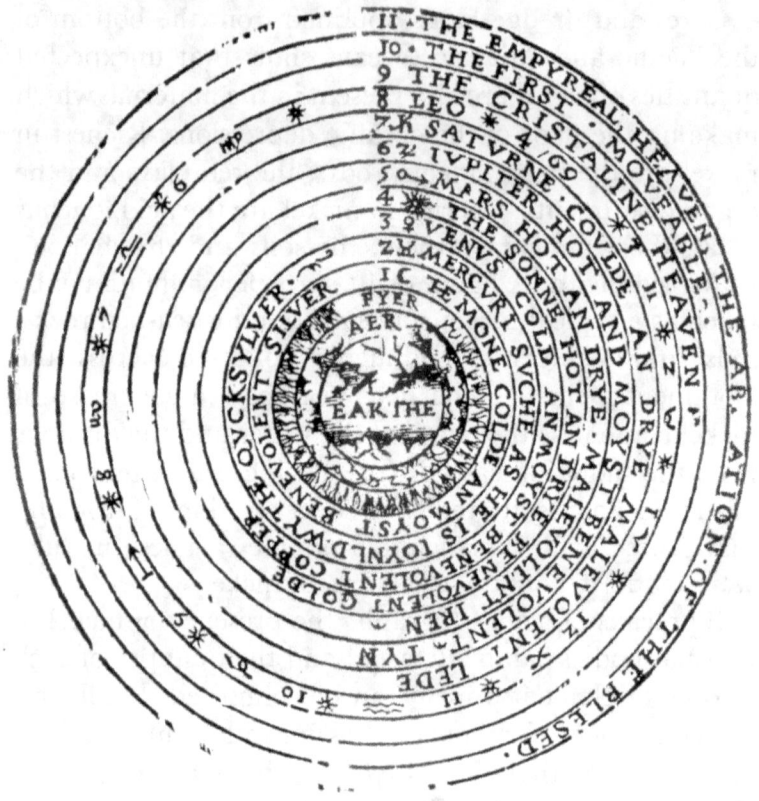

Blundevile's *Cosmographie* 1594

In centuries past the names of metals were symbolized by signs akin to those of the zodiac and linked with the solar system, particularly with the planets. Had nickel been isolated as an element in earlier days, it would probably have been associated with some planet, in the manner shown in this mediaeval drawing. Not only were the fundamental forces of fire (fyer) and air (aer) mentioned, but also each of the metals then known, namely, lead (lede), tin (tyn), iron (iren), gold (golde), copper, quicksilver (qvcksylver), and silver was linked with some specific planet

In the Heart of the Earth

material. If its composition is similar to that of the stony and metallic spherules which are found in dredge hauls in the Pacific Ocean, the lunar surface may prove to hold a substantial amount of iron-nickel.[8]

Anyone who has seen a total eclipse of the sun may recall that just when totality is about to occur there appears a pearly-white halo around the blacked-out disc. This halo is the solar *corona*, the tenuous outer atmosphere of the sun, many hundreds of thousands of miles high. In the innermost parts of the *corona*, at very high temperatures, nickel is spectrographically observed to be present.[7]

The sun is an average star and inasmuch as stellar spectra prove the presence of nickel and other elements identical with those in the sun, it may be reasonably assumed that nickel has found a niche in the no less than one thousand million billion stars estimated to exist in the universe.

(2)

Civilisation Dawns

THE discovery of metals and how to use them in tools and weapons was crucial in human development. It was on a par with the momentous realisation that man could master fire and use it as an aid to a better life and the discovery that he could plant seeds and harvest the yield for food, fodder and, eventually, for clothing.

Laboratory analyses of artefacts made in the two centuries since it first became known that nickel was a separate element have proved that this metal, unknown to mankind in early times, had been useful to him from time immemorial. Although the presence of nickel was probably fortuitous, it occurred not infrequently in early bronze and copper articles.

Among the earliest of such implements known are those found in the plain of Antioch in Syria, where a bronze reamer, believed to date back to 3500–3100 B.C., was found to contain 2·73% nickel.[1]

Other bronze articles from Ur and Kish in ancient Sumer, and from Mohenjo-Daro in the valley of the Indus River, were analysed by the eminent British metallurgist C. H. Desch,[2] for the Sumerian Copper Committee of the British Association, as follows:

Civilisation Dawns

Location	Nickel %
Mohenjo-Daro	9·38
Mohenjo-Daro	3·34
Ur	2·20
Kish	3·34

In all these localities a good number of other bronze objects containing nickel were found, but in each case the amount present was less than 2%. The puzzle of where the metal for these nickel-containing objects came from still awaits solution: nickeliferous ores are known to exist in the territory of Oman, but no proof exists that that area was the source of supply.

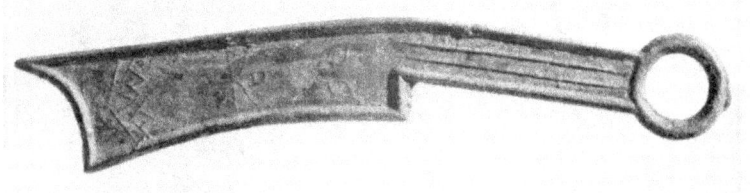

Chinese knife coin used as currency in the late Chou dynasty
(Approximately one-half actual size)

Early bronze objects emanating from China, varying in age from 770 B.C. to A.D. 220, were analysed by Chikashige.[3] Included among them were knife coins, swords and arrow-heads. The first-named objects, unfamiliar to the Western World, were in general use as currency in China, the purpose of the aperture in the handle being to enable a number of them to be strung together. The nickel contents of the various Chinese bronze specimens were as follows:

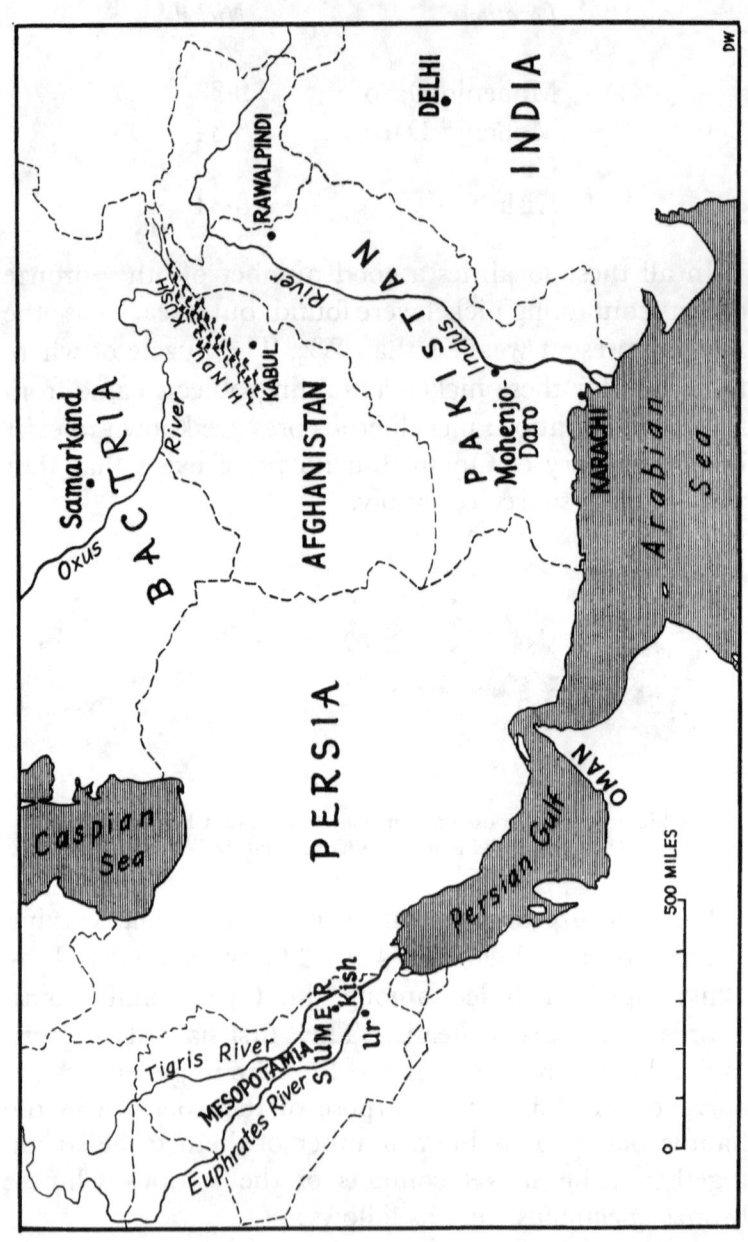

Civilisation Dawns

Objects	Nickel %
Knife coins	5·08, 3·04
Swords	3·52, 2·93, 2·47
Arrow-heads	3·68, 2·04

Ancient bronzes found in the Transvaal of South Africa, have, according to Desch, proved to contain as much as 3% nickel.

The earliest copper-nickel alloy objects which are known to have survived to the present day are coins minted in Bactria, an ancient kingdom situated north of present-day Afghanistan, which may have extended also into what is now Iran. In 327 B.C. the Greeks, under Alexander the Great, superimposed their civilisation upon it, and copper-nickel coins were issued during the reign of sub-kings Euthydemus II, Agathocles and Pantaleon.[4]

The first to discover that there was nickel present in those coins was W. Flight,[4] a mineralogist of the British Museum, who, assaying a coin of Euthydemus II, had found it to contain:

Ni %	Cu %	Fe %	Co %	Sn %	S %	Ag %	Total %
20·038	77·585	1·048	0·544	0·038	0·090	tr.	99·343

Flight stated that he had also found a considerable amount of nickel in a second coin of Euthydemus II, as well as in one of Agathocles, but for these latter coins he gave only a qualitative analysis.

Nearly a hundred years have gone by since Flight made his interesting discovery, and the main constituents of these early Bactrian coins have been confirmed by certain assays carried out recently by the British Museum, details of which are shown on page 10. The standard wet method of analysis was employed.

Ni	Cu	Fe	Foreign matter	Total
Euthydemus II				
18·5	76·7	1·6	3·2	100·0%
Pantaleon				
18·6	77·9	1·7	1·8	100·0%
Agathocles				
20·9	75·5	1·7	1·9	100·0%

Bactrian Coins
(British Museum)

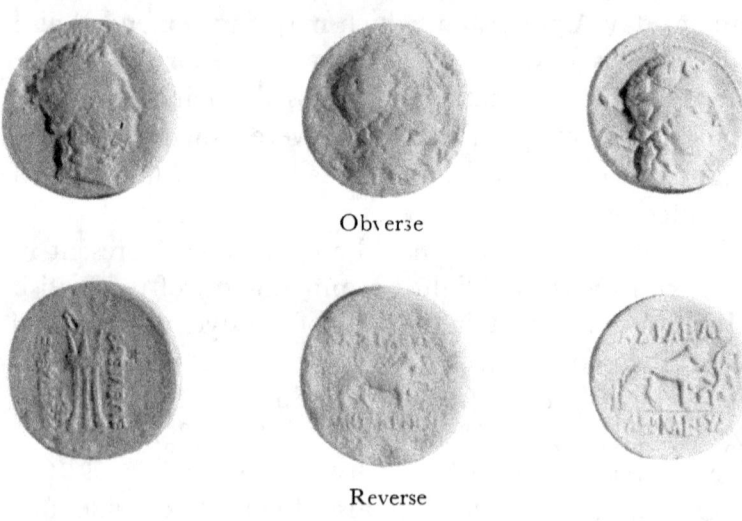

Obverse

Reverse

Euthydemus II	Pantaleon	Agathocles
c. 200–190 B.C.	c. 185–175 B.C.	c. 180–165 B.C.

There are many surmises but there is no sure answer to the question why divinities were displayed on these coins. One suggestion is that they indicate the tutelary deities of the states in which the coins were struck, but what seems more likely is that they were used as family symbols representing the chosen protecting deities of the ruling houses. The symbols are monograms made of Greek letters. They may denote mint towns, but are more probably a form of abbreviation for the names of magistrates or officials responsible for the respective issues

Civilisation Dawns

Numismatists and metallurgists especially will be interested to know that the British Museum say that the coin of Euthydemus II analysed by them cannot be the same as that analysed by Flight in 1868, because the method of analysis used in his day undoubtedly necessitated the complete destruction of the coin.

Confirmation of the composition of ancient coins has been provided by analysis, by the X-ray fluorescence technique,[5] of specimens from a collection belonging to H. de S. Shortt. The results are given below.

	Ni %	Cu %	Fe %	Co %	Cr %	As %
Euthydemus II						
Obverse	12-14	83-87	0·5	0·5	0·1	0·5
Reverse	16-18	78-82	1·0	1·0	0·1	0·5
Pantaleon						
Obverse Reverse	19-21	75-80	1·5	1·0	0·1	0·5
Agathocles						
Obverse Reverse	19-21	75-80	1·5	1·0	0·1	0·2

A number of coins from the American Numismatic Society and the American Museum of Natural History in New York City, as well as one from another collection, were also examined by X-ray fluorescence, with the results shown on page 12.

These analyses, reported for coins of the same era and from the same locality, give interesting confirmation of the relative similarity of the types of alloy then used for coinage. Experts have tried, too, to relate the presence of

Ni %	Cu %	Fe %	Co %	Zn %
Euthydemus II				
8·6	72·5	1·1	0·4	0·3
9·5	79·3	1·6	0·6	0·1
Pantaleon				
10·5	72·0	1·3	0·6	0·3
Agathocles				
13·8	66·2	1·1	0·7	0·3
13·5	62·5	1·8	0·8	0·3

Note: All these coins contained also 0·2–0·5% of arsenic.

nickel in Bactrian coins to the whereabouts of nickel-ore occurrences in China, India and the Middle East.[6] They have gone so far as to suggest that the ores used came from the same source as the nickel-containing 'white copper' of China. Although this interesting possibility is still within the area of controversy,[7] records of the Han dynasty have recently been quoted to show that finished articles of square bamboo peculiar to the same general region in China were also observed in Bactria (Ta-hsia) in about 140 B.C.[8] The almost simultaneous presence of these two distinctive items of commerce in Bactria suggests the existence of some kind of sporadic trade by way of a southern route between China and India, offering additional confirmation of the probable Chinese origin of the ore.

Nearly two thousand years were to go by after the collapse of the early Bactrian kingdom before nickel in coinage appeared once more but, by the long arm of coincidence, the alloy containing approximately 20% nickel and 80% copper, which had been fortuitously hit

Civilisation Dawns

upon in that remote part of Asia, was to prove, centuries later, a material of considerable industrial and strategic importance.

Yet another material in which, for centuries, in the Far East, nickel had unknowingly been used, was 'white copper'.

How long ago the Chinese term *pai-thung* (pronounced phonetically 'buy toong'),[9] or 'white copper', was used for this nickel-containing alloy is left to the experts to settle, but there is abundant evidence that it has been employed by artisans in East Asia for centuries past.[10] There is some reason to think that it may date back as early as the third century after Christ, because the *Kuang Ya* dictionary gives a more ancient word *wu* in a sense which might mean *pai-thung*, but this may have referred only to a high-tin bronze or to speculum metal (Cu 65-70%; Sn 35-30%), which takes so high a polish that from the earliest times women have used it for looking glasses (*Exodus* xxxviii, 8). Other possibilities are that *wu* may have meant tinned bronze or silver-inlaid bronze. J. Needham considers, however, that it is quite safe to say that the Chinese word *pai-thung* mentioned in the *Chiu Thang Shu* (*Old History of the Thang Dynasty*), which Liu Hsü wrote in A.D. 945, refers specifically to the copper-nickel-zinc alloy sent out of China into Europe from the sixteenth century onwards. Since the Thang period centred on the eighth century A.D., it can be said with fair certainty that the metal described as *pai-thung* was being wrought by Chinese craftsmen into objects of art and utility as far back in history as the time when Alfred the Great (A.D. 849–899) was burning his cakes in Britain.

Nickel: An Historical Review

Both the *Pên Tshao Kang Mu* (*Great Pharmacopoeia*) of Li Shih-Chen in A.D. 1596 and the *Thien Kung Khai Wu* (*Exploitation of the Works of Nature*) of Sung Ying-Hsing in A.D. 1637 say that certain 'minerals' were added to the copper. Though *phi-shih*, the word which appears in both these books, normally means arsenious acid, it may here be interpreted, according to Needham, as *niccolite*, the arsenide of nickel (NiAs), because no Chinese word for that mineral exists. The other mineral mentioned in those two references was calamine, or zinc oxide, which is well distinguished in mediaeval Chinese as *lu kan shih*.

Whatever may have been the genesis of the ores from which *pai-thung* was made in the early days, it is beyond all doubt that in comparatively recent times it came from the Province of Yunnan, in China, and that when news of this silvery-looking metal, which was inexpensive and did not tarnish, reached Europe, a great desire was stimulated in the minds of many men to make such a material synthetically. When this material was imitated in Europe, it came to be known as German silver and later as nickel silver. At that time supplies of copper and zinc could be obtained with reasonable ease, but no regular and reliable source of nickel existed, and it was the absence of a suitable source of primary nickel that, in due course, was to encourage enterprising men to set about refining this metal in Europe on a commercial basis.

(3)

'The Thing that fell from the Sky'

THOUSANDS of years before nickel was recognised as an element our ancestors realised that meteoritic iron possessed rare, if not magic, properties. In all probability this 'heaven-sent' metal was the first source of iron used by the human race, although its significance was not appreciated.

Historical research[1] has revealed the interesting fact that in the respective languages the word used for iron by the ancient Sumerians, the Egyptians, the Babylonians, the Chaldees, the Hittites and the Assyrians clearly signifies that it was 'heaven-sent' metal, coming from 'unknown regions of space'. As far as is known, the earliest artefact of meteoritic origin that has survived to the present time is what is believed to be a portion of a dagger found at Ur of the Chaldees (c. 3100 B.C.) which modern analysis has shown to contain 10.9% Ni.[2] Again, iron beads discovered at Gerzah in Egypt, which are of pre-dynastic date, have been found to assay $7\frac{1}{2}\%$ Ni.

Livy (59 B.C.–A.D. 17) reported a shower of stones descending from the sky on Mount Alban, just outside Rome. Then there is the authority of Pliny (A.D. 23–79) who describes the falling of 'stony showers' in various localities, including Mount Ida in Crete, where the local inhabitants were called 'Sons of Vulcan'. Paneth[3] considers that 'the thing that fell from the sky', which was an object of worship by the Ephesians (*Acts* xix, 35), was in all probability a meteorite.

Authorities also attribute to meteoritic origin a holy stone at Delphi, the 'iron shield' of Numa Pompilius, and the 'black stone' of the Kaaba, the holiest of holies of the Mohammedans, at Mecca. The oldest recorded fall of which the actual meteorite has been preserved is believed to be a specimen weighing 235 lbs., which fell near Elbogen, in Czechoslovakia, about A.D. 1400, and was popularly known as 'the bewitched Burgrave'.[4] It is still in a good state of preservation, in the Vienna Museum. Nearly a century later another fall, accompanied by a noise as of a violent explosion, occurred at Ensisheim in Alsace. The Emperor Maximilian I (1459–1519) of the Holy Roman Empire had a portion of the meteorite suspended by a chain in the local church and regarded its advent as a favourable portent for attacking the Turks.[5]

Deliberate use was made of meteoritic iron for the fifteenth-century Malay *krisses*. These fine old blades were made by sandwiching together three layers of iron, or soft steel, separated by thinner ones of meteoritic iron called *pamir*. By reason of the presence of nickel, the meteoritic iron remained bright when the blade was etched, whereas the ordinary steel was blackened by the etching solution.[6]

It is stated that in the reign of King Jahangir sword blades were made from a meteorite which fell at Jalandhar in the Punjab in 1621[7] and there are tales of many other legendary magic blades from Damascus,

'The Thing that fell from the Sky'

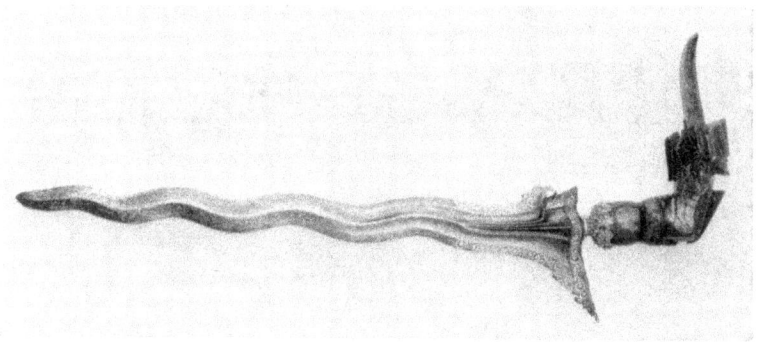

Malay *kris* with welded layers of meteoritic iron in the blade
(The Metropolitan Museum of Art, New York)

Khorassan and Arabia, which were believed to make their owners 'invincible or irresistible'.[1,8]

It is believed that in North America, before the first exploration by Europeans, implements were made from meteoritic iron containing nickel. Similarly, according to Amerigo Vespucci, in South America the natives at the mouth of the La Plata had arrow-heads of that material. When the Spaniards invaded Mexico they were astonished to find that the Aztecs had highly-prized weapons, such as knives and daggers, which, they indicated by pointing upwards, had come from the sky.[1]

Sir John Ross, when exploring Baffin Bay in Greenland in 1818, found out that for ages the Eskimos in the neighbourhood of Cape York had been using knives with handles made of bone but with a blade consisting of flakes of iron, and he realised that these were probably meteoritic iron.

During his expedition in 1892–1895, Robert E. Peary obtained confirmation of the discovery of Ross and, with the aid of the Eskimos, traced four separate masses of

Nickel: An Historical Review

Bone *krisses* with meteoritic iron cutting edges used by Eskimos near Cape York and obtained by Sir John Ross in 1818
Now in the British Museum (Natural History)

meteoritic iron in the neighbourhood of Cape York. Three of these enormous meteorites were transported to the United States and were placed in the American Museum of Natural History.[9] The fourth went to Copenhagen.

Meteorites[10] have been classified into three main divisions, as follows:

I. Meteoritic irons or *siderites*, consisting mainly of nickeliferous iron.[11,12]

According to the percentage of nickel and to the structure shown on etching the meteoritic irons, Division I has been subdivided as follows:
  a. *Nickel-poor Ataxites*, with nickel from $4\frac{1}{2}$ to 7%.
  b. *Hexahedrites*, in which nickel is about $5\frac{1}{2}$–6%.
  c. *Octahedrites* which, according to the width of the *kamacite*[11] bands, and generally to increasing percentages of nickel (from about 7 to 14%) are divided into coarsest, coarse, medium, fine and finest *octahedrites*.

'The Thing that fell from the Sky'

Ahnighito, Cape York Meteorite
Courtesy: American Museum—Hayden Planetarium

    d. Ataxites, with medium percentages of nickel (about (7–11%), probably mostly altered *octahedrites* (*metabolites*).

    e. Nickel-rich Ataxites, with nickel generally greater than 11%.

II. Meteoritic stony irons or *siderolites*, in which iron and stony matter are both present in about equal amounts.

III. Meteoritic stones or *aerolites*. These consist mainly of stony matter and, when present, nickeliferous iron and *troilite* (iron sulphide) are scattered about as small, mostly irregular, grains.

The highest known nickel content of a meteorite is 62·01%; one which fell in Mississippi (Oktibbeha County) and was found in 1854. A meteorite found in

Nickel: An Historical Review

Brazil (Santa Catharina) in 1875 contained 33·97% nickel. It may have weighed originally as much as 25 tons before portions of it were sent to England to be smelted for nickel. A nickel-rich *ataxite*, some 10 in. long by 5 or 6 in. across, was found in 1834 in Lime Creek, Alabama. Its nickel content was 29·99%. Another, with 17·49% nickel, lies where it fell at Hoba in South-West Africa; it is the largest intact meteorite known and its weight was estimated by L. J. Spencer as 60 metric tons.

These examples of nickel-rich *ataxites* emphasise the wide variation of nickel content in that group. In the medium *octahedrites*, in which group the nickel content is lower, the range is narrower.

The arrival of many of these meteorites has indeed been spectacular. Not a few have been described as fireballs, while others are reported as being of great brilliance, often leaving behind a luminous cloud which may persist for some time.

Early in the present century a great meteor was observed in Siberia and its passage was accompanied by earth tremors recorded all round the world. Twenty years later a scientific expedition located the place where the meteorite fell, near the stony Tunguska River. Trees were felled for a distance of 20–30 miles around, but, because of the marshy nature of the terrain, no trace of a meteorite was ever found. It is estimated that it could have been 600 ft. in diameter and its weight must have been immense.

Certain craters in the surface of the earth are believed to have been caused by meteorites. Best known of all is the great Barringer crater in Arizona, originally identified as Canyon Diablo. Located about 75 miles east of Flagstaff, Arizona, the crater is about 4,150 ft. in

'The Thing that fell from the Sky'

Barringer meteor crater in Arizona
Courtesy: Fairchild Aerial Surveys

diameter and 570 ft. deep. Others, discovered in recent years, are in Arabia, Australia, Canada, Estonia, Texas and the Western Sahara.

The velocities at which meteorites encounter the atmosphere (7–50 miles per second) occasion such a high degree of friction that almost immediately the surface begins to melt, or perhaps even to vaporise. The air resistance instantly sweeps away this melted surface, so that the size of the meteorite is rapidly reduced: every day millions of meteorites of relatively small size are in this way reduced to dust and completely destroyed in the atmosphere.

A sufficiently massive meteorite slows down less rapidly. It continues its burning flight into the heavier, lower, regions of the atmosphere before its speed is reduced sufficiently to allow frictional ablation to cease. At that point it usually disintegrates into dust and fragments, or, if it is one of the more resistant metallic types, it may continue on its way intact. In either case, the portion which remains after ablation ceases (usually at heights of 10–15 miles) will continue on its course to the ground, but at a much lower velocity, approximately that of a spent bullet. Small fragments come to rest on the surface of the ground; larger ones penetrate a few inches or a few feet.

As larger and larger meteorites are considered a point is reached at which the mass is so great in proportion to the surface that air resistance effects very little deceleration, and the meteorite continues in its burning flight right down to the earth, striking the ground at velocities measured in miles per second. At the moment of impact resistance is suddenly increased by many thousands per cent; the resulting transformation of energy constitutes an explosion. This explosion causes formation of the crater, and the meteorite disintegrates in the process, scattering fragments and producing a huge cloud of gases and dust. So intense is the heat that in some instances a collar of fused rock has been found at the edge of the crater.

(4)

'I have called it Nickel'

EGYPTIANS, Assyrians, Babylonians, Romans and Chinese, each in the course of time, had utilised cobaltiferous minerals (long before the element cobalt was discovered) for imparting a blue or lapis lazuli colour to pottery. As early as the fifteenth century mining of these ores for silver had taken place around Schneeberg, as well as at Annaberg in the Erzgebirge.

A good idea of how mining was carried on in that vicinity in mediaeval times can be gathered from an oil painting by Hans Hesse, completed in 1521 as the altar-piece of St. Anne's Church in Annaberg, a coloured reproduction of which forms the frontispiece to this book. It is from that town that the mineral *annabergite* ($Ni_3As_2O_8.8H_2O$) took its name. It contains 29·5% nickel, and is also known as 'nickel bloom' or 'nickel ochre'.

Agricola (1490–1555), who lived and worked in the Schneeberg area, warned workmen to wear 'boots of rawhide', to put on gloves 'long enough to reach to the elbow', and to don 'loose veils over their faces', because 'a certain kind of *cadmia*' (of which Latin word the German translation was *Kobelt*) 'eats away the feet of the

Nickel: An Historical Review

GEORG AGRICOLA

workmen' and 'injures their lungs and eyes'.[1] Arsenic was, of course, really the menace.

Now in treating the silver ores from which the *smalt* used by the local potters was made, the Erzgebirge miners had come across a red-coloured ore (later identified as *niccolite*, NiAs), which they had mistakenly thought was copper (*Kupfer*) ore. No copper was forthcoming from it, and as this fume-emitting, reddish ore seemed to have a deleterious effect on the *smalt*, not to mention harmful effects on the health of the miners, they naturally thought that evil spirits or '*Old Nick*'[2] himself had been at work. The foreman miner was even enjoined to eat butter as a precaution.

The archives of the Mines Office of the Electoral Duchy of Schneeberg (Schneeberg Bergamt) for the years 1471–1661, are preserved, in mint condition, in the Freiberg Bergakademie, near Dresden.[3] Phrases in the vernacular originate in phonetic form and, as the following extracts for the year 1654 show, the first opprobrious epithet applied to the ore thought to be copper (*Kupfer*) by these Saxon miners was *Kupper Nicell*.[4] Spelling was far from

'I have called it Nickel'

An illustration from Agricola's *De Re Metallica*, which appeared with the following legend:
'A–Furnace, B–Sticks of wood, C–Litharge, D–Plate, E–The foreman when hungry eats butter, that the poison which the crucible exhales may not harm him, for this is a special remedy against that poison'

standardised and it is not surprising that the second entry, in the year 1660 took the somewhat different form of *Kupfer-Nicklichten* (i.e. *Kupfer Nickel*-bearing). Thereafter the spelling *Kupfer Nickel* came into use.

Facsimiles from the ancient archives of the Schneeberg Bergamt, in the original German handwriting, appear on page 27. Free translations of typical entries are given below but, by reason of the difficulty in interpreting

Nickel: An Historical Review

the archaic German, as well as changes in the significance of individual words in the course of the intervening centuries, only the broad sense of the entries can be given.

From the Schneeberg Mine Office Records, folio 159 ff.

Wednesday, 29th September, 1654, Lucia No. 9.
'... He assisted in working the seam and, in his opinion, not more than 5 or 6 cwt. of *Kobold*, including *Kupper Nicell*, were contained therein ...'

Quartal Reminiscere, 1660.
'... Adam Heber's mine and works are operated by one foreman, one under-foreman, ten miners and four navvies. The high-grade ore is worked night and day, and the main shaft is being driven. It is hoped that the *Kupfer-Nicklichten* (i.e. *Kupfer Nickel*-bearing) *Kobolt* will thin out ...'

Quartal Trinitatis, 1660.
'... In the main shafts a considerable amount of *Kupfernickel* is mined with the *Kobolt*. If only God would turn it into firm red-gold ore ...'

Quartal Crucis, 1660.
'*Kupper Nickel* is still found daily in the *Kobolt* deposits ... The ore contains some *Kobolt*, but is *sehr Kupper Nicklicht* (i.e. of high *Kupfer Nickel* content) ...'

Quartal Lucia, 1660.
'... The two other miners work the *Kupfer Nicklichten* deposits ...'

'I have called it Nickel'

Quartal Reminiscere, 1661.
'. . . Ore of *Kuppernicklichte* type, which interferes with the sample, is found daily . . .'

Wednesday, 29th September, 1654

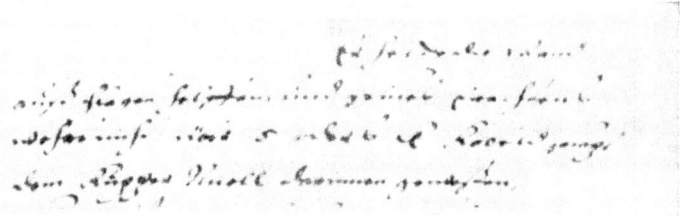

Quartal Trinitatis, 1660

Quartal Crucis, 1660

Nickel: An Historical Review

Forty years went by before the word *Kupfernickel* appeared for the first time in print, in a treatise by the Swedish mineralogist Urban Hjärne.[5]

The frontispiece reads as follows:

> A SHORT GUIDE
> to
> The investigation on ores, rocks, minerals, plants and soils of various sorts, and on a number of singular things
> by
> His Majesty's Most Gracious Pleasure
> addressed to
> All in the kingdom who desire that whatsoever is found in any place shall be brought into the light of day.
>
> ———
>
> Stockholm: Anno 1694.

The paragraph relating to *Kupfernickel* appears below.

A translation is as follows:

'16. A large number of other rocks are omitted, since space does not permit of their enumeration here; such as blendes of all kinds, Wolfram, *Kupfernickel*, Wackensteen, etc. Consequently, will anyone who finds rocks of singular shape, colour or smell, or that melt on heating, etc., kindly describe and report these.'

'*I have called it Nickel*'

Enlightenment as to the adjectival way in which the word *nikkel* or *nickel* had soon become bonded on to the German word *Kupfer* (copper) can be gleaned from the Swedish work of Joh. Gottschalk Wallerius,[6] published in 1750. The statement in that book relating to the mineral species described as *Kupfernikkel* reads:

'*Kupfernikkel*   Species 229
Arsenicum sulphure et cupro mineralisatum, minera difformi, aeris modo rubente. Minera arsenici rubra. Cuprum Nicolai Woodw.

Has a grey, fairly reddish colour, almost similar to copper; contains an appreciable amount of arsenic, but little sulphur and less copper.

Note: Due to ignorance, *kupfernikkel* has been *Cuprum Nicolai* in Latin; perhaps it was thought that the word *nikkel* was equivalent here to Nicolaus, but here it only means spurious, false, etc. *Kupfernikkel* is therefore the equivalent of a spurious grade of copper, *minera cupri spuria*. *Kupfernikkel* often also contains some cobalt, and it is therefore considered by some to come under cobalt ores, but it is also found without cobalt. *Kupfernikkel* gives a dark blue glass.'

Although in the eighteenth century much of the fundamental research upon which modern metallurgy is based had not yet been carried out, there were, in various countries, some brilliant scientists interested in metals. One such was Axel Frederik Cronstedt, born in Sweden in 1722. Nurtured in an atmosphere which gave him a liking for natural science, especially mineralogy, Cronstedt entered the ancient University of Uppsala, but funds ran short and he had perforce to take a salaried post in

Nickel: An Historical Review

Axel Frederik Cronstedt, 1722–1765

the Swedish Department of Mines. Among his colleagues there was a mine-master, G. Brandt, who had reached the conclusion that 'there can be no reason for denying the cobalt a place among the semi-metals', and thus it was described in 1735 by Brandt.[7] While engaged upon a study of the ores of silver, Cronstedt had been investigating some ore from the Los cobalt mines in the parish of Färila, situated in the Province of Hälsingland, Sweden.

Though conceivably Cronstedt's day-to-day research observations may have been jotted down in some journal or laboratory notebook, no such records have survived; it was through a paper published in 1751[8] that the public first became aware of the riddle he had then been attempting to unravel.

Cronstedt first described the appearance of the Los ore (now known as *gersdorffite*, NiAsS) when freshly

'I have called it *Nickel*'

fractured, and then noted that as soon as it became tarnished it had a slightly reddish-yellow colour, almost like that of *Kupfer Nickel*. After giving in considerable detail the various treatments to which he had subjected the ore, he concluded his treatise with these words:

'That, since none of the known metals or semi-metals, pure and unalloyed, has properties similar to those stated, especially in respect of the green colour of the vitriol solution of its *colcothar*,[9] of the calx and of the solution, as well as with regard to its increase in bulk when heated more strongly, and since moreover no metallic mixture possessing such properties is known, *consequently the regulus which remains* when the iron and cobalt are removed, and which gives rise to the phenomena enumerated, *is to be regarded as a new semi-metal*, until some investigator is able to devise a method by which a similar composition can be obtained from the twelve known metals and semi-metals.'

Three years went by before Cronstedt chose a name[10] for the 'semi-metal'; it was not until 1754, when he published *Continuation of Results and Experiments on the Los Cobalt Ore*, that the name *Nickel* actually occurred. He reported his decision in two simple sentences, translated below from the Swedish text.

'*Kupfernickel* is the ore which contains the largest amount of the semi-metal previously described, and of which an account has been published. For this reason, I have given its regulus the same name or, for the sake of convenience, I have called it *Nickel*, until it can be proved to be only a composition of metals or semi-metals previously known.'

Nickel: An Historical Review

The original Swedish texts from which these translations have been made appear below.

> Slutfats:
>
> At fom ingen af de bekante hvarken hela eller halfva metaller rena och oblandade, vifa, et förhållande likt med det anförda, i fynnerhet med den gröna färgen i vitriolens lut (2.), i defs colcothar (3), i kalben (6, 9), och i folution (4, 11) famt med upväxandet i ftarkare hetta (6, 9, 16). Icke eller någon metallifk blanning af fådana egenfkaper är kunnig; altfå lärer den regulus, fom blifver öfrig, när jernet och kobolten är frånfkild (9), af hvilken ock de upräknade phenomena härröra, komma at anfes för en ny half-metall, til defs någon upgifver fätret, at af de kände tolf hel- och half-metaller göra en dylik compofition.
>
> d- 25. Octob.

1751

> Kupfer-Nickel är den malm, fom har ftörfta halten af den förr befkrefne och utgifne half-metallen, hvaraf jag tagit mig anledning, at behålla famma namn för des regulus, eller för mera vighets fkul, kalla honom *Nickel*, til defs bevifas kan, at det icke annat är, än en compofition af förr bekanta Hela eller Halfva Metaller.

1754

Cronstedt added that in his later experiments he had used *Kupfernickel* from the Kuhschacht mine (original Swedish Kuhskaktet) in Freiberg in Saxony.

'*I have called it Nickel*'

Although, in relation to nickel, Cronstedt's publications of 1751 and 1754 were of paramount significance to the world, to him the discovery was no more than incidental. His main ambition in life was to present to the world a systematised classification of minerals. He had collected more than 5,000 specimens and his classification of them, on the basis of chemical composition, was published in Sweden in 1758. Surprisingly, Cronstedt, then only in his early thirties, chose that publication should be anonymous, but the anonymity could not long be preserved and in 1760 his treatise was translated into German and published under his own name. Not long afterwards an English version of the work was prepared by the distinguished Swedish chemist Gustav von Engeström.[11] From that classification the following principal statements on nickel have been taken:

1. Nickel is of a white colour, inclining somewhat to red; it has a solid texture but is shiny upon fracture.

2. Its specific gravity to water is as 8,500 to 1,000, i.e. it is 8·5.

3. It calcines to a green calyx, which is not very fusible.

4. It dissolves in *aqua ortis, aqua fregia* and the spirit of sea salt. It dissolves with greater difficulty in vitriolic acid.

5. It has a great affinity to sulphur.

6. It unites with all metals other than quicksilver and silver.

7. This semi-metal retains its *phlogiston* (i.e. resists oxidation) a long time in the fire.

Though its melting point was not determined, Cronstedt remarked that the new semi-metal nickel melts 'a little sooner or almost as soon as copper or gold' and thus 'sooner than iron'.

Nickel: An Historical Review

In commenting on Cronstedt's comprehensive classification, von Engeström observes that people 'choose rather to retain that definition of the *Kupfernickel* which has received its sanction from the earliest authors than to admit the conclusion to which Mr. Cronstedt's experiments seem to lead'. Von Engeström concludes his remarks by saying that he is tired of the common epithets attributed to unknown bodies, such as 'wild, refractory, rapacious, arsenical, irreducible, metallic-earth, etc., which regard the effect alone and not its cause'. From these remarks it is clear that, despite Cronstedt's conclusions, the consensus of opinion in scientific circles was that he had yet to prove that nickel was a pure metal. Nickel remained in that doubtful category for more than twenty years.

When 35 years of age, Cronstedt turned his talents elsewhere, and, writing to a friend, said:

'I seek my quiet here in the country, in the vegetable kingdom, after the mineral kingdom has deprived me of both courage and money.

'This inclination is increased by the fact that I have found the mineral kingdom unbending and ungrateful since I finished its line-up, which has been the only miner's occupation I have had this spring.'

Cronstedt died in 1765, at the age of 42. The metal which he isolated and named was destined to achieve world-wide importance.

(5)

'On Absolutely Pure Nickel'

MOMENTOUS things had happened during the hundred years between the first separation of nickel by Cronstedt in 1751 and that historic occasion when Her Majesty Queen Victoria, accompanied by His Royal Highness the Prince Consort, and surrounded by a sartorially elegant assembly of colourful crinolines and tall 'stove-pipe' hats, opened in London the Great Exhibition of 1851.

Watt, the pioneer of the steam engine, had put to practical use the earlier idea of 'driving up water by fire'. George Stephenson's railroad 'Rocket' engine had exceeded 15 miles an hour. Early in the nineteenth century Volta (1745–1827), Ampere (1775–1836), Ohm (1787–1854) and Faraday (1791–1867) were exploring galvanic forces and harnessing the electric current. A telegraph line had been established between Baltimore and Washington, and by 1851 the opening and closing prices of stocks were known simultaneously on the Paris Bourse and the London Stock Exchange, through the medium of a submarine cable.

During the hundred years following 1751, however, no worthwhile nickel-ore deposits had been proved, no commercially satisfactory process of refining nickel had been developed, and no assured market for the metal had been established.

The metallurgist, known in the eighteenth century as a 'metallist', was indeed a *rara avis*, while the work of the alchemist or 'chymist', who went before, savoured more of the occult than of science. Admirers of *The Beggars Opera*, written by John Gay (1685–1732) will remember the following stanza in the Soldiers' Chorus:

> 'Let us take the road
> Hark, I hear the sound of coaches,
> The hour of attack approaches,
> To your arms, brave boys and load,
> See the ball I hold,
> Let the *Chymists* toil like asses,
> Our fire their fire surpasses,
> And turns all our lead to gold.'

The announcement by Cronstedt[1] that nickel was a semi-metal was made at a period when the true nature of elements and oxides was only just dawning in the minds of men. More than a century before, the term 'element' had been proposed, in essentially its present meaning, by Boyle (1627–1691). But, in accordance with current practice, Cronstedt described the new element as a semi-metal because the nickel regulus which he had obtained was non-ductile, due to the presence of impurities.

At that period there was a widely held theory of combustion, since disproved by the French chemist Lavoisier (1743–1794), according to which when a substance burned it yielded up *phlogiston*; hence von Engeström's statement that this new semi-metal nickel 'retains its *phlogiston* a long time in the fire', i.e. it

'On Absolutely Pure Nickel'

oxidised only slowly when heated. It is hard to realise that the discovery of nickel antedated by several decades what is now common knowledge, that water consists of two volumes of hydrogen and one of oxygen.

When Cronstedt made his initial announcement many well-known chemists believed that the substance separated by him, and later designated nickel, was in reality an impure regulus of cobalt, containing arsenic, copper and iron. It was not until 1775 that this view was disproved, by the Swedish chemist, Torbern Bergman (1735–1784),[2] Professor of Chemistry at Uppsala, who, in a systematic series of investigations, made a large range of alloys and compounds from the elements which the critics claimed might constitute Cronstedt's 'nickel'. The results of that work, presented by one of Bergman's co-workers, established beyond all doubt that whilst Cronstedt's nickel may have contained some arsenic and cobalt, it consisted essentially of a new element.

☉ Aurum (Sol)
☽ Platina.
☽ Argentum (Luna)
☿ Hydrargyrus (Mercurius)
♄ Plumbum (Saturnus)
♀ Cuprum (Venus)
♂ Ferrum (Mars)

♃ Stannum (Jupiter)
♅ Vismuthum
Niccolum.
Arsenicum.
Cobaltum.
Zincum.
Antimonium.
Magnesium

It was Bergman[3] who, in 1775, first proposed a sign or device for various metals, including nickel, when he published in Stockholm a series of lectures in chemistry given earlier by H. T. Scheffer, who had recommended acceptance of Cronstedt's first paper. Bergman embodied in the text sundry signs, shown above.

Nickel: An Historical Review

Bergman emphasised that when something has to be hastily noted down such devices save both time and space, and he added that in bygone days absurd signs had been used 'to represent things which one thought were not to be generally known' but that these signs not infrequently hid 'ignorance under scholarly airs'.

Though data obtained by the English scientist Priestley (1733–1804) had been employed by the great French savant Lavoisier to ring the knell of the *phlogiston* theory, in 1794 the bell tolled for Lavoisier too, for he was an 'aristo'. With the words 'the Republic has no need of scientists', the French revolutionary prosecutor consigned him to the tumbril. Within a year, however, the French nation realised the gravity of its crime. In atonement, his mortal remains were accorded a proper funeral, at which the *oraison funèbre* was delivered by Fourcroy (1755–1809), also an eminent chemist and a member of the Faculty of Medicine of the University of Paris.

In his *Elements of Natural History and Chemistry* [4] Fourcroy paid much attention to nickel. After alluding to the peculiar 'semi-metal nickel', first made known to the world by Cronstedt, Fourcroy stated 'it is of a sparkling colour, inclining to red, especially on the outside. It is very brittle and its fracture shows it to consist of 'facets', by which it may be distinguished from cobalt'. He went on to refer to the thesis which Arvidsson,[2] in conjunction with Bergman, had previously published, and pointed out that although nickel, as obtained by roasting and fusion of its ores, was so far from being pure that it contained sulphur, arsenic, cobalt and iron, Bergman, by a number of ingenious processes, had successfully removed most of those impurities and

'On Absolutely Pure Nickel'

had obtained a species of nickel differing in many of its properties from that described by Cronstedt. Fourcroy thus felt justified in speaking of nickel as a pure metal.

Using the limited chemical and metallurgical vocabulary of that period, Fourcroy then gave a history of the known ores of nickel, reviewing in some detail the various processes of extraction. He remarked that it was a matter of no surprise that when, in due course, the metal had been extracted, there were still present several impurities, including iron, cobalt and arsenic. He agreed with Bergman and Arvidsson that it was extremely difficult to obtain nickel of a high degree of purity. Fourcroy concluded his thesis with these words:

'Nickel has not hitherto been applied to any use'.

The early years of the nineteenth century saw the rise to eminence, in Sweden, of a great chemist, Berzelius (1779–1848), who himself discovered nickel-containing deposits at Klefva.[5] Even if he had not made other significant contributions to science, Berzelius would probably always be remembered for the system of chemical symbols which he devised. In that system, now universally adopted, nickel was denoted by the symbol 'Ni'.[6] The element was to take its place, too, in the scheme of things developed in England by Dalton in his Atomic Theory. Dalton (1766–1844), the son of a weaver and sponsored by a Quaker, was largely self-educated, being a diligent student of Latin, Greek, mathematics and philosophy. With the background of the thought of the ancients, it is not surprising that in his theory he followed the philosophy of Democritus and the Pythagoreans, according to which nature is composed of indivisible particles, which Dalton designated 'atoms'.

No longer was chemistry the monopoly of the recluse

and the necromancer. It had, in fact, become a topic of social conversation amongst the fashionable throng which entered the dignified portals of the Royal Institution and at the dinner parties and musical soirées given by leading scientists of the day. To quote an amusing aphorism coined in more recent times by the late Lord Cherwell:

'It is more important to know the properties of chlorine than the improprieties of Claudius'.

It was left to Proust (1754–1826),[7] Richter (1762–1807)[8] and Thénard (1777–1857)[9] to obtain pure nickel. In 1804 Richter published a paper entitled *On Absolutely Pure Nickel. Proof that it is a Noble Metal*.[8] He was a methodical investigator, and the importance of his paper, as a milestone in the history of nickel, warrants quotation from it. After explaining the methods by which, after many failures, he had succeeded in obtaining pure nickel, he remarked 'I at last succeeded in obtaining several ounces of metal which I must consider to be absolutely pure nickel, but it took much time, patience and money'. In essence, his conclusions were as follows:

    a. Its colour is half-way between that of silver and pure tin.
    b. It is not affected by air or atmospheric water, that is, it does not rust.
    c. It is perfectly ductile; rods can be made from nickel when it has been heated and one can beat them into very thin plates when cold. Because of this property, nickel cannot be considered a semi-metal and takes its place amongst *'perfect'* metals.
    d. Its specific weight or density is 8·279 for molten nickel and 8·666 for wrought nickel.
    e. Its strength is considerable.

'On Absolutely Pure Nickel'

- *f.* It has a high melting point and so is extremely difficult to melt, at least as difficult as manganese.
- *g.* The metal oxidised very little on being heated until red, when it became a little duller than platinum, gold or silver. Thus 'nickel is not only a *perfect* metal but also a *noble* one'.
- *h.* The action of magnets on nickel is very great, only slightly less than their action on iron.

Richter's paper was prophetic: it forecast nearly all the characteristics which have proved important in the later large-scale applications of nickel. Corrosion-resistance pointed to its use as a material of fabrication and for coinage; its excellent high-temperature properties were shown; its amenability to processing was demonstrated; its magnetic characteristics were noted. However, in spite of this unconscious forecast, nickel remained a laboratory curiosity, and because no commercial demand had yet arisen and the major sources of supply had not yet been tapped, another fifty years went by before nickel started gradually to make its mark.

(6)

'It looks exactly like Silver'

LONG before samples of 'white copper' or *pai-thung* had reached Europe, news about it had filtered through to the West from the far-off Orient. The mention, in 1597,[1] of *aes album* shows clearly that the German philosopher and chemist, Libavius (1550–1616) knew about this whitish metal, treasured because of its resonance when struck and its aesthetic qualities. Again, in 1736, there was published in London a translation of a *History of China* by Du Halde,[2] which describes the alloy:

'The most extraordinary copper is called *pe-tong* or "white copper"; it is white when dug out of the mine and still more white within than without . . . its colour is owing to no mixture; on the contrary, all mixtures diminish its beauty; for, when it is rightly managed, it looks exactly like silver . . .'

According to the *Annual Register* of 1775, one J. B. Blake of Canton sent over to England, from the mines in the Chinese Province of Yunnan, a specimen of what he described as 'the ore *paaktong*'.[3] He sent the sample in the hope that efforts would be made in England to produce a metal equally white and pure, but with more ductility than that made by the Chinese.

'It looks exactly like Silver'

The Swedes also had heard about the white alloy and had succeeded in securing specimens. In 1776 Gustav von Engeström, who had earlier translated into English Cronstedt's work on the classification of minerals, published a treatise on the new material,[4] from which the following paragraphs are quoted:

'Mr. Bladh, who has several times visited the East Indies, has brought this metal with him from there, wrought and mixed, as well as rough and unmixed . . . With the blowpipe, Mr. Bladh had only tried a little of it on coal, but enough to show that it contained nickel. . . . By melting the rough metal with *hepar sulphuris*,[4] I got two separate metals, one that was red and forgeable was real copper, and the other was greyish white, brittle and with a fracture like that of steel. When further experiments were made, the last-mentioned metal turned out to be real nickel containing a little cobalt . . . In this condition the rough metal comes from the mines in the country down to Canton in the form of triangular rings, with an exterior diameter of 8 or 9 inches and with a thickness of about $1\frac{1}{4}$ inches. Consequently, it must have been smelted from copper ore containing nickel, which I dare say is to be found there . . . Some alloying experiments would certainly show in what proportion these three metals ought to be mixed in order to form a real *pak-fong*. My intention was to make it of Swedish nickel . . . '

In the same year, 1776, von Engeström published the following analysis of the alloy:

Copper	Nickel	Zinc
40·60%	18·75%	31·25%

(No figures were given for the 'impurity' constituents, which totalled 9·4%.)

Nickel: An Historical Review

A few years later a statement appeared that those who imported into Europe 'white copper' from China or Japan were sure of a ready market, and that a domestic imitation made by some 'ingenious manufacturer' was envisaged.[5]

In 1822, nearly forty years later, A. Fyfe, a lecturer in chemistry in Edinburgh, examined a basin and ewer made in this 'white copper'.[6] Its cost, in China, was one-quarter of its weight in silver and, according to Fyfe, 'when held in one hand and struck with the fingers of the other, the sound is distinctly heard at the distance of an English mile'. The assay he made was:

Copper	Nickel	Zinc	Iron
40·4%	31·6%	25·4%	2·6%

The saleability of the alloy seems to have dawned on several people, for in 1823 an enterprising Birmingham manufacturer, E. Thomason, made such a material synthetically, using his ingredients in these proportions:

Element	Oz.	%
Copper	85	40
Nickel	65	31
Zinc	55	26
Iron	5	3
	210	100

In a letter which Thomason[7] wrote in that year to the Society of Arts, he said that his product 'is easily cast into large things such as equestrian and other statues, columns, capitals, entablatures and pilasters'. 'Its hardness', he added, 'is so great as almost to resist impressions from a violent blow of the hammer'.

'It looks exactly like Silver'

In 1823 Keferstein, Brandes and Müller[8] had analysed ores from the Henne mine at Suhl in Saxony, from which, for some 60 to 80 years previously, a 'white copper' alloy had been made, and Frick[9] had determined how much nickel was needed to decolourise completely the copper and how much to make that alloy ductile.

In the same year a technical society in Prussia (Verein zur Beförderung des Gewerbefleisses) offered a prize to anyone who would erect, in Prussia, a factory for making an alloy approximating to the composition determined by Fyfe, resembling silver in appearance, and saleable at a price not more than one-sixth that of silver. Apparently there were no entries for the competition, but it was at that juncture that a number of people in Germany started to manufacture commercially a locally made version of *pai-thung*.[10]

J. R. von Gersdorff was one of the first to publish information on the composition of alloys suitable for particular uses: for example, for spoons, ladles and two-pronged forks, an alloy consisting of 25 parts nickel, 50 parts copper and 25 parts zinc was recommended; for knife- and fork-handles, candle snuffers, and sugar tongs, alloys of 22 parts nickel, 55 parts copper and 23 parts zinc were preferred; for plates and wash-basins the recommended alloys were 20 parts nickel, 60 parts copper and 20 parts zinc. It was stated also that addition of 3% of lead to alloys of the last-mentioned type produced a material suitable for casting items such as candlesticks, spurs, bells and horse harness.

Somewhere between 1826 and 1830 P. N. Johnson, the founder of the business which later became Johnson, Matthey and Company, of London, visited the Erzgebirge mining district of Saxony, and, seeing there for the

Nickel: An Historical Review

first time the German equivalent of *pai-thung*, he decided to embark upon its manufacture in Great Britain. Another English firm early in the field was F. and S. R. Topping, of London. But the name which will always be associated with the commercial development of nickel silver in England is that of Charles Askin. Living in Birmingham, Askin had become friendly with his neighbour, one Brooke Evans, a woollen draper, and when, in 1824, he decided to pay a visit to the mining districts of Germany, he included in his European tour a call on Evans' three sons, who were by that time established in Warsaw as merchants and ironfounders.[11] While there Askin saw in a shop window some forks and spoons made from a white metal which was new to him. He purchased some specimens of the cutlery which, he was told, was made from an alloy recently introduced from Germany under the name of *Argentan*. When one of the pieces dropped on the floor it broke, because it was brittle, and that aroused Askin's interest in producing a similar alloy of improved quality.

On his return to England he started experimenting and finally succeeded in casting an ingot in this alloy of nickel, copper and zinc. He showed it to a Birmingham friend, Henry Merry, who suggested asking Mr. Phipson, the owner of a nearby rolling mill, to roll the material. Askin agreed to try it out. He anticipated that when the ingot was placed between the powerful rolls it would fly into a thousand fragments, but to his joy it passed smoothly through the rolls and emerged on the other side as a bright shining ribbon, many feet long. Merry slapped his friend on the back, saying, 'Askin, your fortune is made'.

In 1833 a partnership ensued between Askin and two

'It looks exactly like Silver'

Brooke Evans, 1797–1862

Charles Askin, 1788–1847

members of the Merry family; a plant was set up at Sherborne, Ladywood, Birmingham, and it was there that the first commercial production of ductile nickel silver took place in England. Later that partnership was dissolved, and Askin joined up with his old friend Brooke Evans.[12] By that time the market for the alloy was expanding and, operating from George Street Parade, Birmingham, the new firm, Evans and Askin, concentrated on production of nickel silver and lost no time in establishing itself as a reliable source of supply.

Meanwhile an Austrian chemist had set up a wet refinery on Birmingham Heath, now Wiggin Street, having surreptitiously copied Evans and Askin's manufacturing processes, but, getting into financial difficulties, he offered the works to Evans and Askin. A junior assistant to Askin, named Henry Wiggin, who had studied chemistry, was sent to look at the works, and noticing a large lump of yellow 'mud' tinged with pink, he took in his handkerchief a sample which, upon analysis, proved to be highly cobaltiferous. Evans and

Askin thereupon bought the works, washed all the dump of yellow 'mud' with hot water, and recovered enough nickel and cobalt to pay for the whole works. Upon the death of Askin, Henry Wiggin, whose 'strict and energetic attention to duties and accurate scientific operations' had marked him out for promotion, was taken into partnership by Evans, and when in 1862 Evans died, Henry Wiggin took over the whole business, naming it Henry Wiggin and Company.

About 1841 Webb and Barker, non-ferrous metal manufacturers, of Birmingham (to be followed later by Barker and Allen), entered the field and soon became one of the best-known British manufacturers of nickel silver, meeting the ever-increasing demand. On the Continent of Europe several more firms were stimulated to come into this prosperous trade.[13]

Meanwhile, from the old world the 'know-how' on these alloys had crossed the Atlantic, and about 1835 one Robert Wallace,[14] a Connecticut spoonmaker, bought from an Englishman the 'new formula' for $25. This consisted of two parts of copper, one part of nickel and one part of zinc. The alloy was put through a rolling mill which was working for the brass industry at Waterbury. It fully justified all that was claimed for it, and nickel silver became one more link in the chain of products which were building up New England's rapidly increasing industrial prosperity.

The whiteness of the alloy, its similarity to silver, its ease of casting and fabrication, its relative resistance to tarnish and, above all, its reasonable cost, all served to put it permanently on the map, and for some years during the nineteenth century this justifiably popular alloy was the main outlet for primary nickel. Today,

'It looks exactly like Silver'

the letters 'E.P.N.S.', denoting 'Electroplated nickel silver', are to be found stamped on the tableware in almost every British household, and it is due to these persevering pioneers that so useful an alloy has since found its way into a multitude of other everyday applications.

(7)

'Nickel is very much sought after'

IN Germany, as early as the late fifteenth century, silver deposits were being worked in the Erzgebirge, and so rich in silver was some of the ore in the Schneeberg-Annaberg district that by 1474 as many as 176 mines were being operated in that area.[1] Three hundred years later, after nickel had been separated and named as an element, these deposits were worked for their nickel content also. The supply of the new metal was sufficient to inspire the establishment of a plant in the vicinity for the making of nickel silver. The average assay of the local ores was about 3% Ni, 4–6% Co and 8–10% Bi.

Arsenides of nickel were found at Klaustal in the Harz Mountains. Sulphide nickel ores were known at Dillenburg, Gladenbach and other places, and silicate nickel ores were worked at Frankenstein in Silesia. Nickel was recovered also from ores at Werra in Thuringia, from Richelsdorf and Braunhausen in Hesse, from the famous copper mines at Mitterberg near Salzburg, which were worked at a very early date, and from Dobsina (Dobschau), in Hungary.

In France, a shepherdess discovered veins of silver ore at a height of over 4,000 ft. at Chalanches in Dauphiné.

'Nickel is very much sought after'

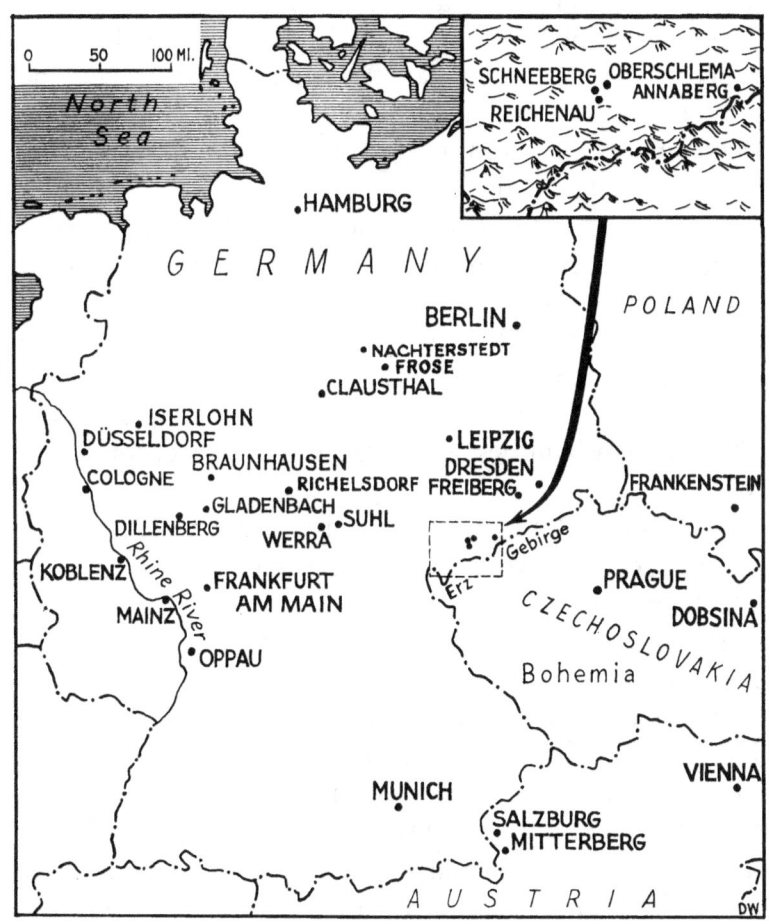

Nickel: An Historical Review

Until 1840 the deposit was worked solely for silver, but over the next fifty years an English company mined ore containing silver, nickel and cobalt, for H. H. Vivian and Company of Swansea. For a while two other small nickel deposits were worked, at Arre near Laruns in the Pyrenees region, and at Chabanne en St. Romain in the Dordogne. Nickel-containing ores were also found at Ste. Marie aux Mines in the Vosges Department, and at Angles and in the district of Riou Majou, both in the Pyrenees.[2]

In Scandinavia, Cronstedt's classic work was initially carried out on material obtained from the Los cobalt mines in Sweden. The first nickel smelter in the world was constructed in Sweden in 1838, soon after Berzelius discovered nickel in ore from the Klefva copper mines. These Swedish mines were worked for nickel for about fifty years.

Nickel-containing ores were found also at a number of other places in Sweden, including Ruda and Slattberg. The Sagmyra nickel works near Slattberg processed ores from both these deposits intermittently, until well into the second half of the last century.

In 1843 Scheerer, then Professor of Metallurgy in the University of Christiania, established that at Espedalen, some 160 miles north of Oslo, in Norway, there existed ores from which a concentrate containing some 22% of nickel could be produced. The Espedalen group,[3] owned by Evans and Askin (subsequently Henry Wiggin and Company), which was in operation during the years 1848–1855, employed many English miners, and erected two smelters. The Ringerike group of mines, which included the Erteli, was about 50 miles from Oslo, and there both mining and smelting took place from 1850 until as late as 1893.

'*Nickel is very much sought after*'

Not long afterwards the Ringerike and Espedalen mines were in commercial operation, and other deposits were being developed. Although the ore in Norway is similar in character to the sulphide ore later discovered in vast quantities in Canada, it is not of comparable grade; the average is around 1·5–2·5% nickel, with approximately the same content of copper, together with precious metals in small quantities. Altogether there are about forty locations in Norway where nickel has been found, but none of these deposits has ever proved to be of much magnitude. The richest of the Norwegian mines was the Evje, or Flaad, as it has often been called, situated some 40 miles north of Kristiansand, on the southern coast of Norway. In 1886 a smelter was erected there.

Nickel: An Historical Review

The material from the nickel mines of Norway was shipped for refining to Britain or elsewhere in Europe. Norway was, in fact, for several decades early in the second half of the nineteenth century the world's principal producer of nickel, but by 1896 production in that country had begun to slow down, and all the mines, with the exception of the Evje, had been closed.

According to *The Mineral Industry* of 1893, nickel deposits were found at various places in the Ural Mountains and in the Caucasus region of Russia in the early part of the nineteenth century, just about the time that the Norwegian nickel mines began to operate commercially. The ore at Revdin in the Urals was particularly rich and the Petrovsk mine was subsequently opened, being then the only place in Europe where oxidised nickel ore, practically free from sulphur and arsenic, was found. A considerable number of years later extensive sulphide and oxidised nickel deposits were discovered elsewhere in the U.S.S.R.

In the Pacific the small island of New Caledonia, discovered in 1774 by the British explorer Captain James Cook, but claimed in 1853 for France, had become of potential mineral importance to that country. Moreover, the French considered it essential to have a naval base in that part of the Pacific. In 1863 the French Minister of Marine and Colonies appointed Jules Garnier, a civil engineer, to be Chief Mining Engineer of New Caledonia, and in the ensuing years he made a thorough study of the mineral resources of the island. In so doing, he noticed, near the Dumbea River, certain cavities in the rock which were filled with silicates of magnesium strongly impregnated with a green substance which coloured these silicates and which, until then, had been

'*Nickel is very much sought after*'

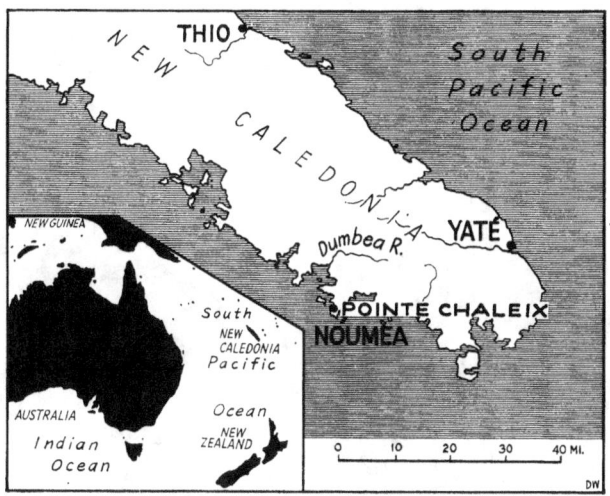

believed to be due to the chromium normally present. Samples were sent by Garnier to the School of Mines in Paris, and were found to be a hitherto unknown variety of nickel ore which, in due time, was named *garnierite*, in honour of its discoverer. Nickel was also found by Garnier accompanying blackish serpentines with nodules of green matter. These hydrous nickel-magnesium silicates contained practically no sulphur, no copper, only a small amount of cobalt, no precious metals, and no arsenic. The absence of those elements differentiated the New Caledonian nickel deposits from the early arsenical ores mined in Europe and from the sulphide occurrences in Scandinavia and in Canada.

In a report which Garnier published in 1867,[4] this passage appears:

'It would be most interesting to study more closely the nickel deposits in New Caledonia and to see if industry could utilise this metal, the price of which, as

Jules Garnier with his guide and his dog
(From a drawing by A. deNeuville)

we know, is high, but the uses of which offer so many advantages in certain cases. To begin with, because of the close mixture of nickel and magnesium silicate, one

'Nickel is very much sought after'

would say that large-scale treatment of this metal would most easily be carried out by the wet method.'[5]

Seven years passed, however, before E. Heurteau,[6] another French mining engineer, visited New Caledonia at the request of the Minister of Marine and Colonies, to examine the mineral deposits and to form a considered opinion on their nature and importance. He reported that nickel was there in abundance and that some samples showed a nickel content as high as 14·95%. 'Nickel today is very much sought after', he wrote. 'Its uses are multiplying for the manufacture of coins and objects of all kinds, especially surgical instruments and even certain machine parts.'

Meanwhile, Rouquayrol, a former director of the Mines de Decazeville, had put Garnier in contact with Henri Marbeau, a distinguished French metallurgist, and as a result they formed, in France, Société des Etudes Coloniales et Maritimes. The difficulties which faced this new organisation were formidable. The ore had to be brought across the ocean to France from an island in the South Pacific over 12,000 miles away; ships were few in number; no economic method of extracting the metal was known; skilled metallurgical labour hardly existed; and, to cap everything, the future outlet for nickel was a complete gamble. It is not surprising that within a year it became expedient to raise new capital and reorganise. The name of the company was changed to Société pour le Traitement de Minérais de Nickel, Cobalt, Cuivre et Autres (système Jules Garnier). The company had a quarter interest in John Higginson and Company, the firm which was financing Fonderies de Nouméa. The assets of the new company included not only those of the earlier Société des Etudes Coloniales et Maritimes,

Nickel: An Historical Review

but also eighteen mine concessions in New Caledonia formerly vested in Higginson himself.

The company had a plant in France, at Septèmes, Bouches-du-Rhône. Commercial production of nickel ore in New Caledonia started in 1875, and in the following year the first blast furnaces were erected, at Pointe Chaleix, near Nouméa. Their active life was destined to be short; within a couple of years mining operations had to close down completely, due to recurrent native insurrections. Writing of those early times, J. Garland[7] remarked:

'the native Kanakas, whose wants are few, seldom work in the mines, holding strong views as to the folly of work and the stupidity of the white man, who is addicted to it'.

The year 1880 was of great importance for the future development of nickel, both for New Caledonia and for the world at large, for in that year there was formed, in France, Société Anonyme Le Nickel (système Garnier), with a capital of $6\frac{1}{4}$ million French francs, which became the owner of all the important known nickel mines in New Caledonia, and of the French plant at Septèmes. Charles Hébert, an industrialist, became first President; Marbeau was made Vice-President; and both Garnier and Higginson were given seats on the Board.

In 1882 there was incorporated Société pour la Fonderie de Nickel et Métaux Blancs, which, two years later, became Société le Ferro-Nickel. Works were acquired at Lizy-sur-Ourcq. Other associates of Marbeau and Garnier were Le Chêsne, chemist and inventor, and Philippe Hébert, a financier, brother of Charles, the first President of Le Nickel.

Notwithstanding a complete shut-down in mining

'Nickel is very much sought after'

Henri Marbeau, 1836–1910

activities in the island in 1886, due to lack of orders, there was later a gradual build-up in the output of nickel emanating from New Caledonia. To permit this greater production, a larger throughput was needed. The richer ores of New Caledonia having been worked first, there was a gradual drop in the grade of ore mined; whereas around 1880 the nickel content was above 10%, by 1892 it had dropped to about 7%. A larger and more up-to-date smelter was erected in 1889 by Le Nickel at Thio, on the east coast of the island, and plants which had earlier been built elsewhere were at the same time closed down.

Meanwhile, alongside all this active quest for nickel in other parts of the world, developments of even greater significance for the future of nickel had been taking place in North America. Early in the eighteenth century nickel ore was mined in the United States, in Litchfield,

Nickel: An Historical Review

Connecticut and, reputedly, shipped to China, probably for the production of *pai-thung*, but that deposit was never of economic importance.

Then again, in Madison County, Missouri, a mine called La Motte was operated, by French explorers, from the early days of the eighteenth century, but it was not until more than a hundred years later that it became known that the lead ore from that deposit contained nickel and cobalt. Spasmodically, a neighbouring nickel-bearing deposit at Fredericktown, Missouri, was also worked. (In recent years that deposit was mined by the National Lead Company for nickel.)

A *pyrrhotite-chalcopyrite* deposit which soon proved to be of relative importance was found in Lancaster County, Pennsylvania. That mine, which was named the Gap, was originally worked for copper only, but in 1853 it was recognised that nickel also was present in the ore. At that time world output of nickel was extremely small, and for about a quarter of a century production from the Gap did, in fact, place it among the leading sources of nickel. Operations at the Gap mine ceased in 1891. (During World War II drilling was again undertaken, but the deposit proved to be too small to have any commercial value.)

By far the most important of the developments in North America was, however, in Canada.[8] As far back as 1848, when only an occasional trapper or prospector penetrated those remote parts, nickel had been discovered in the Province of Ontario, at a spot where the Whitefish River runs into Lake Huron. Though later called the Wallace mine, the deposit was never actually worked for nickel. Eight years later, when making a survey between Lake Nipissing and Sault Ste. Marie, a surveyor named

'Nickel is very much sought after'

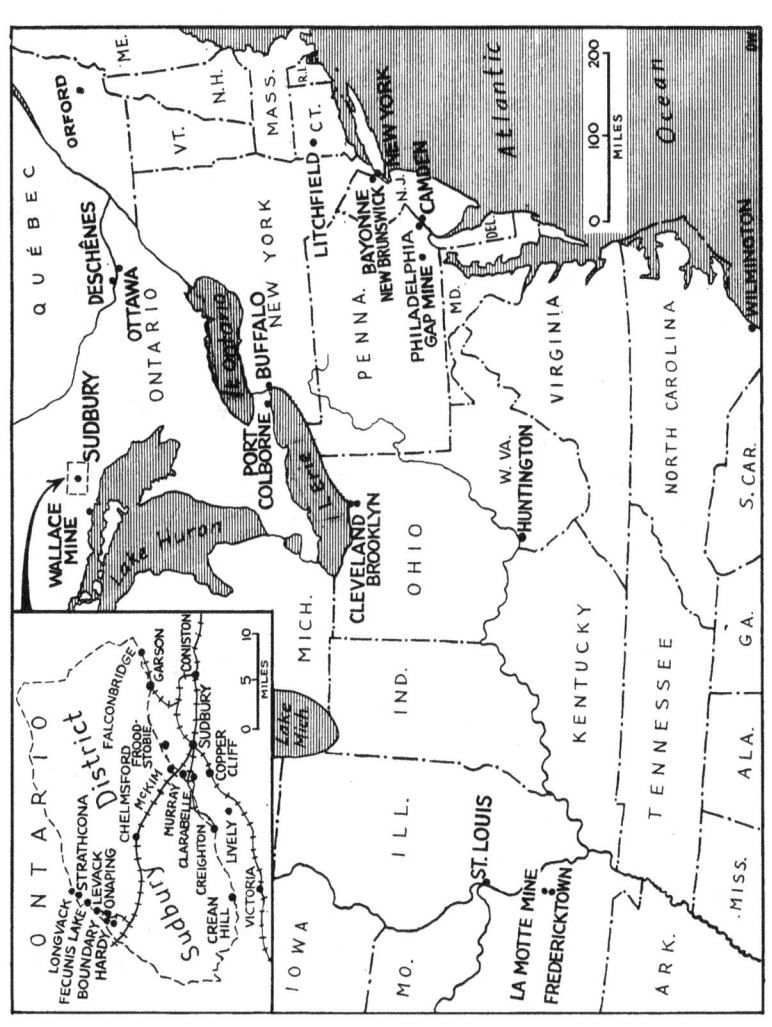

Nickel: An Historical Review

A. P. Salter discovered an area of highly mineralised rocks. He reported the occurrence to Alexander Murray, a geologist in the field, who determined that, accompanying the iron pyrites which was plainly discernible in the rocks, there was nickel as well as copper. However, the value of nickel was not widely realised, and the reports of Salter and Murray were soon forgotten.

It is believed that the location where mining of nickel from Canadian ores first took place, between 1871 and 1873, was the Silver Islet mine on Lake Superior. The ore was very rich in silver and also contained nickel and cobalt. Nickel was extracted as a by-product at Wyandotte, Michigan, where a smelting and refining works was built by the Silver Islet Mining Company to handle the silver ore.

Some time in the 'seventies, at a place in the Province of Quebec, a prospector found a copper orebody which contained small amounts of nickel. This place he named Orford, after his home town in England. An American mining engineer, W. E. C. Eustis, who was intending to buy the property, had taken along with him a young attorney named Robert Means Thompson,[9] to verify the title, and it was thus that Thompson came into contact with the two metals in the future of which he was destined to play so prominent a part.

Born in 1849, the son of a Pennsylvania judge, and a graduate of the United States Naval Academy at Annapolis, Maryland, R. M. Thompson served for a few years at sea before deciding that he wanted to be a lawyer. After graduating at the Dana Law School of Harvard University, he practised law in Boston, and was for a time Assistant Reporter of the Supreme Court of Massachusetts. He served for a few years on the Boston

'Nickel is very much sought after'

Common Council and was the youngest Republican State Chairman in Massachusetts.

Outside his work this promising lawyer and politician channelled part of his dynamic energy into sport, in which he excelled. He liked, as he said, 'amateur sport, where the boys battle for supremacy instead of for money'.

In 1878 an organisation called The Orford Nickel and Copper Company[10] was formed and mining was started. However, attempts to smelt the Orford ore failed, and further experiments to smelt it with some ore from the Crown mine, near Capelton, met with no better success. The Orford mine was therefore abandoned. W. E. C. Eustis was, however, persuaded to acquire a property adjoining the Crown mine and Thompson handled the arrangements in such a masterly manner that he was appointed Acting General Manager.

A modified furnace with which Eustis had been experimenting at Orford was erected for full-scale working, and soon the new company was producing and smelting ore. The operation was successful, but the price of copper fell, and Thompson went to Scotland, where he learned from C. Tennant, Sons and Company Ltd. the process used by Rio Tinto for recovering the sulphur from their copper ores mined in Spain.

Returning with that knowledge, Thompson persuaded Standard Oil at Constable Hook, later called Bayonne, New Jersey, that he could supply sulphur for their use in sulphuric-acid production. He then bought, for only $5,000, four acres of sunken meadow near the Standard Oil plant. By arranging with the New York City authorities to tip ashes and other refuse on to it gratis, he soon had, at an almost trifling cost, a dry, level site, on which he

Nickel: An Historical Review

proceeded to put up a copper refinery. Subsequently, in his search for more copper, he went to Butte, Montana, where, in association with others, he set up a smelter and started making copper matte.

In 1880 the Canadian Pacific Railway had been organised, to build a railroad which would connect the eastern seaboard of Canada with the Pacific. Two years later construction was begun at Pembroke, Ontario. By 1883, working westward, the construction engineers had pushed forward, mile by mile, a new line as far as the place now known as Sudbury, so called after the town in Suffolk, England, where the wife of one of the construction engineers had been born.

As the track for the new line was being cleared about three miles to the west of Sudbury, a gossan, a form of iron oxide capping or hat on the top of massive pyrites, was struck by one of the workmen, a blacksmith named Thomas Flanagan, while wielding his pick. When the rest of the gang started digging, a highly mineralised outcrop was exposed; incidentally, at a spot only a few miles from the place where A. P. Salter and Alexander Murray had reported nickel ore twenty-seven years before. In the following year two merchants from Pembroke, Ontario, Thomas and William Murray, sought title to the particular mineralised area through which the new railway route ran. That property became the Murray mine.

Other characters gradually appeared on the stage, including one Rinaldo McConnell. He started as a lumber man, turned to prospecting, and, becoming interested in copper, sought mining claims. Another early prospector was Thomas Frood, who, after leaving his Scottish home in Renfrewshire, set up a drug store, tried his hand at teaching, and subsequently worked as a timekeeper on the railway. In due time, accompanied by A. J. Cockburn, another prospector, he located the deposits which were to become the famous Frood mine and Frood extension. Yet another individual active in that field was Francis Charles Crean, who had had the fortune to discover the Crean Hill, Elsie and Worthington deposits. By the mid eighteen-eighties local prospectors were numerous and, as a result, other significant deposits were located, among them the Stobie, discovered by J. Stobie in 1885, and the Victoria and Creighton, located by H. Ranger in 1886.

Another personality who had come on to the scene was S. J. Ritchie, a persuasive promoter described as 'extravagantly optimistic, desperately pugnacious, generous as a prince, and possessed of no degree of caution whatever'. He was a man of great ability and was most ambitious: his impoverished upbringing had made him decide that he would make his millions and never again become poor. He dabbled in several ventures, and when visiting an executive of the Canadian Pacific Railway he saw some samples of ore. Realising the rich copper content, Ritchie set about buying up most of the promising properties in the Sudbury region.

Before long Ritchie had obtained the support of several wealthy backers who had been behind him in his earlier, less profitable, ventures. On 6th January, 1886 there was incorporated, in Ohio, the Canadian Copper Company and legal steps were taken to enable it to operate in Canada. S. J. Ritchie became its first President. The principal assets of the company were the copper properties in the Sudbury area which Ritchie and his wife had purchased.

Nickel: An Historical Review

Early in 1886 the Canadian Copper Company started production of ore, from the Copper Cliff mine; later the Stobie, Evans and Frood deposits were added to the company's holdings, and during the first years of operations, by hand-sorting, some 3,000 tons of high-grade copper ore were ready for treatment.

In those early days the ore from Canada was shipped for refining to three firms: the Orford Copper Company[11] of R. M. Thompson at Bayonne (Constable Hook), New Jersey; the Nichols Copper Company, whose smelter was on Long Island; and H. H. Vivian and Company, of Swansea in Wales. However, all three refiners failed to extract copper effectively from this Canadian ore. In the interim R. M. Thompson, upon having the ore assayed, had found that instead of a copper content of 7%, the copper was only $4\frac{1}{2}$% with some $2\frac{1}{2}$% nickel. H.H. Vivian and Company had also discovered the presence of nickel in the ore. Clearly the future of these extensive Canadian orebodies, hitherto regarded as being solely a source of copper, depended upon development of an economic method for separating out the intractable, potentially valuable, nickel content.

Although it was not long before the Orford Copper Company was scraping the bottom of the barrel for further funds, the worth of the nickel accompanying the copper in the ores mined by the Canadian Copper Company was by then fully recognised and it became of primary importance to find some way to separate the two metals.

These many and varied mining activities had directed the attention of the Ontario Government to the potentialities of the mineral resources in their Province and, following a Royal Commission Report in 1890,[12] the

'Nickel is very much sought after'

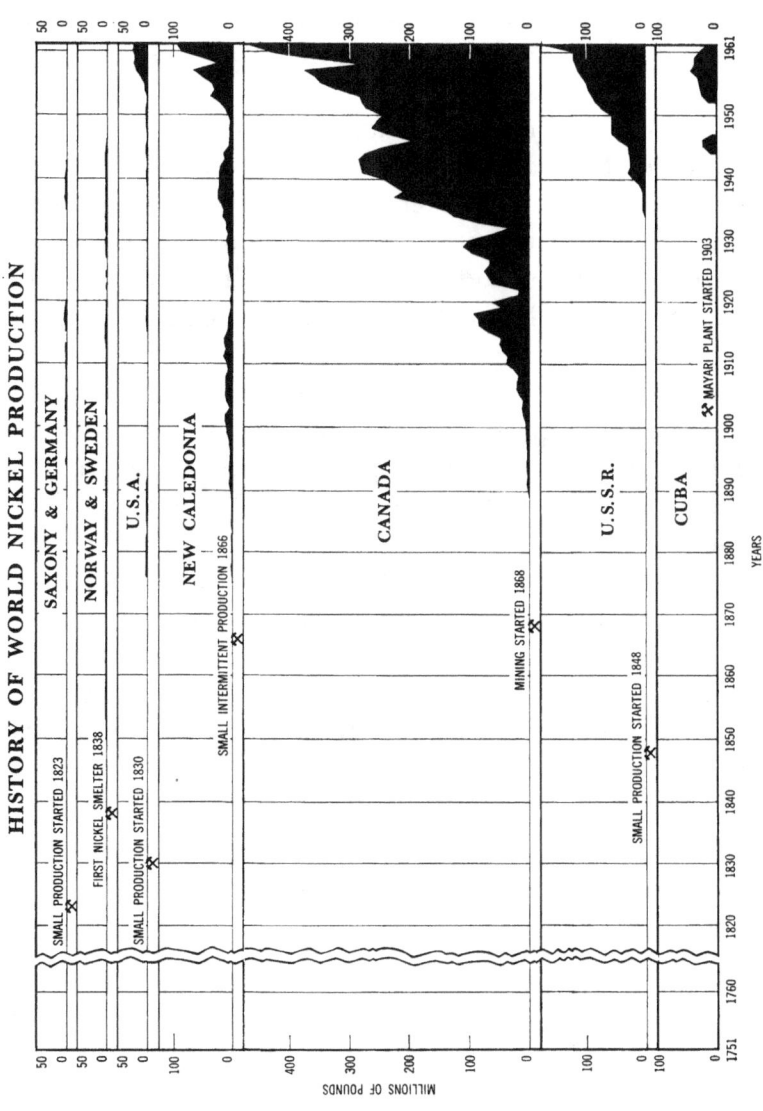

Ontario Government for a time withdrew all its nickel-bearing lands from sale. There was an attempt to interest the British Government in them, but Britain declined the proposition and the withdrawal order was rescinded.

Although prospectors were numerous in Canada, no geologists having experience with nickel ores were available, and it is not surprising that in 1890 Garnier, the French engineer after whom *garnierite* was named, was called to Sudbury to report upon the new nickel discoveries. It is said he arrived in immaculate frock coat, with the ribbon of the Légion d'Honneur adorning his lapel, a model of courtesy and suavity. Garnier diligently studied all the new orebodies and in due time, under his supervision, with the help of his associate Michaud, there was erected, at Copper Cliff, a plant for production of a high-grade matte (80% copper-nickel). Garnier himself described the sequel. 'The manufacture was taken up with the vigour natural to the Anglo-Saxon race, and the necessary plant was installed at a great cost.'

The nickel industry was on the threshold of an assured future. Canada's amazing mineral wealth was just beginning to be recognised.[13]

(8)

'Men not easily Baffled'

BEFORE 1838 the arsenical deposits from Central Europe were, for practical purposes, the only source from which the intractable metal nickel was wrested from its ores. Both J. R. von Gersdorff, of Reichenau, near Schneeberg and E. A. Geitner, also of Schneeberg, had started in 1824 to treat these complex nickel ores. A patent dated 26th August, 1824 was obtained in Austria by von Gersdorff, and it would appear that he and Geitner went into this new business almost simultaneously; these two men may thus share the honour of being the first two persons in the world who refined nickel direct, by metallurgical methods. For both of them the primary interest in the refining of nickel was the production of a metal suitable for making, synthetically, a *pai-thung* type of alloy.

The operations involved in the Geitner extraction process used on the complex cobalt-nickel-iron-arsenic ore which the Saxons were then mining were as follows: the gangue, or non-valuable portion of the ore, was first removed, following which the ore was roasted. Much of the arsenic was thereby volatilised, while the iron, the nickel and the cobalt, were converted into oxides.

Nickel: An Historical Review

The resulting product was mixed with twice its weight of siliceous sand and some of it was sold to pottery makers as *zaffre*.[1] The rest of the *zaffre* was melted with soda and sand, so that the cobalt was separated from the nickel and other metals and passed into the slag, giving it a distinctive blue colour. This slag, a blue pigment or glass consisting of silica, potash and cobalt, was used by the potters, under the name of *smalt*, to impart a blue colour in the decoration of ceramics. The crude, half-melted, by-product of the preparation of *smalt*, which consisted of a *speiss* of nickel, and contained nickel, iron and arsenic but relatively little cobalt, was known as 'pottery nickel' and from that *speiss*, by a wet treatment, Geitner had produced refined nickel. Some twenty years later extraction technique in Saxony had advanced to a stage permitting systematic production of primary nickel from the pottery *speiss*. Closely associated with that development was K. A. Winkler, a member of one of the leading pigment-producing firms in Saxony.

The Englishman P. N. Johnson,[2] who was one of the first to manufacture nickel silver in England, bought his 'pottery nickel' from Geitner in Germany. When the material reached London it was ground to a fine powder before mixing it with potassium nitrate (nitre) and potassium carbonate (potash). The mixture was then heated in a reverberatory furnace until all the arsenic had combined with the potash or had been driven off. The resulting cake was 'washed free from potassium arsenate and sulphate and dried on chalk stones'. When nickel silver was to be made, this cake, consisting mainly of impure nickel oxide, was mixed with charcoal and borax and, along with sheet copper, melted in a crucible. Zinc was added, and the whole was cast into

'*Men not easily Baffled*'

Percival Norton Johnson, 1792–1866

28-lb. ingots. (The usual composition of the nickel silver P. N. Johnson made was 55% copper, 18% nickel, 27% zinc.) Alternatively, when primary nickel was required, the cake was reduced, with charcoal and borax, to metallic nickel.

Shortly afterwards G. Hallett also began to refine nickel in London. Hallett was a refiner of antimony, and because for over twenty years he was a manufacturer of nickel silver in England, selling it under the name of *albata*, it is presumed that he likewise followed the technique that had been worked out and operated in Saxony.

Evans and Askin were at that time trying out the possibility of refining nickel by a wet process. Since nickel and cobalt, both present in the arsenical deposits, are chemically very similar, they respond in similar fashion to many chemical treatments, and this presented Evans and Askin with a difficult problem until Edward

Nickel: An Historical Review

W. Benson,[3] then Managing Director of the British White Lead Company, of Birmingham, suggested adding bleaching powder to an acid solution of the mixed metals, to cause selective precipitation of cobalt oxide. The story goes that Benson was dining with Askin and they worked out a chemical equation for separating nickel and cobalt by means of bleaching powder and lime. Each went home to try it out independently. Askin put in the correct calculated quantity of the two ingredients, but found that the oxides of both nickel and cobalt mixed together and were precipitated. Benson, however, did not happen to have the calculated quantity of bleaching powder, so threw in all that he had and thus, purely by accident, obtained a highly satisfactory separation of the salts of the two metals. Certain modified forms of the process, which had been used in Saxony, were still in operation in the United Kingdom late in the nineteenth century.[4]

World consumption of nickel was then only a few million pounds a year, but with the discovery of the richer orebodies in New Caledonia and, later on, in Canada, supplies of nickel from the deposits of Central Europe and Scandinavia gradually dwindled.

Whereas shaft-sinking and underground mining were necessary for winning the nickel ores which emanated in the early days from Europe, most of the mining in New Caledonia has been by open-cast work. After removing the overburden, the ore is quarried out, layer by layer, down the hillside.

According to a report made by E. Glasser,[5] a French mining engineer, to the French Government, there were four varieties of ore deposit in New Caledonia: vein-like deposits, brecciated deposits, masses of altered serpentine

'Men not easily Baffled'

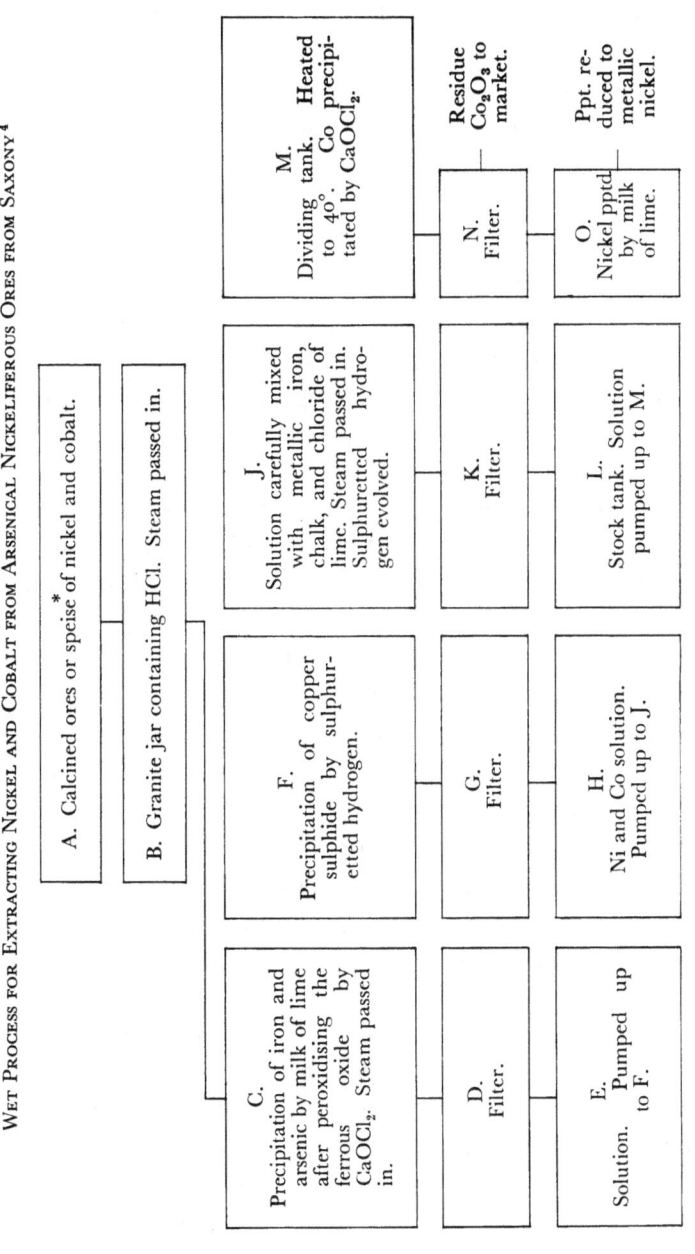

WET PROCESS FOR EXTRACTING NICKEL AND COBALT FROM ARSENICAL NICKELIFEROUS ORES FROM SAXONY [4]

A. Calcined ores or speise* of nickel and cobalt.

B. Granite jar containing HCl. Steam passed in.

C. Precipitation of iron and arsenic by milk of lime after peroxidising the ferrous oxide by $CaOCl_2$. Steam passed in.

D. Filter.

E. Solution. Pumped up to F.

F. Precipitation of copper sulphide by sulphuretted hydrogen.

G. Filter.

H. Ni and Co solution. Pumped up to J.

J. Solution carefully mixed with metallic iron, chalk, and chloride of lime. Steam passed in. Sulphuretted hydrogen evolved.

K. Filter.

L. Stock tank. Solution pumped up to M.

M. Dividing tank. Heated to 40°. Co precipitated by $CaOCl_2$.

N. Filter. — Residue Co_2O_3 to market.

O. Nickel pptd by milk of lime. — Ppt. reduced to metallic nickel.

* now known as speiss

Nickel: An Historical Review

impregnated with nickel, and nickeliferous earths. Referring to the practice in the nineteenth century, Glasser stated that pure *garnierite* was very rich in nickel, but most of the ore was lower in grade. The miners therefore mixed together rich and poor ore and then dried the product at 100°C. (212°F.). The average nickel content was about 7%. Neither copper nor precious metals occurred in such ore.

In the 'seventies Garnier put up his first smelting furnace in Nouméa, to make ferro-nickel (60-70% Ni), but the alloy proved to be too high in sulphur. Garnier's method, which he patented in France, involved production of ferro-nickel pig or 'fonte', and the refining of that material in a Bessemer or open-hearth furnace, with a view to utilising the resultant product solely in the production of iron and steel. The 'fonte', originally made in water-jacketed furnaces, contained 21-25% nickel.

That technique was replaced by cupola smelting in New Caledonia, followed by bessemerising in Europe. (At a much later date both operations were carried out in New Caledonia.) The process used in the final decade of the last century is outlined in the table facing this page. Nickel oxide of French origin assayed at that time about 78% nickel; the pure nickel averaged 98-99%.

In the early eighteen-nineties the mining of nickel ores in New Caledonia was carried on almost exclusively by Le Nickel and Société Anonyme d'Exploitation des Mines de Nickel. A contemporary review[6] of mining operations in the island stated that the miners included a few Englishmen, and some Kanakas, together with 'Annamite and Tonkinese prisoners, galley slaves and convicts obtained by contract from the Government'.

At that time nickel and nickel oxide were being

EUROPEAN PROCESS FOR EXTRACTING NICKEL FROM SILICATED ORES IMPORTED FROM NEW CALEDONIA[8]

(Low water jackets are exclusively used in this process.)

STAGE I—SMELTING FOR MATTE

Materials	Reactions	Products
1. The ore 2. Gypsum 3. Ground coal 4. Fuel } Ground together and pressed into bricks.	1. The silica unites with the Mg and part of the Fe of the ore and Ca of the gypsum to form a slag. 2. The Ni and part of the Fe of the ore unite with the S of the gypsum to form a matte.	1. A slightly nickeliferous slag, which goes to waste. 2. A highly nickeliferous matte, which goes to the next stage.

STAGE II—REMOVAL OF IRON

Materials	Reactions	Products
1. The roasted matte from the first and fourth stages. 2. Sand. 3. Fuel.	1. Most of the Fe and part of the Ni are oxidised by roasting. 2. The silica combines with the Fe and NiO to form a slag, while most of the Ni retains its S.	1. A slag which goes to the next stage. 2. Nickel sulphide, which goes to the fifth stage.

STAGE III—RESMELTING FOR MATTE

Materials	Reactions	Products
1. The slag from the second stage. 2. Sand. 3. Gypsum. 4. Fuel. } Ground together and pressed into bricks.	1. The silica unites with the lime and part of the Fe to form a slag. 2. The Ni and part of the Fe unite with the S to form a matte.	1. A slightly nickeliferous slag, which goes to waste. 2. A nickeliferous matte, which goes to the next stage.

STAGE IV—REFINING THE SLAG MATTE

Materials	Reactions	Products
1. The matte from the third stage. 2. Sand. 3. Gypsum. 4. Fuel.	1. The silica unites with the lime and part of the Fe to form a slag. 2. The Ni and part of Fe retain their S.	1. A slightly nickeliferous slag, which goes to waste. 2. A highly nickeliferous matte, which goes to the second stage.

STAGE V—REMOVAL OF SULPHUR

Materials	Reactions	Products
1. The nickel sulphide from the second stage. 2. Nitrate of soda in small quantity. 3. Fuel.	1. The Ni and S are both oxidised.	1. Gases which escape. 2. Ni oxide, which goes to the next stage.

STAGE VI—PRODUCTION OF METALLIC NICKEL

Materials	Reactions	Products
1. The nickel oxide from the fifth stage. 2. Charcoal, flour or other carbonaceous substances.	1. The oxide is made into a paste with flour and baked. 2. The baked mass is broken into fragments or molded into cubes, disks,* etc., and is strongly heated: parts with the C and O and becomes metallic.	1. Gases which escape. 2. Metallic "grain", "cube", or "disk"* nickel, which goes into the market.

* "Disks" are now called "Rondelles": see page 132

'Men not easily Baffled'

produced from New Caledonia material by refineries situated, in France at Le Havre and in England at Erdington, near Birmingham. There was also the Kirkintilloch plant in Scotland, equipped with water-jacketed furnaces and converters. In addition, the nickel works at Iserlohn in Germany, formerly owned by Theodor Fleitmann, which originally had obtained its nickel ores from Europe, had later, when the works were sold to the French company, switched over to New Caledonia as its sole source of supply.

The discovery of nickel in the ores from the Gap mine at Lancaster, Pennsylvania, midway in the nineteenth century, stimulated a desire for refining in the United States and a plant was built by Joseph Wharton at Camden, near Philadelphia. Although this ore contained only about $1\frac{1}{2}\%$ nickel, Wharton claimed that his product was 'of singular purity and uniformity'. Like everyone else in the nickel business at that time, he kept the details of his refining process a closely guarded secret, but it is believed to have involved wet treatment by dissolving the nickel-iron matte in hydrochloric acid, precipitating the iron by lime, and separating the nickel and cobalt by the old method which used bleaching powder. His commercial interests lay more in nickel salts and cobalt oxide than in metallic nickel.

By 1877 Wharton's annual output of primary nickel was about 200,000 lbs., or one-sixth of the total world output at that period and during the following decade. In Wharton's own words 'all the processes of extraction and refining are complicated and costly; although considerable improvements have been made, advancing decidedly the quality of the product, great skill, care and diligent attention are demanded in all stages of this

Nickel: An Historical Review

Joseph Wharton, 1826–1909

tedious manufacture'.[7] He used to say 'I am alone in the business simply because no other man in America has dared to embark on so difficult and hazardous a trade'.

The ore reserves of the Wharton organisation, corporately known as the American Nickel Works, were meagre, and in 1891 the Gap mine was closed down, although Wharton continued to refine nickel from imported ores.

The early history of mining around Sudbury in Canada is inextricably tied up with copper. Were it not so, the locality where so many nickel developments have occurred would today be known as Nickel Cliff, not Copper Cliff.

Many were the newcomers who went to the wall, but the Canadian Copper Company, in spite of frequent financial crises, managed to keep its head above water. In 1888 sites for a roast yard and smelter were chosen in Copper Cliff. The first furnace of the Canadian

'Men not easily Baffled'

Copper Company was started up, and by 1889, 80 to 100 tons of ore a day were being treated, yielding a matte containing 50% of copper and nickel. Most of the matte was shipped for refining to H. H. Vivian and Company in Wales, and to C. Tennant, Sons and Company Ltd. in London. A little went to Wharton in Camden, New Jersey. Subsequently shipments were made to the Orford Copper Company, at Bayonne in New Jersey. There was at that period no complete refining of nickel in Canada, though it was the policy of the Canadian Copper Company to do in Canada all that could economically be done in the processing of nickel and copper ores.

Following the erection, at Copper Cliff, of a bessemer-matte plant, under the supervision of Garnier, a plant was also built at Brooklyn, near Cleveland, Ohio, for the reduction of oxide to nickel. Although a considerable sum was spent on the venture, Garnier's efforts did not achieve the company's goal of making its own primary nickel. Garnier returned to France and the Canadian Copper Company continued to conduct its own experiments to find the best way of extracting nickel from the matte.

In heap roasting, amounts up to 3,000 tons of ore were stacked out-of-doors on top of cord wood and, after being set alight, were allowed to burn for as long as twenty weeks, thus partly oxidising the iron and reducing the sulphur to about 7%. The roasted ore was then charged into a water-jacketed blast furnace. The furnace matte, containing 20–25% copper, 18–23% nickel and 25–35% iron, was re-melted in a cupola and then bessemerised to a matte containing about 45% copper and 40% nickel. As the Orford Copper Company's method of refining at Bayonne was improved, more and more of this matte was shipped there for treatment, but some was sent by the Canadian Copper Company to its own plant at Cleveland, Ohio, where they made a 50:50 copper-nickel alloy.[8]

In spite of the fact that brilliant technologists were engaged by the Canadian Copper Company, they failed to find a satisfactory and profitable method for recovering nickel as well as copper from the Sudbury ores. That failure was certainly disappointing, but in the meantime the Orford Copper Company had a great stroke of luck.

In the eighteen-nineties the United States Navy placed an order with the Canadian Copper Company for nickel in the form of matte. R. M. Thompson, though at that time still experimenting on matte from the Canadian Copper Company, was doubtful whether he could undertake to deliver the metal and, being aware that Joseph Wharton was the only nickel refiner in the United States, he suggested to the U.S. Navy that Wharton should refine the matte. However, the U.S. Navy, realising that Wharton's costs were high and that R. M. Thompson was doing his utmost to perfect a process for refining nickel at the lowest possible cost, decided to ship to the latter, in New Jersey, a considerable quantity of the Canadian Copper Company's matte, and in due course he delivered to the U.S. Navy a nickel oxide of a quality approved as being suitable for steel-making. The refining had been achieved by using a technique consisting in treatment of the uncalcined matte with dilute sulphuric acid, a process which led to removal of the iron and the nickel as the sulphates, leaving the copper sulphide behind. These sulphates were calcined, producing an oxide of nickel and iron quite free from copper.[9] Unfortunately the costs even then exceeded the toll which the Navy had agreed to pay for extracting the nickel, but at long last R. M. Thompson's pertinacity had its reward.

Adjacent to the works in Bayonne, New Jersey were the Bergenport Chemical Works. Supplies of nitre cake (acid sodium sulphate) or 'Sally Nixon', as it was facetiously named after its nomenclature of *sal enixum*[10], were obtained from the chemical works and some of it was put into the crucible with matte and coke, preparatory to melting. When the melt cooled and had been tipped out of the mould, it was found that the bottom portion of the melt had a silvery appearance, and the top portion was black and flaky. Hence the phrase 'tops and bottoms'.[11] Upon analysis, the bottom portion proved to be impure nickel sulphide, whilst the top portion was a mixture of copper sulphide, iron sulphide and nickel sulphide.

A method of separation had thus been discovered. To quote R. M. Thompson's own words at the time: 'It is due to Mr. J. L. Thomson and Mr. C. C. Bartlett to state that there has been no metallurgical work in the last decade carried out more thoroughly or scientifically than the working out of this process. Time after time it seemed as if the process must be abandoned, but Mr. Thomson's scientific scent always brought him back to the right path, and the indefatigable practical work of Mr. Bartlett made a combination which it was impossible to defeat.'[12] At that time John L. Thomson was superintendent of the Orford Copper Company and on 4th May, 1891 a patent for a *Process of producing and separating sulphide of nickel from ores containing nickel*, a claim which for the first time covered those 'tops and bottoms'

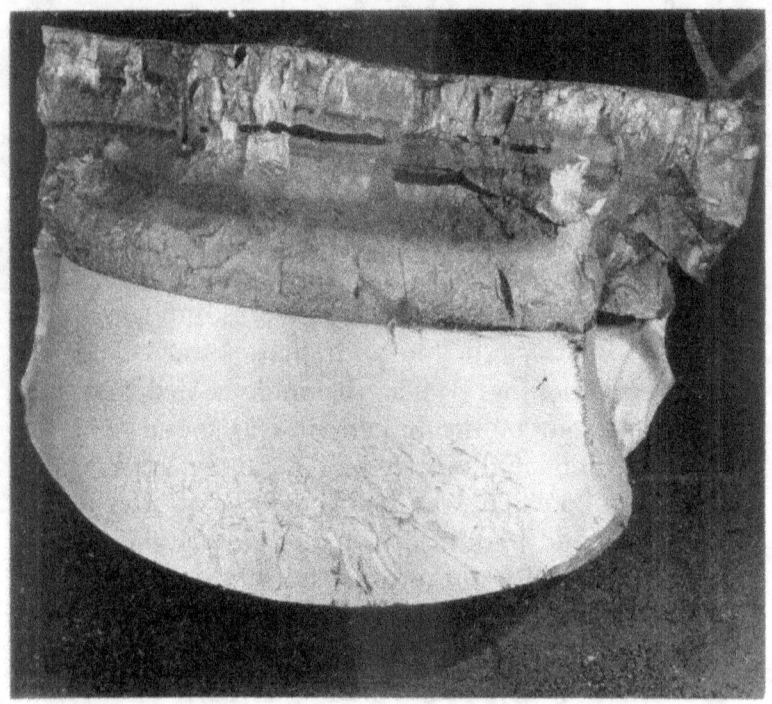

'Tops' and 'Bottoms'
Top layer: Copper sulphide
Bottom layer: Nickel sulphide
(Approximately three feet high and five feet wide)

and used that phrase, was filed in the name of his assistant, Charles C. Bartlett[13] (described in the patent as 'a subject of the Queen of Great Britain', though residing in the State of New York). The patent was assigned to the Orford Copper Company.

The concept was not entirely new. More than a century before, the Swedish scientist G. von Engeström had published a treatise in which he stated that by using *hepar sulphuris* he had obtained a separation into two layers—the one layer high in copper and the other layer high in nickel.[14] In 1824, when J. R. von Gersdorff applied for an Austrian patent, he specified that nickel may be separated as a heavy layer from its impure matte by addition of specified quantities of sulphur and blue glass, at elevated temperatures. Since glass is essentially sodium silicate, the two chemicals sodium and sulphur, as required by the Bartlett patent, are present. However, it is not wrong to attribute principal authorship of the 'tops-and-bottoms' process to the Orford workers, for they were indubitably the first to obtain a real grasp of the mechanism of the reaction and apply it to operating the process flexibly and efficiently on an industrial scale.

During 1892 five more patent applications were filed, all concerned in one way or another, with the 'tops-and-bottoms' process.[15, 16, 17] Not long afterwards it was announced[12] that since 1891 the Orford Copper Company, which had become the principal refiner of nickel-copper matte in the United States, had been employing, at Bayonne, this new 'tops-and-bottoms' process, which was a notable improvement in the metallurgy of nickel.

Commenting on the Orford method, R. M. Thompson said: 'The metallurgical world at large must benefit greatly from the cheapening of nickel which this process will give, and I may add that a further extension of the process is being perfected, which has already, in a laboratory way, given metallic nickel of 99·9% purity'. He further claimed 'When this process shall be put on working scale, it seems as if very little will remain to be done in the metallurgy of nickel'. Thompson's somewhat naïve concluding observation may not be without humour for those who in later years have laboured untiringly to improve extraction efficiency.

Nickel: An Historical Review

ALKALINE SULPHIDE PROCESS FOR EXTRACTING NICKEL FROM CANADIAN MATTE[8]

The 'Tops-and-Bottoms' Process

STAGE I—CONCENTRATION SMELTING

Materials	Reactions	Products
1. Matte. 2. Sulphate of soda. 3. Coke.	1. The Na_2SO_4 is reduced to sulphide. 2. Part of the iron and copper unite with the sodium sulphide.	1. "Tops", consisting of highly cupriferous and ferruginous matte, which goes to the next stage. 2. "Bottoms", highly nickeliferous matte, which goes to the third stage.

STAGE II—"TOPS" SMELTING

Materials	Reactions	Products
1. Weathered "tops" from the first and third stages. 2. Matte. 3. Coke.	1. The soda in the tops takes up some S from the Ni in matte and forms a sulphide which unites with part of the iron and copper.	1. "Tops" as in first stage. 2. "Bottoms" as in first stage.

STAGE III—"BOTTOMS" SMELTING

Materials	Reactions	Products
1. "Bottoms" from first and second stages. 2. Sulphate of soda. 3. Coke.	1. The sulphate of soda becomes reduced to sulphide. 2. Most of the iron and copper unite with the sodium sulphide.	1. "Tops", which go to the second stage. 2. Highly nickeliferous sulphide, which goes to the fourth stage.

STAGE IV—REMOVAL OF IRON

Materials	Reactions	Products
1. Sulphide from the third stage. 2. Sand. 3. Fuel.	1. Most of the iron and part of the nickel are oxidized by roasting. 2. The silica combines with the oxides. 3. The nickel retains its sulphur.	1. A ferruginous and slightly nickeliferous slag, which goes to waste. 2. Nickel sulphide, which goes to the fifth stage.

STAGE V—REMOVAL OF SULPHUR
(Finishing Roast)

Materials	Reactions	Products
1. Nickel sulphide from the fourth stage. 2. Nitrate of soda in small quantity. 3. Fuel.	The sulphur and nickel are both oxidized. A little salt may be added to convert lime adhering to the bottoms as slag or sulphide into $CaCl_2$, which is afterwards removed by washing.	1. Gases which escape. 2. Nickel oxide, which is sold to nickel steel makers, or is reduced direct to refined metal.

In the Old World there had occurred, back in 1839, an event which was to prove of great significance for the nickel industry. Ludwig Mond was born in Cassel, Germany. He studied chemistry under Kolbe and later became a pupil of Bunsen, then Professor of Chemistry in the University of Heidelberg, whose Bunsen burner is known to every schoolboy.

His first job was in an acetic-acid factory near Mainz, where his inventive mind evolved a profitable process for manufacturing basic copper acetate (verdigris). While working there, he frequently spent the weekends at his uncle's house in Cologne and there he met his cousin Frida, whom he ultimately married. 'Happy is he who can combine verdigris with romance!'[18]

When only twenty-three Ludwig Mond came to England, where he was soon immersed in the chemical industry, founding Brunner, Mond and Company. In 1872 he became a British citizen. The story of his spectacular success as a great chemical industrialist is told in his biography.[19] Nothing daunted Ludwig Mond, and he was a man who rarely allowed a problem to remain unsolved. Those who knew him well described him as a man whose mind was often miles away, wrestling with some scientific poser.

His prime interest had always been research, and in the early 'eighties he had set up, in the stables of his London house, a research laboratory, where he had as assistant a young Austrian chemist, Carl Langer. While working alone there late one evening in October, 1889, Langer noticed that in some apparatus in which carbon monoxide was being passed over finely divided nickel, cooled to a temperature below the boiling point of water, the blue flame became highly luminous. Furthermore, the flame, from its usual lambent blue, had turned a sickly green. Langer at once summoned Ludwig Mond to see this interesting phenomenon. At first they suspected that arsenic had been present, and that the formation of a volatile hydride of arsenic had tinged the flame. That assumption was easily tested; a cold porcelain tile was thrust into the flame and immediately became coated with a shining metallic mirror, significantly different from the brown or black spots left by arsenic in the well-known Marsh test. When the neck of the combustion tube was heated, a bright mirror formed on the glass and the luminosity of the flame disappeared. Analysis of the mirror showed it to be nickel and the gas to contain a previously unknown compound, nickel carbonyl $(Ni(CO)_4)$.

The colourless nickel carbonyl has the property that when heated to around 180 °C. (356 °F.) it breaks down, yielding carbon monoxide and pure nickel which is practically free from carbon. Thus, if, into this gaseous carbonyl, small granules of pure nickel are continuously introduced and heat is applied, each nodule will increase in size, just as inside an oyster the continuous excretion of nacre causes the growth of a pearl. Such, in essence, was how the carbonyl process ultimately came to be applied to the refining of nickel.[20]

By 1892 a Lilliputian model plant had been set up in Ludwig Mond's laboratory and after it had been working for some time he announced that by means of that apparatus he had successfully extracted nickel from a great variety of ores, in a time varying, according to their nature, between a few hours and several days. Before the year-end, so he said, the process was going to be tried out, in Birmingham, on a scale that would conclusively prove its industrial capacity.[21] He forecast that in a few months' time nickel carbonyl, a substance quite unknown two years before and still a laboratory rarity, would be in bulk production and would play an important rôle in metallurgy.

This prediction aroused the keenest interest in North America, and, in fact, throughout the world. Commenting on the Mond carbonyl process, an American journal[22] remarked: '*If this process proves practicable on a*

'Men not easily Baffled'

large scale it should supersede all others'. However, after expressing some doubts, the article continued '*Mr. Mond, however, and his colleague, Mr. Quincke, are not men to be easily baffled by any difficulties of operation, and it is to be expected that the Mond nickel will soon enter the market*'.

After a great many teething troubles in a pilot plant established by Mond, by 1895 nickel was being produced from Canadian matte at the rate of 3,000 lbs. per week.

Eager as Ludwig Mond was to see his discovery developed commercially, his highly successful chemical interests were by then keeping him so fully occupied that he hesitated to launch out into a new, and probably financially hazardous, metallurgical venture. At that time nickel was, to him, only a side line and it is not surprising therefore that he decided to offer the carbonyl process, lock, stock and barrel, to the Canadian Copper Company, who had no efficient process for separating nickel and copper.

In the autumn of 1896 the Canadian Copper Company sent their metallurgist, D. H. Browne, to England and, as a business precaution, the company took an option to purchase the whole of Mond's patents and know-how for a million and a half dollars. D. H. Browne, who had shipped over with him for trial about 75 tons of the Canadian Copper Company's bessemer matte, remained for nearly twelve months studying the pilot plant in Birmingham and, when commenting on it afterwards, remarked 'this process is one of the most beautiful known to metallurgy and the comparative simplicity of the operation constitutes its chief charm'.

The negotiations between Mond and the Canadian Copper Company dragged on for nearly two years but the Canadians decided not to exercise their option on

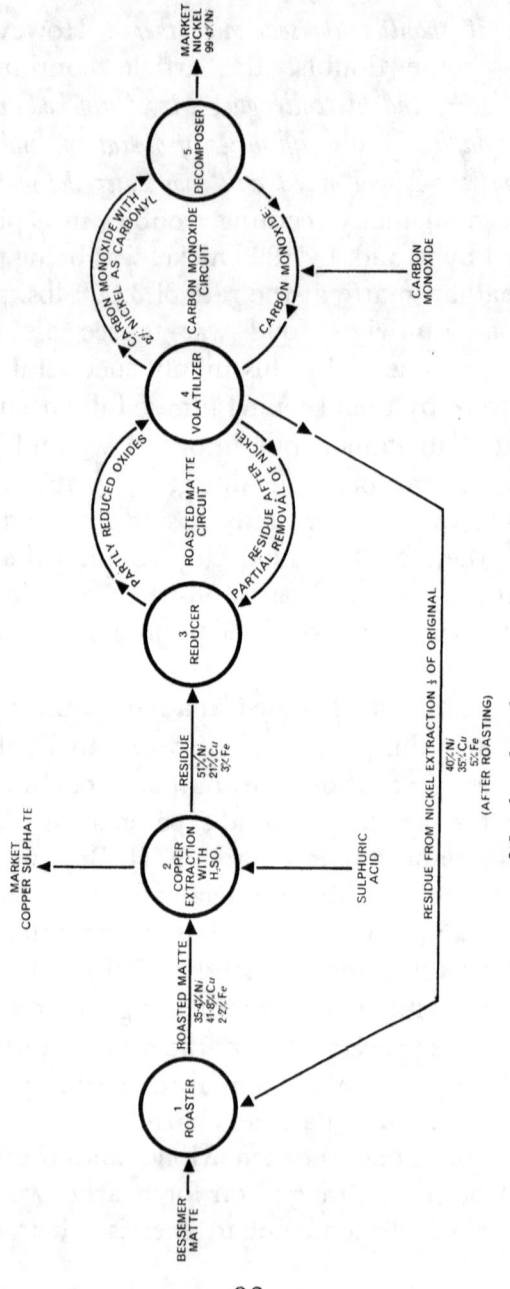

Mond carbonyl process for refining nickel

'Men not easily Baffled'

the carbonyl process. There were three main reasons for their turning it down: (i) mechanical problems involved in large-scale production, (ii) the poisonous nature of the nickel carbonyl, and (iii) the unsuitability of the Canadian climate, where wide variations in temperature would make it difficult to handle large quantities of gases.

Undaunted, and with a complete disregard for the train of troubles that he well knew lay ahead, Mond took a momentous decision. He would enter the nickel field himself.

He then made an arrangement with Henry Wiggin and Company whereby part of their land at Smethwick, with some buildings standing on it, was placed at his disposal and there, in 1892, he built a complete experimental plant. Details of the pilot-scale nickel-extraction plant were given in 1898, in a paper by W. C. Roberts-Austen,[23] Professor of Metallurgy in The Royal School of Mines and Deputy Master of the Royal Mint. As he pointed out, the process possesses unusual interest, in that it is the only one in the whole range of metallurgy in which a metal is obtained from its ores by causing it to combine with a gas, to form a gaseous product from which it is subsequently released. Lord Kelvin spoke of it as 'giving wings' to nickel. Moreover, the operation, being a regenerative one, is continuous, thus minimising labour costs.

A milestone had been reached in the history of nickel and there had been laid the foundations of an essential industry of immense importance.

Everything has to have a beginning, and as it may be of interest to future generations, there is reproduced below a letter which Ludwig Mond received from H. H.

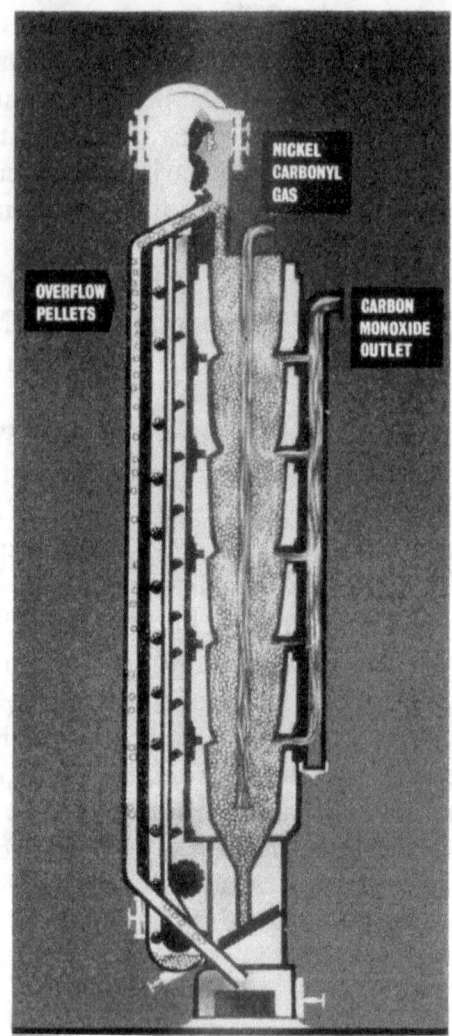

Sketch of original Mond decomposer

The nickel pellets move continuously by gravity through six gas-heated boxes and are elevated by buckets. The pellets grow and the excess volume overflows through the down pipe into the box at the base

'*Men not easily Baffled*'

Vivian and Company, dated 9th March, 1897.

'Your name was handed to us as a Maker of Nickel, and we should like to try some of your nickel for special work. Could you oblige us with a small sample lot, as we think it might lead to further business'.

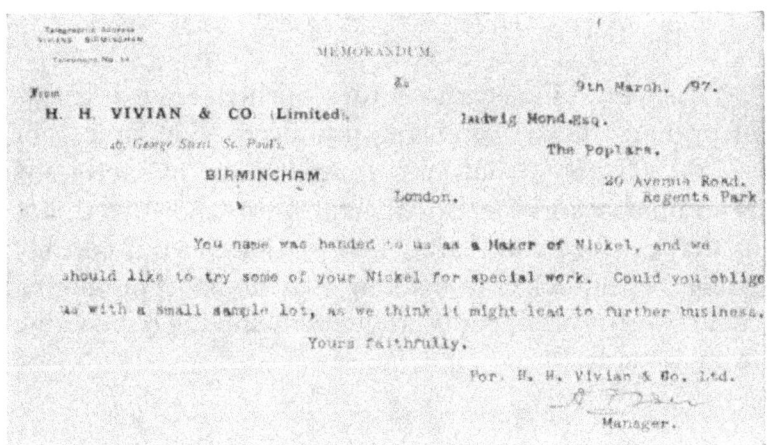

Qualms about Mond's venture into the nickel business certainly existed at that time, as is evident from a letter he received on 19th May, 1897 from Henry Gardner,[24] then Managing Director of Henry R. Merton and Company, the well-known London metal merchants.

> '*Dr. Ludwig Mond,*
> *The Poplars,*
> 20 *Avenue Road, N.W.*

Dear Sir,

We are in receipt of your favour of yesterday, but we find some little difficulty in selling the nickel referred to, more especially as we are unable to tell the buyers

that the supply will be regular. We are however doing our best to dispose of it and we hope you will allow the nickel to remain at the works for the present. We were not at all aware that you were being inconvenienced by it, or we should have made greater efforts in the matter.
Yours faithfully,
per pro. Henry R. Merton & Co.,
(*Signed*)   *H. Gardner.*'

When the nineteenth century opened only a trickle of primary nickel was being produced. The figures for 1775–1900 show that nickel production in Germany, Scandinavia and the United States was short-lived, but as that century came to a close production was steadily rising, with nickel from New Caledonia representing some two-thirds of world production, and the rest coming from Canada.[25]

(9)

Here was a Material Second to None

In prehistoric times iron ore was heated in a charcoal 'furnace', to obtain lumps of iron which could be shaped crudely into weapons or implements. Pure iron melts at about 1,535°C. (2,795°F.) and the heat used in bygone days was sufficient to remove the oxygen but insufficient to fuse the iron, which remained in workable form because it did not absorb more than a small percentage of carbon. With the introduction of coal and coke as fuel for the furnaces, higher temperatures were obtained and a molten product resulted. At these higher temperatures, however, carbon and other impurities were absorbed, and in the modern blast furnace, which has a maximum operating temperature approaching 1,600°C. (2,910°F.) the molten metal produced is of such a composition that on solidification it forms brittle material known as pig iron.

In the late middle ages wrought iron was made by refining a bath of molten cast iron by passing air above it. Carbon and other elements were removed, thereby raising the melting point of the product. The process was accelerated by adding iron oxide in convenient form and rabbling it in, but, since the temperature was insufficient to maintain the higher-melting-point mass in molten form, the product was a sticky ball of iron. This ball was forged under primitive hammers, thereby ejecting some slag. The worked product, wrought iron, was a forerunner of steel and was extensively used in engineering applications.

As nickel was not separated until 1751, prior to that date no one could have tried out its effect on iron intentionally. In 1799, however, one S. S. Hickling of Birmingham, England, obtained a British patent for improving and beautifying certain vessels and utensils used for 'chymical' and other purposes made of hammered iron, cast iron and cast iron united with a semi-metal called nickel. He fused together nickel and cast iron, in various proportions from 40 parts iron and one part nickel to four parts iron and one part nickel, so the nickel content could have been as low as $2\frac{1}{2}\%$ or as high as 25%. He claimed that in addition to beautifying the articles, the presence of nickel preserved them.

The year 1791 was of immense significance in relation to the use of nickel in association with iron, for in that year, in England, a son was born to a blacksmith named Faraday. That son was christened Michael.[1] When nearly 22 Faraday went 'to fag and scrub' for Humphry Davy, who was then Professor of Chemistry at the Royal Institution. The research carried out by Bergman and Richter, proving that nickel was a pure metal, would naturally have been a topic of current discussion there, and it was not long before Faraday's interest was aroused. In 1812, in a letter to a friend, he wrote 'I was going to Knight's to obtain some nickel . . . I inquired and bought some—have you seen any yet?'

Here was a Material Second to None

Faraday became intrigued by the infinity of different metallic combinations that are possible, particularly when pure iron is combined with minute portions of carbon and other elements, and his imaginative mind soon led him to wonder why meteoritic iron had unusual qualities. Little did he realise that his experiments would inspire investigations which, in the subsequent century and a half, would have a prodigious effect upon the demand for nickel.

In a letter to Professor de la Rive, Faraday wrote:

'*June* 26, 1820—We have been induced by the popular idea that meteoric (*sic*) iron would not rust, to try the effect of nickel on steel and iron. We have made alloys of iron and nickel . . . But nickel alloyed with steel gave us no hopes . . . So for the present we have dismissed that metal from our experiments, though I expect, as we go on, we shall find many occasions to resume thoughts and intentions which we may have laid down. Mr. Children has obliged us with an accurate analysis of the Siberian meteoric (*sic*) iron, and he finds it to contain a very large proportion of nickel. In the mean of three experiments it amounts to 8·96 per cent.'

Fortunately for the world, Faraday and Stodard, who were collaborating in the research, persevered in their imitations of meteoritic iron by synthetic methods. In their first experiment, reported in that year, they added to good horseshoe-nail iron about 3% of pure nickel. They heated the ingredients in a crucible for some hours and, on forging the alloy, found it 'to be quite as malleable and pleasant to work as pure iron'. A like success attended the making of an alloy to match some Siberian meteoritic iron, which contained 10% of nickel: 'the metals were found perfectly combined, but less malleable, being disposed to crack under the hammer'.

In 1824 the Swiss metallurgist J. C. Fischer, who was visiting his son in Vienna, saw an exhibition of meteorites at the Imperial Museum of Natural History, and the crystal structure of the polished surfaces aroused his interest. He had the idea of producing a synthetic meteoritic iron, and when he also saw some Turkish damascened blades exhibited there he became firmly convinced that their characteristic appearance was due to the nickel content of the meteoritic iron.

On returning to Schaffhausen, Fischer succeeded in producing meteoritic steel by the addition of nickel. The qualities of this material exceeded those of the best cast steel he had ever produced, and he forthwith obtained patent privilege for it in Austria. In the following year Fischer visited London, and showed specimens of his 'meteor steel' to Faraday, who was greatly impressed by its hardness and elasticity. It was Fischer's discovery which formed the subject of a patent by two then unknown Londoners, J. Martineau the younger and H. W. Smith, for an invention communicated 'by a certain foreigner residing abroad' for producing the 'beautiful wavy appearance exhibited on the best Damascus sword blades'. It was claimed that 'meteor steel' was made by adding to 'blister steel' the patentees' 'meteor powder', consisting of 24 parts of zinc, 4 parts of 'purified nickel' and 1 part of silver. About that time a German manufacturer named Wolf, in Schweinfurt, also produced meteoritic steel which could 'be readily damascened', but no market for it developed.

In 1845 a British patent was granted to M. Poole for 'adding to cast iron in its various compositions of cast metal and steel' various metals, including nickel in proportions varying from 2% to 10%. Whereas pure iron is a comparatively soft metal, the specification of this patent is interesting because it makes clear that by then it was appreciated that the amount of carbon present determined whether the resultant metal would be steel or cast iron. (Carbon in amounts varying up to about 1·7% produces steel. If the carbon is above that figure, the material is cast iron.)

In the United States, in 1851, Otis Boyden obtained patent coverage for a process of making wrought or malleable iron by adding, either to the ore or to ordinary cast iron, zinc or an alloy of zinc and nickel.

In 1853 one W. Fairbairn, an English engineer, used some No. 3 Blaenavon pig iron to which he added nickel, with the object of improving the strength of the cast iron made from it, and seven years later he reported further work with the same aim. His first results, determined on bars made by use of nickel ore from a small occurrence at Inveraray in Scotland,[2] indicated that deterioration in strength resulted from introduction of nickel. Subsequently he 'obtained from London a number of other bars, consisting of iron and nickel, which on being submitted to the same tests as before, gave better results than those obtained in the previous experiments'. This led him to conclude that 'probably a totally different process of manufacture will have to be adopted before a sufficiently strong and satisfactory compound can be obtained'.

Although for centuries steel had been produced in small quantities by cementation or by the crucible process, nothing was yet known about bessemerising or the open-hearth method. W. Kelly, an ironmaster in

Kentucky, and Henry Bessemer, an English engineer, however, independently evolved a novel process of steelmaking which came to be known as bessemerising. This method involved blowing air into molten pig iron, to remove impurities and thereby make the material malleable. The process was rendered even more practicable by R. Mushet, an English metallurgist, who proposed the addition of *spiegeleisen* after the blow, to introduce manganese and carbon and to remove the oxygen. This technique was supplemented soon afterwards by the invention, by the Brothers Siemens, of the 'open-hearth' process, whereby large quantities of metal could be handled in a single charge. Finally, a method for removing phosphorus came from two Welshmen, S. Thomas and P. Gilchrist. The names of many other scientists and engineers could be added[3]; men who also helped to give the world what it wanted, namely, strong steel of consistent quality, which could be produced rapidly in large quantities, at a cost of little more than that of iron.

During the Crimean War, at the bombardment of Kinburn, east of Odessa, three French marine batteries, shielded for the first time in history with compound or plated-iron armour, succeeded in silencing the Russian forts in the short period of four hours. This led the French to design their first armoured warship, the steam frigate *Gloire*, with iron plates up to 4·7 in. thick. Firing tests by the British, at Woolwich, soon demonstrated the superiority of wrought-iron armour plates over cast iron, though the Royal Navy continued for a time to launch 'ships of oak'. In 1859 the *Warrior* and the *Black Prince* were built in Britain with $4\frac{1}{2}$-in. wrought-iron plates affixed to teak 18-in. thick amidships, and American

Here was a Material Second to None

vessels constructed then had 6-in. laminated iron plates. Armour tended to become progressively thicker as improvements in naval ordnance were made.[4]

Such an innovation could not fail to upset the 'diehards'. Rear-Admiral R. D. Evans, a member of an Advisory Board set up in 1882 to discuss modernisation of the United States Navy, wrote: 'I shall never forget, as long as I live, the trouble I caused in that small convention by proposing that we should build steel ships. I was the original steel man, and when I proposed that all ships in the future should be built of steel, Admiral Rogers adjourned the Board for three weeks to prevent a fight'.

In the British Isles several manufacturers of steel had commenced producing naval armour. Particular interest then centred on compound plate consisting of a tough backing of wrought iron and a facing of carbon steel. The steel portion, comprising about one-third of the total thickness, was welded on to the iron back.

In 1885 the Bethlehem Iron Company sent over a representative to visit all the great gun and armour-plate plants of Great Britain and the European Continent, with the result that at their works in South Bethlehem, Pennsylvania, there was set up a forging plant duplicating that of Whitworth and Company of Manchester, England. About that time, too, a contract was made between Bethlehem and J. Schneider of Le Creusot, by which the French armour-plate patents and special machinery were bought for use in America.

Before long compound armour was replaced by homogeneous steel armour but, with the improved penetrating power of the armour-piercing shell developed shortly afterwards, still stronger plate was necessary. It is

Nickel: An Historical Review

believed that nickel-steel armour-plate was first commercially produced in 1885 at the Montataire works in France, where Marbeau and Le Chêsne were closely collaborating on steelmaking. Shortly afterwards it was being produced in France by Schneider, in Italy at Spezia, and, by 1889, at various steelworks in Great Britain. Tests showed that a steel containing 3% of nickel developed remarkable projectile-breaking qualities, coupled with tremendous toughness. Here was a material second to none for armour plate.

In the interim the pioneer work done by Marbeau in France on various steels containing nickel had been protected by patents in several countries abroad, including Great Britain, where a brilliant young metallurgist, James Riley, Manager of the steelworks of C. Tennant, Sons and Company Ltd., was working on alloy steels. Riley was fully aware of those patents, but it was not until he actually examined some of Marbeau's products that his interest became 'much excited', so much so that shortly afterwards he paid a visit to the Montataire works, in order to satisfy himself that consistency in properties was obtainable from crucible cast steel. Soon afterwards Marbeau visited Riley in Glasgow and heats were made to show that composition could just as easily be controlled when the steel was made in an open-hearth furnace.

The striking mechanical properties of these previously unknown nickel steels were described in some detail in a paper Riley presented to the Iron and Steel Institute of Great Britain in 1889.[5] In this historic announcement Riley also said that, by hardening and tempering, exceptionally high mechanical properties had resulted, including breaking strength up to nearly 96 tons per sq. in. (215,040 p.s.i.). He gave figures showing the greatly improved torsional properties obtained from nickel steel, as compared with unalloyed carbon steel. He confirmed that 'steels rich in nickel are practically non-corrodible', and that 'those poor in nickel are much better than plain carbon steel'.

After remarking that 'it requires no powerful imagination to conjure up a most bewildering number of applications' for these previously unavailable materials, particularly where non-corrodibility coupled with high elasticity and phenomenal strength is desired, Riley concluded with these words:

'I find some difficulty in not becoming enthusiastic on the point, for in the wide range of properties or qualities possessed by these alloys, it really seems as if any conceivable demand could be met and satisfied'.

As can be well imagined, Riley's pronouncement unloosed a spate of enthusiasm for alloying nickel with steel.

Benjamin F. Tracy, then U.S. Secretary of the Navy, became interested in Riley's report and, hearing also of the Schneider tests at Le Creusot, he arranged for comparative trials of armour-plate to be carried out at the Naval Ordnance Proving Ground, Annapolis, Maryland. Within a few years the Bethlehem Company, the only large forging plant in the United States, was also making, in nickel steel, guns up to 8-in. bore for the United States Navy, and even 12-in. guns for the Army.

At about the same time Hayward Augustus Harvey, an American steelmaker, invented a process for treating nickel steel in a way which added a hard face to its inherent toughness, thus greatly improving nickel steel for armour plate. Parallel developments took place in

Nickel: An Historical Review

Great Britain. On 19th August and 4th November, 1892, there appeared articles[6] on certain trials carried out at Portsmouth, England, on high-carbon nickel-steel armour made by Vickers, which had been surface-hardened by 'Harveyising'. The most remarkable result achieved was the holding together of a piece of armour plate under the wedging strain of five 8-in. projectile heads which had penetrated to a considerable depth. This testimony to nickel then followed: 'In fact, the hard face due to the "Harvey" process caused the projectiles to break, and though the heads had impressed energy enough on the plate to penetrate to a considerable depth, the plate, as we suggested, probably thanks in a great measure to the nickel in its composition, held wonderfully well together'.

Subsequently the power of armour and ordnance was still further enhanced by the introduction, into the steel, of chromium as well as nickel. At the St. Chamond steelworks in France, owned by Compagnie des Forges de la Marine, steel containing 0.4% carbon, 2% nickel and 1% chromium was produced for the French Government.

What all this meant to the producers of nickel may be gathered from the report made by the Secretary of the United States Navy in 1892, when he said that the quantity of armour plate needed for an ordinary war vessel, such as the United States was then constructing, was some 3,200 tons, and as there was $3\frac{1}{4}\%$ nickel in the steel of that armour each vessel required about 100 tons of nickel. The nickel needed in heavy ordnance was obviously not included in that figure.

Nor were these the only Governments contemplating the vast potentialities which these nickel-containing

Here was a Material Second to None

Armour-plate tests, Annapolis, 1890
The nickel-steel plate kept out all the shell and remained without cracks
Courtesy: National Archives, Washington

steels were opening up. Testing of armour plate was taking place at Russia's proving ground at Ochta, near St. Petersburg, and in other countries.

Meanwhile, a less belligerent outlet for nickel was about to make its appearance. The age of steel and steam, in which mammoth mileages of railway track linked one coast of a continent with the other, and in which ships, framed and clad in steel, steamed regularly across the oceans, had brought in its train yet another age, that of the horseless era. The horse was to be replaced by a machine that

> '... never kicks or bites, never tires on long runs and never sweats in hot weather. It does not require care in the stable and only eats while on the road...'
>
> R. E. Olds, *Scientific American*, 1892, May 21.

No one person invented the petrol-driven automobile, or 'car', as it soon came to be called. A Frenchman, J. Lenoir, early in the 'sixties, had been the first to demonstrate the practicability of the internal-combustion engine, using illuminating gas as fuel. N. A. Otto, in Germany, had followed up an idea of A. Beau de Rochas, in France, that the internal-combustion engine could operate on a four-cycle system. Many men, indeed, were working independently on the idea of a petrol-driven road vehicle; amongst them were S. Markus, an Austrian, who had road-tested an automobile in 1865; the Bostonian, G. Brayton, who had designed a two-cycle petrol-powered motor, and G. B. Selden of Rochester, New York, who had obtained a patent for 'a safe, simple and cheap road locomotive, light in weight, easy to control, possessed of sufficient power to overcome an ordinary inclination'. In Germany K. Benz and G.

Here was a Material Second to None

Daimler had independently built, respectively, a bicycle and a tricycle (petrol-powered forerunners of today's automobiles) and in France E. Levassor, under patent rights from Daimler, had adapted the automobile for highway use.

Particular honour should be accorded to C. E. Duryea of Springfield, Massachusetts, who evolved what is recognised as having been the first successful petrol-driven automobile in America, incorporating a four-horse-power, four-cycle, water-cooled engine, a spray carburettor, make-and-break ignition, two forward speeds and one reverse. Many others also played their part in the evolution of the automobile, including R. E. Olds, Henry Ford and Will Durant in America; A. de Dion and G. Bouton in France; Ferdinand Porsche in Austria and Germany; F. W. Lanchester, H. Austin and others in England.

(10)

Nickel Plate denotes Quality

THE upper reaches of the River Schmollnitz in Hungary trickled through a disused copper mine and some pieces of iron which had been accidentally dropped into the stream became coated with copper. The alchemists of those days erroneously thought that there had been transmutation of iron into copper, but it is now obvious that it was no more than the deposition, on iron, of metallic copper from an aqueous solution of a salt of that metal.[1]

Use was doubtless made, at an early date, of the method of heating one metal, such as copper, and coating the surface with another metal with a lower melting-point, such as tin, by the process known as 'wiping', or by the related process called 'close plating'. Ever since the beginning of the eighteenth century coating with silver by the close-plating method had, in point of fact, been practised, and in 1830 the first patent for introducing, *inter alia*, a layer of nickel silver between silver and copper, or copper and brass, had been granted in the United Kingdom to S. Roberts. 'Close plating' consisted in taking a base-metal article, dipping it into molten tin, fitting closely over the surface a thin foil of silver, and then passing a hot soldering iron over the composite. W. C. Hutton, of Sheffield claimed to have been the first to use this process in production of plated *Argentan* spoons and forks, and he applied the method to other articles also.

Again, using a solution of a metal in mercury, i.e. an amalgam, and applying heat, one metal could be coated with another. The Romans had applied gold to base metals in this way ('fire gilding'). Also, it was possible by hammering a thin foil or leaf of metal, such as gold, on to another metal, to obtain a clad article.

None of these methods, however, involved the use of electricity. In 1803 Berzelius,[2] working with Hisinger, 'ascertained by a numerous series of experiments the transfer of the elements of water and of neutral salts to the respective poles of the battery'. In 1806 Brugnatelli[3] mentions that he 'had gilt in a complete manner two large silver medals by bringing them into communication by means of a steel wire with the negative pole of a voltaic pile and keeping them one after the other immersed in ammoniuret of gold, newly made and well saturated'.

One scientist after another[4] added his quota of knowledge to these important electrical developments, but it needed the master mind of Michael Faraday to formulate the laws of *electrolysis*,[5] as this technique soon came to be called.

Although in his many records Faraday makes frequent reference to nickel and its salts, nowhere is there any indication that he personally tried to deposit nickel by means of an electric current. It was nevertheless his basic research which set other minds thinking along the same lines.

Michael Faraday, 1791–1867
Courtesy: British Broadcasting Corporation (Radio Times Hulton Picture Library)

Nickel Plate denotes Quality

The electrodeposition of metals from aqueous solutions of their salts soon became a subject of prime interest in scientific circles, superseding the process of 'close plating'.

In 1837, Golding Bird[6] described the electrodeposition of nickel, lead, iron, copper, tin, zinc, bismuth, antimony, silver, manganese and silicon, in crystalline form, by the action of long-continued currents of low voltage on solutions of metal salts. For example, after electrolysing solutions of nickel chloride or nickel sulphate for some hours, he had obtained a crust of metallic nickel on a platinum cathode. Bird's paper thus emerges as the first published reference in the world to the *de facto* electrodeposition of nickel.

Then came Joseph Shore, who in 1840 was the pioneer in applying for a patent relating to nickel-plating.[7] After disclaiming any novelty for the employment of a galvanic battery to deposit copper on to a metallic surface (wherewith to obtain copies of engraved designs, etc.), Shore specified his invention as a mode of treating manufactured articles by obtaining a permanent covering of copper or nickel to give a superior and preservative external surface. He advocated a solution of nitrate of nickel.

A French inventor, Henri-Catherine, Count of Ruolz-Montchal, composer and chemist, obtained as many as seventeen patents of addition to his basic one of 1841[8] and one of these additions, the twelfth, relates to the nickel-plating of copper, brass, bronze and iron, using a nickel-chloride solution. Ruolz-Montchal had studied electrolytic gilding and, on finding that process satisfactory, he generalised it by applying it to the electrodeposition of other metals, such as silver, platinum, cobalt, copper, zinc, and, in particular, to nickel, under the name of 'nickelising'. In a report made to the Paris Academy of Sciences, he stated that 'nickel can be applied very well to iron, and this might become an important application for high-quality locks, and above all for use in the clock- and watch-making industry, for meters, and even for machine parts which should be protected from the effect of air, thus avoiding the necessity for greasing these parts frequently'.[8] Although the use of nickel chloride was disclosed in the patent mentioned above, in his report to the Paris Academy of Sciences Ruolz-Montchal described the use of an insoluble anode with a nickel-nitrate solution, employing batteries as the source of current.

Meanwhile a German chemist, R. Böttger,[9] of Frankfurt am Main, writing in 1843, claimed that, of all the known salts of nickel, 'none is so suitable for nickel plating as the complex acid ammonium sulphates'. Böttger used this type of solution for coating copper, explaining how he made the nickel solution from 'impure metallic nickel', then the only grade available. Apparently the quality of the nickel coating Böttger obtained was excellent, but, primarily because continuous use of the bath was not feasible owing to the variable and unreliable grade of the nickel, and secondly by reason of its high price, many years went by before the process was commercially developed in Germany. It was, however, reported that in 1849 Alfred Roseleur of Paris plated cutlery, using the Böttger type of electrolyte.

In 1862 A. C. Becquerel[10] reviewed the work on electrochemical phenomena which he had initiated thirty years earlier, alluding to the electrodeposition of nickel from a sulphuric-acid solution of nickel oxide.

Nickel Plate denotes Quality

Becquerel is alleged to have been the first to make known a process of galvanic nickel plating by means of a neutral solution of the double sulphate of nickel and ammonia.[11]

A name pre-eminent in relation to the establishment of nickel plating as a commercial technique is that of Isaac Adams. Adams worked for some years in his home in Boston, Massachusetts, and in the eighteen-sixties paid a visit to Europe, during which he made contact with others interested in plating. In 1866 he took out a patent for the nickel-plating of gas-burner tips, but after initial success with his process, he found difficulty in repeating his results. This led him to study the effects of impurities in his anodes and solutions and in the following year or two he took out many patents describing methods of preparing pure nickel salts and casting nickel anodes. Among these was one claiming the use of nickel-ammonium sulphate as the principal constituent of the plating solution, and although other investigators had previously used that salt, this type of electrolyte came to be known as 'the Adams solution'.

Adams gradually developed the commercial side of his business, establishing plating shops in Boston, New York, England, France and Germany. He formed the United Nickel Company and that company licensed platers in America and Europe to work under the patents held by Adams and his collaborators.

Another pioneer in the nickel-plating field was Edward Weston,[12] from Shropshire, England. When only 16 years of age he delivered a lecture on electricity, illustrated by apparatus made by himself, and in 1870, after emigrating to New York, he joined the American Nickel Plating Company.

Galvanic batteries had until then been employed as

the source of electricity, but Weston replaced them by dynamos. He also improved the plating solutions; he made anodes by mixing grain nickel with a small amount of carbon and a binder of tar or pitch and subjecting them to hydraulic pressure, and he introduced various other innovations. But perhaps his principal contribution was the addition of boric acid to the plating electrolyte.

In England one of the first nickel-plating vats installed was at the Birmingham works of Bouse and Muncher, about 1874: they used the Adams solution, containing nickel-ammonium sulphate, imported from the United States, and cast nickel anodes containing as much as 6–10% iron. Up to fifteen hours were necessary to obtain a good deposit. Soon afterwards the manufacture of nickel salts in Great Britain was started.

Some seven years later John Thornton joined the old-established drysaltery business of W. Canning in Birmingham, which then became W. Canning and Company. The first catalogue published by the firm described preparation of a nickel solution, and also offered nickel anodes, nickel sulphate and nickel-ammonium sulphate. Two years later Canning started to supply concentrated nickel salts, and their nickel anodes and nickel salts were guaranteed 'free from copper, iron and foreign matter'. By 1894 Canning were giving in their catalogue practical information on the operation of nickel-plating solutions. Two grades of solution and salts were listed, one made up from specially pure double nickel salts, another prepared from double salts of ordinary quality. The catalogue also gave information on the use of cast and rolled nickel anodes, the purity of which was guaranteed at 98–99%.

Nickel Plate denotes Quality

Courtesy: W. Canning and Company

Nickel: An Historical Review

Knowledge of nickel plating soon spread elsewhere and in 1873 there was founded in Vienna, by Wilhelm Pfanhauser,[13] the organisation which later became Langbein-Pfanhauser.

Before long pure nickel anodes, in both cast and rolled form, were being produced by several firms, and by the 'eighties the composition of nickel baths had been considerably improved and the citric-acid nickel solution had been developed.

In Switzerland F. Müller in Zürich started up a nickel-plating plant but, owing to financial difficulties, it was closed down in 1884. Meanwhile, between 1882 and 1884 the Swiss Telephone Company started to develop nickel plating, and continued to operate the process for some twelve years. In 1895 Jean Zolliker, who had worked with both these firms, opened up his own nickel-plating house, which still exists. Simultaneously there were developments in Italy, where about 1879 Fratelli Bratke and Fratelli Chiodoni, both of Milan, started nickel plating on a commercial basis, for use in the manufacture of tableware and other items. In 1887 the industry spread still further, when Pertile Cesare e C. joined the ranks of Italian platers.

With the advent of the bicycle, nickel-plating of handlebars, spokes and rims soon created a growing and steady market. Furthermore, it was not long before many household fittings previously made in brass were plated, and acquired the nickname of 'nickel plate'. It had by then become a habit to call any article or project of a commendable character 'nickel-plated', and thus it came about that The New York, Chicago and St. Louis Railroad, because of its high-grade potential engineering status and the immense money backing of the concern,

Nickel Plate denotes Quality

gained the name of the 'Nickel Plate Road'.[14] 'Nickel plate' had come to denote 'tip-top' quality.

* * * * * *

Outlets for nickel other than in the electroplating industry had meanwhile been developing. One was nickel for coinage. As long ago as 1837, one Dr. Lewis Feuchtwanger,[15] in New York, had had the idea that an alloy of nickel would be suitable as a replacement for the small bronze coins then in circulation in the United States. He had made up two sample coins which were exhibited at the time in the United States Mint and elsewhere. Although the samples were marked 'Feuchtwanger's composition', it is stated in a letter which the Director of the United States Mint wrote on 4th January, 1838, to Senator Thomas H. Benton, that they were made of nickel silver. Dr. Feuchtwanger's proposal that his metal should be used in place of the copper coinage of the United States was not accepted.

The next development occurred in Europe in 1848–49. During a period when coins of all sorts were scarce the Austrian firm Berndorfer Metallwarenfabrik had made up, for use within its own organisation, tokens in an alloy consisting of 25 parts nickel and 75 parts copper. These tokens were withdrawn as soon as the dearth of small coins was over.

Switzerland was in fact the first country to pass, in 1850, an enactment officially adopting a nickel alloy (*Argentan*) for its coinage.[16]

About 1869 Theodor Fleitmann,[17] who had set up as a small refiner of nickel at Iserlohn, and had recently

Nickel: An Historical Review

Theodor Fleitman, 1828–1904

withdrawn from a joint enterprise with Joseph Wharton of Camden, near Philadelphia, decided to put up, at Schwerte in the Ruhr, a mill for making semi-manufactured products in alloys of nickel and possibly also in pure nickel. Fleitmann eventually got into production and managed to secure the bulk of the order for the cupro-nickel blanks required by Germany for its new 5- and 10-Pfennig pieces. A portion of the order was executed by Henry Wiggin and Company of Birmingham. The composition was 25 parts nickel and 75 parts copper. The coins were struck at the Mints of Berlin, Frankfurt am Main, Munich, Hamburg, Stuttgart, Karlsruhe, Dresden, Hanover and Darmstadt. The 'planchets', as they were called, met with approval because they took a good sharp impression from the dies: moreover, the alloy was acclaimed as durable in wear and difficult to counterfeit.

The next task to which Fleitmann applied himself was to improve the malleability of pure nickel, because the metal available up to that time often fractured when hammered, rolled or drawn. He found that castings resulting from the addition of metallic magnesium to molten nickel were amenable to working by hammer in both the cold and hot conditions and that they possessed a high elongation and could be readily polished.[18] In the ensuing years nothing has proved more effective than magnesium for combining with the trace of sulphur which causes most of the brittleness.

Fleitmann did a lot of research on the properties of nickel, in the course of which he demonstrated its resistance to corrosion in various media, and this led to its development for kitchen- and table-ware, and to widespread use in chemical plant.

The hygienic aspect too had been carefully studied, in many countries. In the light of present knowledge it is somewhat amusing to record that when, in 1886, the Emperor of Austria had been smitten by some inexplicable illness, its onset was mistakenly attributed to food cooked in utensils made in malleable nickel, and within a year a decree was made in Austria forbidding the use of that metal for such purposes. Subsequent investigations by Roos[19] however, categorically demonstrated the fallacy of that assumption, and, as a result, a resolution was passed in 1887, by the 6th International Conference for Hygiene, affirming that such prohibition was entirely without justification. The Austrian decree was repealed in 1897, and thereafter permission was unhesitatingly given to use nickel for cooking utensils. Later research and practical experience have amply confirmed the hygienic suitability of the metal.

Finally, a great debt is due to Fleitmann for his pioneer work on cladding various non-ferrous materials, as well as steel, with malleable nickel. The nickel used for cladding was customarily one-tenth, by weight, of the composite. It was applied to each side of the basis material, and, to secure good bonding, the steel or other material, before cladding, was flattened and cleaned. A pile or pack was made with outer facings of sheet iron, to protect the nickel from scaling, and the whole pack, after heating, was hot-rolled. This treatment so firmly united the two metals that they could afterwards be cold-rolled down to whatever thinness was desired.

Over in America, too, Joseph Wharton had been striving to make nickel malleable, and at the Vienna Exhibition in 1873 he displayed some pure nickel 'in the form of axles and axle-bearings'.[20]

At an exhibition in Philadelphia three years later Wharton displayed a series of objects made of wrought nickel, including 'bars, rods, a cube, a horse-shoe magnet and magnetic needles of forged nickel'. Nor did he intend to let the grass grow under his feet with regard to the vast potential outlet for nickel in cupro-nickel for coinage. In a memorandum[15] which he circulated privately, after naming the countries which had already adopted cupro-nickel coinage, he laid the spectre about the inadequacy of the world supply of nickel then available. He went on to indicate what conversion profit Russia, for example, would derive were it to substitute cupro-nickel for its various existing denominations in silver and copper coinage. Although Russia was unimpressed, Wharton did a valuable service to the future of nickel.

In quite a different field other applications for nickel alloys had been born. Alloys of nickel and iron (as distinct from nickel steel and nickel-containing cast iron) appear to date from 1754, when Cronstedt announced that 'among the metals proper, iron has the greatest affinity for nickel'. In the 1853 New York Exhibition articles made from nickel-iron alloys were shown by P. Thurber, who had produced them from nickeliferous limonite from Marquette, Michigan. Some time later J. Percy[21] referred to a number of nickel-iron alloys made in his laboratory in England, by one Richardson. The next step was in 1870, when a patent for the production of alloys of iron and nickel was granted to A. Parkes of Birmingham, England, but no practical results followed that work.

In France, as early as 1876, Maison Boulenger et Cie. of Paris had been making iron castings containing nickel. One such casting, containing 70·60% of nickel and 16·0% of iron, took the form of an artistic statuette of Venus de Milo, about one metre in height.

The opening-up of the nickel deposits in New Caledonia revived interest in expanding applications for the metal, and it is believed that Le Ferro-Nickel were among the first to produce, in a crucible, satisfactory alloys of nickel and iron. These experiments were carried out in France, at Montataire and Imphy, under the supervision of Ferro-Nickel's technical staff.

At an International Mining and Metallurgical Congress held in connection with the Paris Exhibition of 1889, a paper on ferro-metallic alloys, including those containing nickel, was presented by F. Gautier,[22] and in 1896 a Berlin scientist, M. Rudeloff,[23] reported investigations on nickel-iron alloys with nickel ranging from 0·05% to 98·39%. Although elaborate data on tensile tests, resistance to shear, and behaviour under forging and rolling were given, no mention was made of one of the most important of the elements, namely, carbon. But for that omission, this interesting and exhaustive set of experiments would have been of far greater value.

As the last century was drawing to a close, R. A. Hadfield, the eminent British steelmaster and metallurgist, carried out a research on a wide variety of alloys with nickel ranging from 0·27% to 49·65%, and, apart from minor impurities, containing iron as the balance. The paper which he read before the Institution of Civil Engineers in 1899[24] records his informative results.

A very important contribution was made by a Frenchman, C. E. Guillaume,[25] Directeur du Bureau International des Poids et Mesures. In 1889 iridio-platinum standards of weight and measure were introduced for the purpose of establishing uniformity in the metric system throughout the world. They were excellent standards in every way, but were expensive and, since the common measuring rules of brass or bronze were not accurate enough, Guillaume was given the task of finding metals or alloys which would have greater stability than brass, together with the other necessary properties. Working closely with the Société de Commentry Fourchambault et Decazeville, in 1898, he made the remarkable discovery that nickel-iron containing about 30% nickel had a lower expansivity than platinum. He also found that under thermal changes iron alloys with nickel contents between 15% and 25% had expansion characteristics similar to those of glass and were consequently invaluable materials for use in lens mountings, telescopes and microscopes. Shortly afterwards he found that the minimum expansivity occurred at 36% nickel. This alloy, which came to be known as Invar (short for invariable), was useful for the pendulum of a clock or the escapement of a watch, for chronometers and all kinds of precision instruments. (Since this discovery the expansion characteristics of the iron-nickel system throughout the entire range of nickel contents have been very fully investigated and there are now available alloys with a great variety of ranges of expansivity.)

Guillaume also found that certain nickel alloys lost their magnetism on heating but recovered it on cooling, thus providing a material suitable for circuit breakers and automatic fire alarms.

The first comprehensive investigation of the magnetic properties of these nickel-iron alloys, in various conditions of heat-treatment, was carried out by Burgess and Aston[26] who also studied the electrical characteristics of the alloys. Other workers who had been investigating these alloys reported that if a rod containing 25–30% nickel, balance iron, was drawn down into fine wire, it had a resistance to electricity 48 times greater than that offered by an ordinary copper conductor.

It was not long, however, before it became evident that yet higher electrical resistivity was obtainable in non-ferrous alloys of nickel. The copper-nickel-zinc alloys and later the 45% nickel, 55% copper alloy Constantan were quickly adopted for electrical-resistance uses and an alloy containing 84% copper, 12% manganese and 4% nickel, marketed under the name of Manganin,[27] with very low thermal electromotive force versus copper, was developed for shunts in direct-current instruments. Later other nickel alloys with 10% or more chromium, alone or with iron, which had been shown by A. L. Marsh[28] to have not only high resistivity but also good strength and resistance to oxidation at high temperatures, came into increasing use. These alloys led to the development of electric irons, toasters and industrial furnaces. It was also found that Constantan coupled with iron or copper made a good thermocouple for measuring temperature; and that a couple of 10% chromium, 90% nickel alloy, with a 95% nickel, 5% aluminium alloy was suitable for use up to higher temperatures.

One name of that period which cannot be left unmentioned is that of Thomas Edison (1847–1931). Although earlier workers had made some suggestions regarding the use of nickel in storage batteries, Edison was the first to propose this as a large-scale application. His patents[29] referred to the use of nickel receptacles and nickel plates to carry the elements and to hydrated nickel oxide as galvanic element. He used in his storage battery nickel flake produced by electrodeposition on very thin starting sheets.

Thus, in the early years of the present century, while nickel was in great demand for armour plate and ordnance steel, the metal, due to its versatility, was gradually proving its value also in the workshop and the home.

(11)

Foundations of an Industry

BY the time the nineteenth century was coming to a close the most valuable of the nickel-ore deposits then known to exist in the Sudbury district belonged to the Canadian Copper Company. That company, though its mines were in Canada, was still working at its experimental electrolytic nickel refinery near Cleveland, Ohio, on various methods of recovering nickel from matte, including treatment of bessemer-matte anodes by the Hoepfner electrolytic process and refining from a chloride electrolyte, using a method developed by D. H. Browne[1]. However, it had not yet been found possible to recover primary nickel at a realistic cost. Refining at Joseph Wharton's plant at Camden, New Jersey, by a chemical process, had turned out to be not only complicated but costly.[2] Consequently, the Canadian Copper Company had to continue shipping its nickel and copper matte to the Orford Copper Company at Bayonne, New Jersey, where, by the 'tops-and-bottoms' process,[3] nickel could be produced at a profit.

In 1893 Ludwig Mond had commissioned Bernhard Mohr, a mining engineer, to study the nickel-silicate deposits at Frankenstein in Silesia, as well as certain nickel ores in Nevada and Oregon, in America. Some nickel showings in North Carolina had also been examined. Learning, however, that the nickel and copper sulphide ores in the Sudbury district were preferable, Mohr went to that area, where he visited and reported on almost all the mining properties of the companies then in operation. The survey indicated that the majority of the nickel deposits in Sudbury—and those believed to be the best—had already been acquired by the Canadian Copper Company; a number were owned by small operators, including the Dominion Mineral Company, the Drury Nickel Company, H. H. Vivian, and others, and the rights to the others were held by a Canadian named Rinaldo McConnell and his associates.

Of the many nickel-ore bodies inspected, the deposits in the townships of Denison and Garson were adjudged to be the most promising, and Rinaldo McConnell, who was in a position to offer title to them, was invited by Ludwig Mond to visit him in Rome. McConnell, a robust and husky sort of fellow, of unusual intelligence, accepted the invitation. As a result of discussions held there, Mond acquired options over the Denison property (later named the Victoria Mine) and over the Garson deposit, a one-eighth interest in which had to be acquired subsequently from the Canadian Copper Company. Later he obtained an option on Levack.

In addition to the mass of details involved in such an undertaking, there were troubles. Problems of rights of way and apportioning of constructional costs had to be resolved; results of long negotiations with the Ontario Government and the Canadian Pacific Railway had to be awaited; property titles had to be investigated; and

Foundations of an Industry

Ludwig Mond, 1839–1909

finally a site suitable for a roast yard and smelter had to be found somewhere near Sudbury. Nevertheless, Mond forged ahead with his venture. Orders for equipment were placed and, despite all obstacles, mining and smelting on a regular basis began at the Victoria mine in the summer of 1901.

In the interim there had been incorporated in England, on 20th September, 1900, a company called The Mond Nickel Company, Ltd. Its first Chairman was Ludwig Mond and his two sons, Robert and Alfred, were among the Directors. A seat on the Board was deservedly given to Carl Langer, who had not only designed and operated the pilot plant at Smethwick, in which the carbonyl process had proved its worth, but had prepared the principal plans for the new refinery at Clydach.[4]

A freehold site of some thirty acres had been acquired at Clydach, four miles from Swansea, in Wales, chosen because each ton of nickel produced by the Mond carbonyl process required several tons of high-calorific-value coal, and good-grade anthracite was mined in that vicinity; a reliable supply of water was at hand; adequate metallurgical labour was available locally; and Swansea was a convenient port for shipping the main by-product, copper sulphate, to France and the other Mediterranean countries, where it was in demand as a fungicide in the vineyards.

Early in the present century the first flow of nickel pellets emerged from the new refinery at Clydach, but barely a fortnight had passed when several of the workers there were poisoned. While the dangers of carbon monoxide had been well realised, the nature of this new invisible gas, nickel carbonyl, was then almost unrecog-

Foundations of an Industry

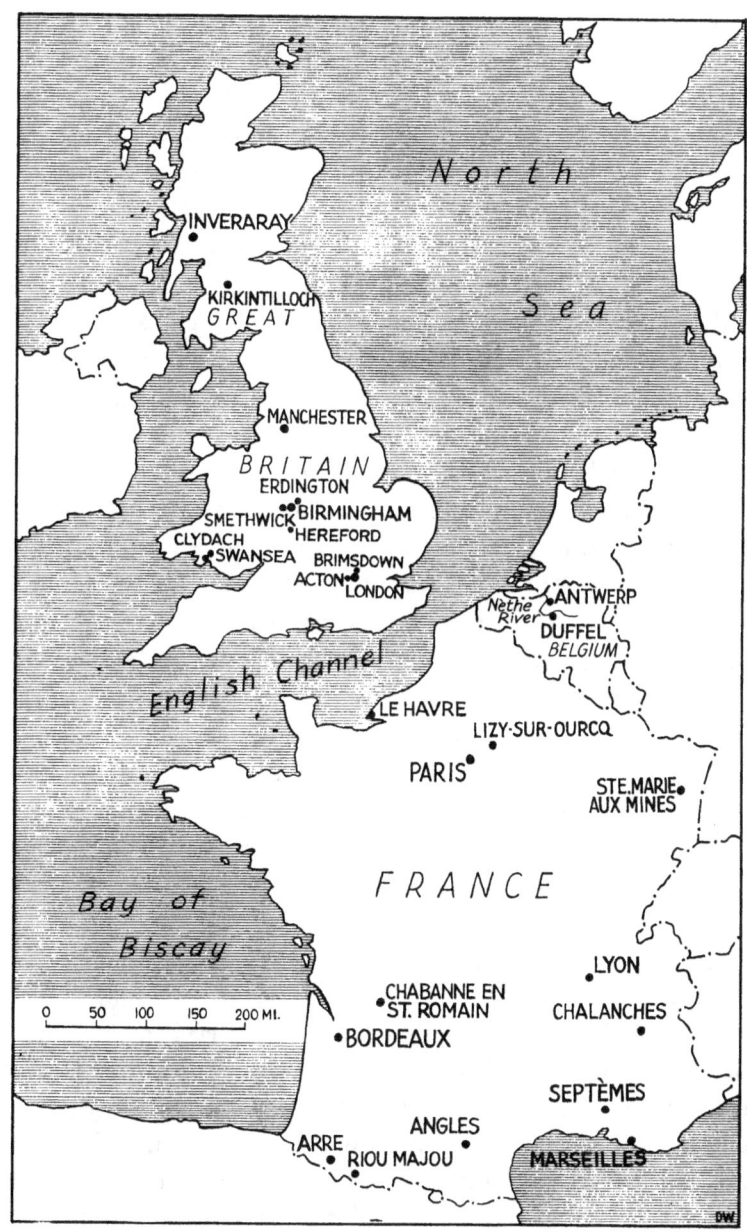

nised. Effective remedial measures were promptly devised. Labour disturbances culminated in 1902 in a strike at the refinery, and at the end of that year no more than £2,095 remained to be carried forward to the credit of the Profit and Loss Account. The Chairman himself paid the accrued Preference Dividend.[5]

By 1900 Ludwig Mond had become world-famous. A great lover of art, he had amassed a superb collection of old masters, which adorned the walls of his home in London and his Palazzo Zuccari in Rome. He entertained generously, and many of the savants of the day found pleasure in his company.[6] Ever a pioneer, he was among the first in England to install electric light in a private residence, having found in his stables, already choc-à-bloc with laboratory equipment, a corner for a gas engine to drive the electric generator. Unperturbed by the lack of space for horses and carriages, he hired a carriage and pair to drive him from his home to his offices in Westminster. For his visits to the ever-spreading works of Brunner, Mond and Company in Cheshire he reserved a special train from London, in which he and his staff would work, surrounded by blue prints, estimates and correspondence, until the express drew up in the private railway siding inside the plant at Winnington.

In the United States, on 29th March, 1902, R. M. Thompson, with Charles M. Schwab, brought into existence the first of the corporations carrying the name of International Nickel. This new organisation served essentially to unify the Canadian Copper Company, which was solely a mine-owning concern, with the Orford Copper Company, where the refining facilities existed. A few other smaller companies, including

Foundations of an Industry

Wharton's American Nickel Works at Camden, New Jersey, were brought into the organisation, but none of these contributed to the earnings of the newly formed company.

Thompson became the first Chairman of the International Nickel Company. By then he could look back on almost a quarter of a century of tenacious development of the industry, in which he had taken a decisive part. His administrative ability was matched by his enthusiasm for activities outside his work, particularly in the sphere of athletics.[7] He was, in fact, an international figure in more than one sense, and many of his friends were world personalities.

The Presidency of the International Nickel Company had been offered initially to Henry Gardner, at that time Managing Director of Henry R. Merton and Company (afterwards Henry Gardner and Company), the well-known London metal merchants, but, as he had not felt able to accept, the choice had fallen upon Ambrose Monell. Born in New York, Ambrose Monell had graduated as an electrical engineer at Columbia University. Joining the Carnegie Steel Company, he had risen rapidly, attracting favourable attention from the renowned steelmakers Carnegie and Schwab. At the unprecedentedly early age of 28 he was made President of International Nickel. He was a man of strong and decisive character, but had a pleasant, approachable and well-balanced personality. His wide range of human contacts was further extended by his competence at fly fishing, for which he gained an international reputation.

President Monell, in his first report to his stockholders (26th May, 1903), did not mince words in describing the far from satisfactory condition of the plants that formed

Nickel: An Historical Review

Robert M. Thompson
1849-1930

Ambrose Monell
1873-1921

part of his new organisation. He said that the Canadian Copper Company's smelting plant was 'badly located'; its furnaces were 'small and costly to operate'; there was a 'total lack of machinery for handling ores and materials economically'. The locomotives and cars were 'old, inadequate and practically worthless'. Of the Orford Copper Company he expressed the view that 'conditions here are not as bad as in Canada, but the plant is old, badly arranged, and expensive to operate'. He described Wharton's American Nickel Works as 'old and not arranged to the best advantage'.

The President then announced that all the plants of the constituent companies would be reconstructed and brought up to 'the highest standard of metallurgical and economic efficiency'. During the year a new nickel refinery had been constructed in Bayonne, New Jersey; a new smelter would be built in Canada.

Robert C. Stanley was appointed Assistant Superintendent of the Camden plant of the American Nickel Works. He had been educated as a mechanical engineer at Stevens Institute of Technology at Hoboken, New

Foundations of an Industry

Jersey, and as a mining engineer at the Columbia School of Mines. Going directly from college to the S. S. White Dental Company, he passed the few months after graduation in working on platinum and palladium alloys and in examining some platinum-containing placer sands in British Columbia.

Local scarcity of labour compelled the International Nickel Company to close down all its mines during the summer months of 1903. There was, however, sufficient ore stacked on the roast heaps to keep the existing smelter operating continuously, and such men as were available concentrated on the construction of the new smelter. Plans for the new plant included blast furnaces and converters to bessemerise the furnace matte to about 80% nickel-copper.

In 1904 two serious fires put part of the new Copper Cliff smelter out of action temporarily and during the period when, in consequence, smelting facilities were inadequate, some of the furnace matte was bessemerised at the Victoria smelter of Mond Nickel. By the summer, however, the first matte was tapped at Copper Cliff and it was in the same year that hydraulic power was harnessed at High Falls, on the Spanish River, in Ontario.

In New Caledonia in those early days labour was exceptionally cheap because it had been a French penal settlement, and, as the ore was then extracted merely by means of pick and shovel, no degree of skill was needed. Later, natives from adjacent islands in the Pacific took the place of the French convicts, and Japanese and quite a few Javanese natives worked at the mines. On the smelters, where the heat was intense, many Arabs were

Nickel: An Historical Review

employed. All the supervisory staff were, however, European.

The ferro-nickel or 'fonte' produced at first by Le Nickel could not be bessemerised and a second operation had been required to sulphidise it. As the present century opened, furnaces were installed at their smelting works at Thio in New Caledonia with a view to making a matte (62% Ni) by mixing limestone and gypsum with the ore. Cupola smelting was next tried, but in due time this was replaced by water-jacketed blast furnaces.

In 1904 war broke out between Russia and Japan and, after various engagements, the battle of Tsushima in the Sea of Japan took place on 27th May, 1905. Nickel-containing armour plate and huge guns made from nickel-chromium steel had by now become standard on battleships. A report on the battle of Tsushima stated, with reference to the six Russian battleships sent to the bottom, that there was no reason to believe that their principal armour had been pierced. Due to the injuries received above the waterline, the ships had been invaded by high waves which, pouring in above their unprotected decks, had destroyed the stability of the vessels. It was found that in the *Orel*, which was captured, the lightly armoured portions had been shattered, but that the chief armour had remained quite sound. The account of the battle[8] concluded by saying that the value of nickel-chromium steel armour was thus in no way challenged, though the manner of its distribution might require reconsideration.

This armada of armour in the conflict in the East unquestionably had a significant effect on the construc-

Foundations of an Industry

tion programmes for the navies of other great powers, notably the United States, Great Britain, France and Germany. The great race in the building of 'dreadnoughts' had begun.

Le Nickel had a substantial share interest in the Anglo-French Nickel Company, whose works were at Hafod Isha, near Swansea, and the Welsh refinery obtained its matte from New Caledonia. Other shares were held by the leading armour-plate and steel companies in Great Britain. There existed, too, the Steel Manufacturers' Nickel Syndicate, which was closely connected commercially with Le Nickel and the Anglo-French Nickel Company. That Syndicate had acquired options on certain nickel properties in New Caledonia, but instead of interesting itself in production, it entered into a long-term contract with Le Nickel, under which supply of material from New Caledonia was assured.[9] The principal British and European armour-plate firms had obtained their nickel supplies from the Steel Manufacturers' Nickel Syndicate, and that proved initially a formidable obstacle when, during the first few years of its existence, Mond Nickel tried to find a market for its carbonyl nickel pellets.

A second French organisation, financed by Maison Ballande, the shippers of Bordeaux, had meanwhile started operating in New Caledonia. Though prior to 1904 nickel ore had been shipped by Ballande to Germany, he had in 1906 built a smelter in New Caledonia, under the name of Société Hauts-Fourneaux de Nouméa, and had set up a nickel refinery at Duffel in Belgium, on the Nethe River not far from Antwerp, where he made a 75% nickel matte practically free from

Nickel: An Historical Review

Nickel Cubes
(each cube is about ¾" thick)

Nickel Rondelles
(each Rondelle is about 1" in diameter)

Foundations of an Industry

Nickel Pellets
(each pellet is about ⅜″ in diameter)

Nickel Shot
(under 1″ and over ⅜″)

Nickel: An Historical Review

Carbonyl Nickel Powder

iron. That matte was then refined by a process similar to that in use at the Le Havre refinery of Le Nickel. In order to take advantage of the increased call for nickel in the United States, Ballande later (1909–10) formed, in that country, a subsidiary called the United States Nickel Company. The company had a refinery at New Brunswick in New Jersey, where the iron-free converted matte from Duffel was roasted and reduced to metallic nickel. At first it was produced in cube and rondelle form, but subsequently only nickel shot and ingots were made by Ballande, for the American market.

Nickel silver at that time was a major outlet for nickel, and someone had had the idea that it might be possible to make, direct from matte, a nickel-copper alloy suitable for the manufacture of nickel silver. A prime mover in this significant development was Robert C. Stanley, who had been transferred from the Camden Works to the Orford Copper Company works at Bayonne, where he had materially improved the efficiency of the Orford process, lowered costs, and stepped-up production.

On 30th December, 1904 the Orford Copper Company enquired whether the Canadian Copper Company could supply a carload of bessemer matte 'free from iron or blown down to as low an iron content as possible'. When the carload of matte arrived at Bayonne, Stanley started calcining, saying 'we will draw the furnace only when it is right and after we have learned how to make the material, then we will work on increasing the draw'.[10]

The experiment was successful from the beginning, and to Stanley belongs the credit of being the man who first converted the idea into a material, thus becoming the 'father' of the nickel-copper alloys thereafter marketed under the trademark Monel. The first batch of oxide so made was taken to the refinery, put in a crucible with some charcoal, brought to the right carbon content and malleablised by the addition of metallic magnesium. Some of this metal was cast into a test bar, hammered out on the forge, and sent to Ambrose Monell in the New York office: the test piece made from that first melt was in fact stamped 'Monell Metal'. This was soon changed to 'Monel' with one 'l', in connection with trademark registration. Other nickel-copper alloys were later added to the Monel series, and this first alloy is currently designated Monel alloy 400.

The composition, as originally announced, consisted of 68–72% nickel with the balance copper, except for trifling impurities (0·5–1·5% iron, 0·073–0·15% carbon and 0·014% sulphur).[11] It was further stated that 'the proportion of nickel to copper are those of the ore now worked by the Canadian Copper Company, so that the alloy may be produced directly from the matte, at a cost not much greater than that of copper'.

Having this new alloy, it was necessary to learn its properties and possibilities, so that it could be developed commercially. As a consequence, in 1906 John F. Thompson, who at that time was teaching in the metallurgical department of the Columbia University School of Mines under Professor Henry M. Howe, was engaged to design, build and operate the company's first Research Laboratory, originally called the Physical Laboratory, which was to be located at the Orford Works.

It became apparent at once, however, that it would be fruitless to investigate the properties of the alloy until economic methods of manufacture had been stabilised. The two lines of research were therefore carried out side by side, and the alloy thus became the first material to benefit simultaneously from a broad and balanced programme of determination of properties and methods of manufacture, along with a search for markets which its properties would justify. Naturally, since this was the first time that such an activity had been undertaken, the 'broad and balanced' programme was a matter of gradual growth as the company felt its way along a hitherto unexplored, even untrodden, path. One activity after another was initiated and developed as the need for it became clear. These efforts resulted in many applications of this white metal having sufficient strength and ductility to make it suitable for engineering and structural uses where corrosion-resistance and

Foundations of an Industry

permanence were required; for example, some 300,000 square feet, in the form of sheet, was used to roof the Pennsylvania Railroad Station in New York City.[12] It may be mentioned, in passing, that over half a century later that roof is still in excellent condition.

In the United Kingdom no less important progress had been made. By 1905 the capacity at Clydach had been doubled, and nickel sulphate was being produced, followed, a year later, by the marketing of nickel-ammonium sulphate, both of which salts were needed for the ever-growing electroplating industry. Two copper-sulphate plants were soon in operation and the stage was set to develop concentrating operations for the recovery of the valuable precious metals present in the Sudbury ore. Within two years a reverberatory furnace and cupola were installed, as part of the cycle of operations of the process and to clean up wet-treatment and other residues, and in the following year still further expansion was being contemplated.

Ludwig Mond died on 11th December, 1909, at the age of 70. He had won universal recognition in the field of science and established himself, against heavy odds, as a successful producer of nickel. No one can deny his lasting influence also on the heavy-chemical industry in Great Britain.[13]

Alfred, the younger son of Ludwig, succeeded his father as Chairman of the Mond Nickel Company. After graduating at the Universities of Cambridge and Edinburgh, he had been called to the English Bar. From his earliest days he had been drawn to politics, and this led to his representing, at various periods, three constituencies in the House of Commons. He possessed great financial acumen, and industry soon claimed him.

Nickel: An Historical Review

Alfred Mond, Lord Melchett, 1868–1930

Foundations of an Industry

His mind dealt in terms of large-scale planning and, surrounding himself with able men, he was content to leave to them the working out of detail. When, in 1909, he became Chairman of the company, his star can be said only just to have appeared on the horizon, since he is remembered, first and foremost, for his part in subsequently bringing into being Imperial Chemical Industries.[14]

The mark which Alfred Mond made in the spheres of politics and commerce was matched by the distinction with which Ludwig's elder son, Robert, maintained the scientific tradition set by their father. A graduate of Cambridge University, Robert Mond, in the course of a lifetime's devotion to science, made an important contribution to progress in the chemical, metallurgical and other fields. His name will always be associated with the fundamental research which he directed on the carbonyl compounds of certain metals. Although his abiding preoccupation was with science, this elder son of a famous father was singularly versatile. Multilingual, he was an expert conversationalist; he will be remembered as a tireless peripatetic, to follow whose flow of words involved the listener in perpetual motion. A discriminating lover of the arts, he was endowed with an exuberant capacity for enjoying life and people.

About the turn of the century an imaginative young fellow from Sweden, N. V. Hybinette, who was accustomed to say that 'slag heaps were his playground', because he was born of a metallurgical family, also played a part in the progress of the nickel industry. He had been trying for some years, though at first without success, to refine nickel electrolytically. R. M. Thompson thought highly of Hybinette's technical ability, and had

Nickel: An Historical Review

Sir Robert Mond, 1867–1938

Foundations of an Industry

appointed him superintendent of the nickel department at Bayonne, but the two did not work easily together, and they ultimately parted company. Convinced, however, that there was a future for the refining of nickel by the technique of electrolysis, Hybinette obtained patents,[15] and for a while operated his process on the complex ores of the North American Lead Company[16] at Fredericktown, Missouri. In 1911 he started to produce nickel in small quantities in a refining plant at Kristiansand in Norway. This electrolytic method of refining nickel later came to be developed commercially on a substantial scale and with great success.

Up till 1911 most of the ore mined by the International Nickel Company came from the Creighton mine, but by 1912 the company had again started shaft-sinking and development at the Frood mine, where the existence of a large orebody was later proved. Even after the approximate position of an orebody has been determined by various preliminary means above ground, diamond drilling is nevertheless necessary to outline its actual extent. As it is easy for a bore hole to miss such a peculiarly-shaped mass of ore, a great number of drill holes need to be put down.

Five blast furnaces were in operation at the new smelter at Copper Cliff and a sixth was under construction. Five basic-type converters had been installed, to replace the original ten acid-type units. At Bayonne, where Stanley had become General Superintendent, the Orford plant had been considerably enlarged, and was producing about 35 million lbs. of nickel per annum.

Meanwhile Mond Nickel had raised its output in Canada, having replaced the original smelter at Victoria by a new one at Coniston. By 1913 two blast furnaces were in operation, space was available for a third one, and there were two basic converters similar to those at Copper Cliff. Although the main production of ore by Mond Nickel continued to come from the Victoria and Garson mines, its North Star mine had been re-opened, Worthington had been developed for mining, a programme of development had been completed at Frood extension, and diamond drilling was taking place at the Levack, the Kirkwood and the Blezard deposits.

In the United Kingdom rapid expansion was likewise taking place. The small ball-bearing-like nickel pellets, the shape of which at first had proved such a handicap, though their quality had never been challenged, had by now become highly popular with steelmakers and producers of non-ferrous alloys, and so pressing had become the demand for them that a third production unit had already been installed at Clydach. The first two plants there had had combined volatilisers and reducers, but in the new unit the volatilisers were separate from the reducers, and similar changes were made in the two earlier units. At the beginning of 1913 plans were in hand for still further increasing the output of the refinery at Clydach, from 4 to 10 million lbs. per annum.

Whereas in the early years of the century New Caledonia was producing almost double the amount of nickel mined in Canada, by 1905 the Canadian output had completely outstripped that of New Caledonia, where the annual rate of production over that period had increased hardly at all. Among the other producers, the principal ones were in Norway and Germany and a small amount came from other countries. World requirements of nickel had, however, increased at such

Photograph of an original painting by Simon Greco of a three-dimensional scale model of a nickel-ore body

Such scale models are used by mining engineers to visualize the size and shape of ore bodies and plan the most efficient methods of extracting the ore

Foundations of an Industry

a rate that although at the beginning of the century a total annual output in the region of 20 million lbs. had been ample, on the eve of World War I about three times that amount of primary nickel barely sufficed to meet the demands of the munition factories of the various nations, as they inexorably prepared for war.

(12)

An Unparalleled Demand

ON 28th July, 1914 Austria-Hungary declared war on Serbia. On 1st August Germany declared war on Russia and, two days later, on France. On 4th August Great Britain declared war against Germany and on 12th August against Austria-Hungary. Canada and Australia followed the lead of Great Britain. Eleven days later Japan declared war against Germany. Italy, Portugal, and Rumania and the United States subsequently joined forces with the Allies, and Turkey and Bulgaria came in on the German side.

The outbreak of war brought critical problems to the four largest producers of primary nickel: International Nickel, Mond Nickel, Le Nickel and Ballande.

Three thousand miles of German-submarine-infested Atlantic separated Canada from the Clydach refinery of Mond Nickel in Wales. Still more remote from the refinery of Le Nickel at Le Havre in France and that of Ballande in Duffel in Belgium was New Caledonia. The risks of war imperilled, too, the shipment of New Caledonian nickel matte to plants in the British Isles which belonged to the Anglo-French Nickel Company and Le Nickel. The French-owned nickel refinery at

An Unparalleled Demand

Iserlohn in Westphalia fell into German hands; so also did the plant of Ballande at Duffel.

Including her proven, probable and possible nickel-ore reserves, Canada had at that time the sizeable potential of 150 million short tons.[1] In 1915 the output of the Sudbury district was one and a third million short tons of ore, yielding some 68,000 tons of bessemer matte containing roughly 7 million lbs. of nickel. Both before and after the United States joined the Allies on 6th April, 1917, supplies of nickel matte from Canada were delivered to the refinery of the International Nickel Company at Bayonne, New Jersey, free from the hazards of war.

For some considerable time, however, there had been political agitation for refining of nickel in Canada, and early in the war a Royal Commission was appointed to study and report on all aspects of the nickel industry in the Province of Ontario.[2] At that period there were no nickel-refining facilities in Canada and the Royal Ontario Nickel Commission was called upon to report, among other things, whether any insuperable difficulty would prevent the refining of the nickel-copper ore of Sudbury within the boundaries of the Province in which the ore was produced.

The Commission took more than two years to produce its report. Its findings ultimately were:
   a. the nickel-ore deposits of Ontario were more extensive than those of any other country and facilities were available there for the economic refining of primary nickel;
   b. the richness and uniformity in metallic content of the nickel-bearing ores in the Province strongly pointed to the conclusion that Ontario nickel had

Nickel: An Historical Review

little to fear from competition; *and*

c. the electrolytic process appeared to be the most attractive for domestic refining of primary nickel in Ontario, better than all of the other methods of nickel refining studied by the Commission.

The International Nickel Company had also come to the conclusion that development in the art had reached a point where it became advantageous to have refining facilities in Canada, near the abundant supply of power from Niagara Falls. A site for a nickel refinery was chosen at Port Colborne, Ontario, with a planned annual capacity of 15 million lbs. of nickel. Construction was started in the autumn of 1916 and the refinery went into operation two years later.

The war had created an unparalleled demand.[3] A new company, British America Nickel Corporation, Ltd. (known as 'Banco'), in which the British Government had a large interest, was formed to produce nickel in Ontario. Acquiring certain deposits in the Sudbury area from the Booth-O'Brien Company (Dominion Nickel-Copper Company), Banco started to construct a smelter at Nickelton, Ontario, and a refinery at Deschênes, Quebec, not far from Ottawa, where they used the Hybinette electrolytic process, to which the company had secured the rights for North America.

Also, to meet the ever-growing need for nickel, the annual capacity of the Orford plant at Bayonne in New Jersey was extended to include 5 large nickel furnaces, 31 calcining furnaces, 5 refining furnaces, 2 copper-blast furnaces, 5 copper reverberatory furnaces, and the necessary associated converting equipment.

Once the United States had joined the Allies,

An Unparalleled Demand

Electrolytic Nickel Cathodes, cut into 4" × 4" squares

industrial uses in America were drastically restricted, so that ordnance requirements might be fully met. The United States Nickel Company's refinery at New Brunswick, New Jersey, owned by Ballande, was able to continue drawing matte from New Caledonia without interruption and throughout the war its nickel capacity remained at about 5–6 million lbs. per annum, thus giving strong support to the Allied effort.

In August, 1914 the annual refining capacity at Clydach had been slightly less than 7 million lbs. of primary nickel. Shortly before that date the Mond Nickel Company, the only nickel producer whose mines and plants were situated entirely within the British Empire, had carried through an important financial reconstruction, with the result that there were ample funds in its treasury. This meant that as the war developed the company was able to equate its constantly expanding capacity with the sharply rising requirement for nickel. Early in the war all strategic materials in the United Kingdom, including nickel, had been put under the control of the Ministry of Munitions, in order that they could be directed into the channels where they were most needed for support of the national effort.

For some years there had existed in Great Britain two nickel refineries other than Clydach; Erdington, near Birmingham, and another refinery at Hafod Isha, near Swansea. Further, at a partly-processing plant at Kirkintilloch, in Scotland, ore and crude matte from New Caledonia were treated and the bessemerised matte produced there was sent either to Erdington or Hafod Isha, where the matte was roasted and reduced with carbon, to produce nickel in the form of cubes or rondelles.[4] New Caledonian matte also was shipped direct to Erdington and Hafod Isha. The Kirkintilloch and Erdington works were owned by Le Nickel and it was from Erdington that the French nickel producers supplied primary nickel, mainly to users in the Birmingham area, for manufacture of nickel alloys. The Hafod Isha works had an annual capacity of 7–8 million lbs. of nickel.

At the outbreak of war there had been fairly considerable stocks of nickel ore and matte in Europe, but labour shortages and transport difficulties soon made themselves felt. Shipments of coal and coke to New Caledonia, and of ore and matte to Europe, were insufficient to satisfy the needs of the plants. The longer hostilities continued, the more difficult it became for

An Unparalleled Demand

Le Nickel to maintain production in Europe and New Caledonia; at least five ships bringing matte to Europe were torpedoed, and vessels which Le Nickel had bought were progressively requisitioned by the British Admiralty. Freight charges reached a high level, fuel prices increased considerably, and it was almost impossible to get spare parts for maintenance purposes. These considerations, and the fact that production was irregular and was dependent on the arrival of cargoes of matte, ore and fuel, caused a substantial rise in costs.

The Le Havre refinery of Le Nickel, and its plants in Great Britain, were forced to make successive reductions in production. In 1918 the plant at Le Havre was closed; in the following year the Kirkintilloch works, where it had been possible to carry on rather longer due to the arrival of a cargo of Greek ore, were likewise shut down. The refining plants of Erdington and Swansea worked-up nickel oxide brought from Canada, and deliveries to British steelmakers were supplemented by supplies of nickel bought by Le Nickel from International Nickel.

Near the southernmost point of Norway, four years before the outbreak of the First World War, an electrolytic refining plant had been built at Kristiansand, to treat nickel-copper matte from the Evje smelter. The company formed to operate that undertaking, Kristiansand Nikkelraffineringsverk Aktieselskap, had started in a small way by producing only about a million lbs. or so of nickel per annum, but had subsequently doubled that output, and meanwhile several improvements had been made by N. V. Hybinette, whose electrolytic method of refining nickel had now been well established on a sound commercial footing.[5]

In the Hybinette process the bulk of the sulphur in the

matte was first removed by roasting. The next step was to remove most of the copper, by leaching with sulphuric acid. The residue remaining was then melted and cast into anodes which assayed about 65% nickel. From these anodes cathodes of pure nickel and cobalt were obtained by electrolysis in special cells divided into separate compartments. When the anodes dissolved, not only nickel but also copper, cobalt and iron went into solution. The foul electrolyte was then circulated through purification stages whereby the contaminating metals copper and iron were removed prior to the return of the purified electrolyte to the cathode compartments of the electro-refining cells.[6] Not least among the advantages of this process was the recovery, from the anode sludge, of the highly valuable precious metals present.

The output of the Kristiansand refinery was, until the middle of the war, made available wholly to Germany, but later part of the Norwegian output of nickel was diverted to the Allies, under a long-term contract. Towards the close of hostilities the Kristiansand nickel refinery was partially destroyed by fire, and ceased production, though at a later date it was rebuilt and its capacity was considerably enlarged.

The wartime need for nickel was a serious problem also for the Germans and their co-belligerents. The metal was especially needed for armour plate; it was required also for torpedo compressed-air vessels, periscope tubes on submarines, gun barrels, projectiles, certain types of rifle barrel, bullet envelopes, parts of aircraft, engines of lorries, mine throwers, and numerous other types of munitions.

From the outbreak of hostilities the responsible authorities in Germany had prohibited all civilian uses

An Unparalleled Demand

of nickel.[7] First the German Chancellor issued a decree prohibiting the export of nickel, either as a metal or in semi-manufactured form. Soon afterwards the War Office established a Raw Materials Department, whose investigations indicated that altogether no more than about 6 million lbs. of nickel in ore or in partly-processed material were available in Germany. The Raw Materials Department formed an organisation entitled Kriegsmetall A.G., in which were included the principal German firms connected with the nickel industry. Kriegsmetall was under strict Governmental supervision, in order to unify the purchase and distribution of all nickel and nickel-containing materials. Moreover, to prevent rise in prices, the German authorities not only fixed ceilings for all nickel products but themselves purchased, at fixed prices, such nickel-containing steel scrap as came on to the market.

In Germany the shortage of nickel rapidly became so acute that early in 1915 all wrought and unwrought nickel products were requisitioned. On 1st May, 1915, all nickel anodes were compulsorily bought by Kriegsmetall A.G. and on 31st July of that year all household utensils having a nickel content of over 90% were called in.

The German 25-Pfennig coins in pure nickel, which had been issued before the war, proved to be a welcome reserve of metal, although it is stated that not more than about 220,000 lbs. of nickel were made available from that source. There were in addition over 24 million lbs. of nickel in the cupro-nickel coins (5- and 10-Pfennig), and although these coins were withdrawn from circulation in the third year of the war, they were later re-issued. Many were hoarded as a hedge against inflation.[8] Even

Nickel: An Historical Review

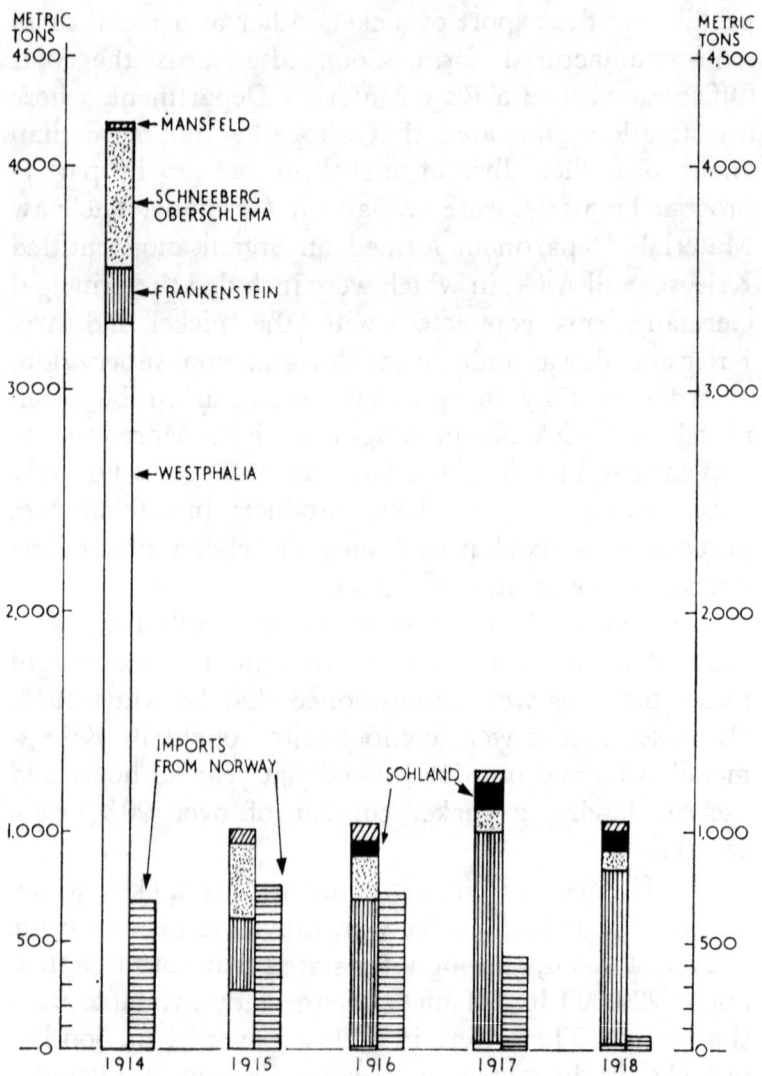

German production and imports of nickel, 1914–1918

An Unparalleled Demand

cupro-nickel objects and nickel silver goods were requisitioned. Yet another source of scrap was the nickel-chromium steel armour-piercing shells and their cupro-nickel driving bands, captured in Belgium and Serbia.

In order to increase the production of nickel in Germany, ores assaying as low as 0·8% nickel, together with certain refinery slags, were smelted by Friedrich Krupp A.G. in Frankenstein. The low-nickel-containing material was smelted into ferro-nickel, together with nickel-steel scrap, by Hermannshütte in Neuwied and by Mühlhofener Hütte in Engers. Altogether about 6 million lbs. of nickel content came from that source.

The State Saxon Blaufarbenwerke in Oberschlema, near Schneeberg managed to add to the wartime domestic production of Germany a further 3 million lbs. of nickel. Moreover, the Mining Department of Kriegsmetall A.G. re-opened certain abandoned nickel deposits in Germany, as well as in Austria-Hungary and in the conquered territories of the Balkans. Apart from the limited tonnage of primary nickel available in Germany when hostilities broke out and what was collected through requisitioning, Germany managed to produce from her own territory, in each of the war years, only a relatively small amount of nickel.

Notwithstanding all the hazards of importing nickel from Norway, in view of the constant vigilance of the Allied submarines, Germany did obtain from the Kristiansand refinery, in each of the first three years of the war, an additional 2 million lbs.

Despite the shortage of manpower consequent upon so many Canadians joining the Armed Forces, Canada's

Nickel: An Historical Review

effort in the nickel industry unquestionably made a significant contribution to the victory of the Allies. An indication of what was accomplished can be obtained from the figures given below for the expansion in output of nickel and copper from the Province of Ontario:

Year	Nickel in products produced lbs.	Copper in products produced lbs.
1914	45,517,937	28,948,211
1918	92,507,293	47,074,475

Although nearly two decades had passed since the three economic processes for extracting nickel had been discovered, only one new method, namely that of Hybinette at Kristiansand, had been added to that list. The French, in France and at their refineries in England and New Jersey were still using their process for treating New Caledonian ore; the matte made in Canada by the Mond organisation was still being treated in South Wales by the carbonyl process, while at Bayonne, New Jersey, the 'tops-and-bottoms' Orford process of International Nickel was still being used.

As the war came to a close new refineries were being constructed in Canada for the International Nickel Company at Port Colborne and for British America Nickel Corporation at Deschênes. As a result of the unparalleled demand for nickel while hostilities lasted there had been an impressive expansion in refining capacity. (See the table on page 156.)

An Unparalleled Demand

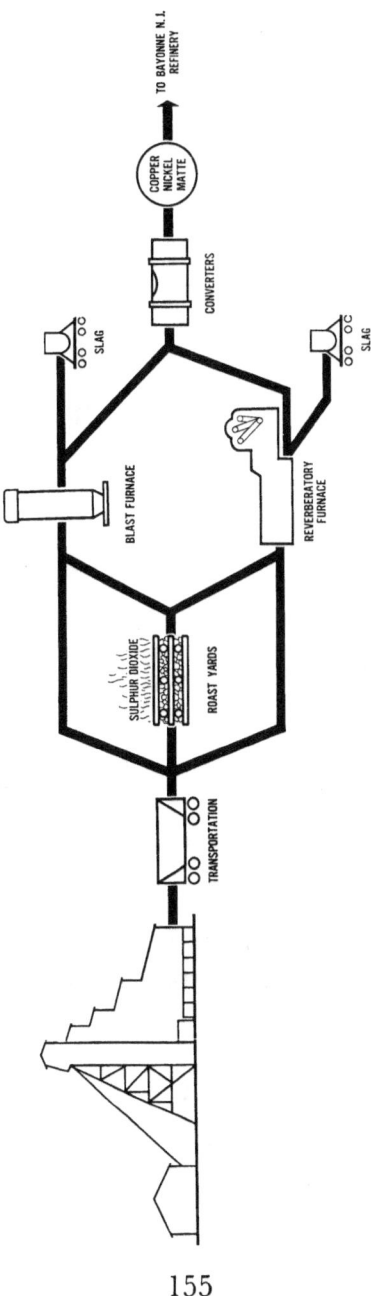

Flow sheet of Orford Process, 1918

Nickel: An Historical Review

Refinery	1914 Output million lbs.	1918 Output million lbs.
Bayonne, New Jersey (International Nickel)	35	60
New Brunswick, New Jersey (Ballande)	2	2
Port Colborne, Canada (International Nickel)	Not built	Construction nearing completion (target 15 million lbs.)
Deschênes, Canada (British America Nickel Corporation)	Nil	Construction not quite complete (target 15 million lbs.)
Clydach, Wales (Mond Nickel)	7	10
Le Havre, France (Le Nickel)	8	2
Erdington, England (Le Nickel)	7–8	Closed in 1919
Hafod Isha, Wales (Anglo-French)		Closed in 1922
Duffel, Belgium (Ballande)	8 approx.	Nickel production had ceased at end of 1914: refinery not rebuilt until 1921
Kristiansand, Norway (Kristiansand Nikkelraffineringsverk)	2	4

Anxious days were, however, ahead for those whose responsibility it was to see that peacetime requirements could absorb so great a spate of the metal.

(13)

The Bottom falls out of the Nickel Market

WHEN at last hostilities ceased, the task of healing the wounds of war faced victor and vanquished alike. Civilian employment was needed by millions of men discharged from the forces, and the situation was further complicated by the levels to which wartime wages had risen. Vast munition factories had to be re-tooled for the production of peacetime goods. Hundreds of thousands of tons of shipping sunk at sea had to be replaced. The pattern of life had also changed: the internal-combustion engine had ousted the horse, and sundry electrical appliances were finding a place in the home.

The nickel industry was hard hit. In the munitions race which culminated in the First World War fully four-fifths of the world's supply of nickel had gone into armaments.[1] Under pressure of the requirements of war, world production of nickel had trebled in a decade. Nickel had been needed for armour plate on battleships and tanks; for guns and projectiles; for bullet envelopes; for use in the vast quantities of alloy steels in trucks, tanks and cars. Nickel anodes had been consumed in great quantities for electroplated components; nickel-copper alloys, as well as considerable quantities of nickel silver, nickel-iron and other nickel alloys, had proved very useful in armaments. Malleable nickel, too, had been in constant demand, for sparking-plug points, meters, electric-light-bulb suspension wires and other equipment.

At the peak of the struggle the combined annual smelter production of the chief Canadian producers had soared to just on 92 million lbs. of nickel. When the long-awaited armistice was declared, huge stocks of nickel were on hand and the peacetime outlets for nickel, though important in their potential, were as yet incapable of absorbing the metal on the vast production level which had by then been built up.

Drastic economic retrenchment and curtailment of production were obviously the first step. In 1919 the ore hoisted in Canada was reduced by 62% compared with the previous year, and the tonnage smelted fell by 55%. One solitary mine in Sudbury, the Creighton, sufficed to supply the meagre quantity of ore required to feed the throttled-back smelter of the International Nickel Company.

By 1920 the total annual smelter output from Canada had been only about 60 million lbs. of nickel; early in 1921 the annual rate had fallen to a trifling 20 million lbs. and half-way through that year every operation at the mines and smelter of the International Nickel Company was completely shut down. Activities at the Mond Nickel mines and smelter were kept going, but things were only just ticking over. Finally, it was felt that a great saving could be effected by concentrating nickel refining at Port Colborne. During that year the Orford nickel refinery at Bayonne, New Jersey, was closed down permanently.

So deep was the trough of depression that the nickel refinery at Port Colborne, which had started up only in

The Bottom falls out of the Nickel Market

the concluding months of the war, was closed in the autumn of 1921. As that year ended the International Nickel Company announced that its sales of primary nickel had fallen off by 60%, and that sales of Monel alloy 400 had decreased by a third.

The ephemeral British America Nickel Corporation came into production only in 1920, but in the following year the demand for nickel had fallen to such a low ebb that the company was compelled to close down. A brief effort to reactivate it two years later failed, and ultimately its assets were sold at a foreclosure sale brought by the bondholders.

Although the Mond Nickel Company had managed to keep operations in Canada going on a diminutive scale during 1922, the International Nickel Company did not restart its smelter until late in that year, when it opened up with only two furnaces operating. The Creighton mine had returned to production a few weeks before the smelter, and the nickel refinery at Port Colborne had meanwhile re-opened in the spring of 1922.

At Clydach the high wartime rate of production had continued barely into 1919, but then had come the lean years of 1920–22, when only two nickel units were working and production of primary nickel in the form of pellets had dropped from 10 million lbs. to 4 million lbs. per annum.

In New Caledonia the depression was no less marked. Whereas during the peak war years the annual nickel-ore production had reached over 170,000 metric tons, by 1922 the yearly rate of output had fallen to 45,000 metric tons.

The earnings of the three principal producers had fallen off in an alarming manner. For example, those of

Nickel: An Historical Review

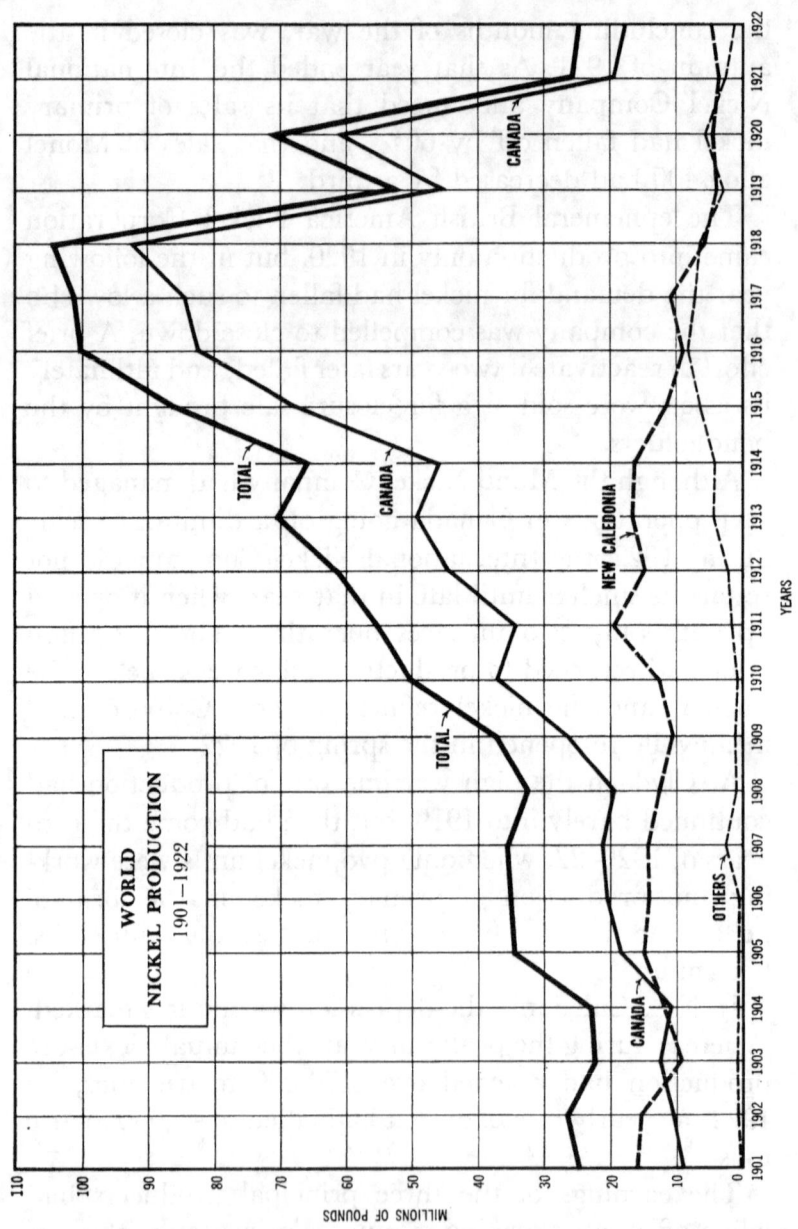

The Bottom falls out of the Nickel Market

the International Nickel Company, which in 1921 had dropped to $2,029,700, became actually a *loss* of $797,747 in 1922. The Mond Nickel Company's earnings, which for the year ended 30th April, 1918 had been £505,254, before allocating £250,000 to reserve, fell away for the year ended 30th April, 1921, to £138,165, though in the following year they partly recovered, to £247,423. For several years Le Nickel declared no dividends.

And just as the last straw broke the back of the camel, so it came about that a final blow bedevilled the plight of the nickel industry. In 1923 the United States, Great Britain, France, Italy and Japan entered into a Naval Disarmament Treaty which provided for the scrapping of large numbers of battleships and armoured cruisers and the abandonment or cancellation of similar vessels already under construction or still on the drawing board.

As the result of that Treaty, and the subsequent London Treaty in 1930, the United States scrapped warships of a gross tonnage of 1,018,000 short tons, containing 190,000 short tons of armour.[2] Taking a minimum average of 4% nickel contained in armour, such a tonnage would represent no less than 15 million lbs. of nickel.

In Great Britain, before the Washington Treaty, the Royal Navy had already sold capital ships of 550,000 long tons displacement, containing 148,000 tons of armour.[2] As a result of the two treaties, however, additional ships to a total of 676,000 long tons were scrapped, containing 167,000 tons of armour, and it is estimated that the total quantity of nickel involved in these ships of the Royal Navy amounted to yet another 21 million lbs.

Nickel: An Historical Review

Again, to the quantity of nickel in the ships scrapped by the United States and Great Britain, there should be added substantial tonnages for the ships scrapped by other signatories, including France, Italy and Japan. Furthermore, probably as much as twice that total of nickel went into the ingots from which so huge a tonnage of armour plate, guns and projectiles had been forged. A factor which further aggravated the situation was that the scrapping of so much armour on naval vessels inevitably threw on to the market thousands of tons of nickel-containing scrap.

This, then was the desperate plight in which the industry found itself. Only imagination, foresight and resolution could restore the balance. Fortunately, in the industry there were many men of great initiative and courage who had the conviction that new and diversified peacetime uses could be created for the metal.

First among the wholly civilian uses were the low- and medium-alloy steels containing nickel, with or without small amounts of chromium, the properties of which were being increasingly utilised in highly stressed components used in sea, land and air transport, as well as for structural engineering, such as long-span bridges.[3]

Transcending every other use as a potential outlet for nickel was, however, a material which at that time was not fully recognised or developed. That material was chromium-nickel stainless steel. The history of chromium steels, *per se*, goes back a long while. Over forty years earlier, the improved corrosion-resistance of chromium-containing steels had been pointed out by Boussingault,[4] and a few years later R. A. Hadfield had studied steels containing up to 17% chromium.[5] Early in the present

The Bottom falls out of the Nickel Market

The Quebec Bridge spanning the St. Lawrence River. Completed in 1917, it is the largest cantilever span ever erected. It contains 16,300 tons of structural nickel steel in eyebars, pins and trusses

century L. Guillet[6] had investigated the metallurgical characteristics of chromium steels to which nickel had been added and, shortly before World War I, E. Maurer and B. Strauss, both of Krupps, had obtained patents for a steel which was subsequently marketed under the name of 'V 2A'.[7] Two years later H. Brearley[8] patented the results of his researches covering 9–16% chromium steels, which, though containing no nickel, became popularly known as 'stainless steel' and were much used for cutlery. In America E. Haynes[9] was working on high-chromium alloys containing iron and other elements. Stainless-steel development in those early days has been reviewed in detail by Krainer.[10]

It soon became evident that the chromium-nickel stainless steels would find much wider applications in industry than had been open to the plain chromium steels. Tanks for transporting nitric acid and valves in the same service were among the first commercial uses to which this new class of steel was put, but in the early nineteen-thirties, even though some ten years had gone by since the basic patents had been applied for, the quantity of nickel needed for stainless steels was barely perceptible.

Another promising direction in which nickel was being introduced in association with iron was in the instrumentation and cognate industries, where materials of closely controlled and consistent physical properties were essential. Based on the work of Guillaume, in France, nickel-iron-base alloys of low thermal coefficient of expansion, developed by Société Anonyme de Commentry Fourchambault et Decazeville,[11] under the names of Invar and Elinvar, were proving ideal for watch-regulating mechanisms and other precision instruments, to obtain immunity from the effects of temperature fluctuation. In the nineteen-twenties certain nickel-iron alloys having high magnetic permeability were in the early stages of development, for use in telecommunications engineering.[12,13]

Among foundrymen there was already a growing realisation that the properties of engineering cast irons could be enhanced by the addition of small amounts of nickel, and there was also considerable interest in higher-alloy cast irons, to provide corrosion-resistance and non-magnetic properties. At that date, however, the use of nickel in the foundry was in its infancy.

Among engineers the original Monel nickel-copper

The Bottom falls out of the Nickel Market

alloy (Monel alloy 400) was justifying its early promise, and copper-nickel alloys were continuing to be popular for coinage; non-ferrous electrical-resistance materials were increasingly needed, and the market for the well-established nickel silvers remained steady. In the realm of pure nickel there was a large potential awaiting development, in anodes for electroplating and in wire and sheet for water meters. Nickel was finding applications, too, in components of thermionic valves, although the radio industry was then only in its cradle.

But even when the requirements for all these promising peacetime outlets were aggregated, the over-production of primary nickel (including inventories built up during the war) was staggering.

Nickel: An Historical Review

Robert C. Stanley, 1876–1951

(14)

The Metallurgist comes into his own

WHEN, in the early nineteen-twenties, the bottom had fallen out of the nickel market, Robert C. Stanley was at the helm of the leading producer, the International Nickel Company. This was most fortunate. In Stanley the company had a trained engineer who had had experience in mining and also in alloy development when he worked on the platinum alloys for the S. S. White Dental Co. He had also operated the Camden Works and had been successively Assistant General Superintendent and General Superintendent of the Orford Works, where he had done much to improve the processes and equipment. A man of great common sense and of the very highest integrity, he had the complete confidence of everyone who worked for the company, which gave life and force to his technical and professional equipment and enabled the company to unite in its time of deepest distress. A man of few words, Robert Stanley had a way of communicating his rock-like resolution through his eyes, set beneath heavy black eyebrows. He possessed an almost uncanny prescience, and once he had reasoned out the solution of a problem, seeking the best advice he could get, he backed his own judgment unswervingly and nothing could prevent him from driving his plan through to completion. Alongside him at that critical juncture was John F. Thompson.

More nickel business had to be created. This was not an entirely new concept, although it had not as yet been applied to nickel. Monel alloy 400 had paved the way for this since 1906, when it was a new metal. There were therefore men who had had fifteen or more years of experience in doing exactly this work, with all the history of unsuccessful and successful attempts to create a market, together with the knowledge that this involved a great many steps which, to be successful, must be correlated. Accordingly, the two largest producers set up research laboratories and each attacked this problem in its own manner. From the beginning the Mond activities were more largely controlled by the technical and scientific aspects, whereas the International Nickel Company had a more commercial approach, due to the experience gained through their work on the problem of developing markets for the '400' alloy. Their programme was based on the premises that all proposed applications had, of course, to be technically sound, and that assistance must be given to users of nickel in improving their products and finding markets for them. This outlook logically called for matching of properties to uses and a continuing concern with the details of service performance.

In the International Nickel Company's organisation this campaign of development based on research was entrusted to Albion J. Wadhams, a graduate of the U.S. Naval Academy, who had served at sea before becoming connected with the production side of the nickel business. He had started at the Orford Copper Company, and

The Metallurgist comes into his own

was later transferred to the Wharton works at Camden. He then became Superintendent of the refinery of International Nickel at Bayonne. In 1922 he was called to take charge of a newly named Development and Research Department, which took over the old research laboratory and made formal the activity of developing new products or adapting old ones to changing markets, as well as the rendering of technical service to customers and the dissemination of technical literature.

He chose as his assistant Paul D. Merica who had joined the company in 1919 as a physical metallurgist. Merica had already made his mark at the United States Bureau of Standards, and in the course of his work he had developed an extensive knowledge of nickel. Merica's work had been carried out to form the basis of an important Bureau of Standards Circular which, from the time of issue of the first edition[1] in 1921, has been recognised as one of the most reliable and comprehensive sources of information on the physical and mechanical properties of nickel and its principal alloys.

Not only did Merica bring to the new projects most competent scientific direction, giving stimulation and guidance to staff working on many and varied subjects, but his prestige attracted other first-rate metallurgists, resulting in the development of a research team of outstanding ability.

Although the initial research effort was a modest one, Merica's brilliant selection of topics for research during the next several years led to the opening of important markets for nickel in cast iron, bronzes and steel, as well as a number of nickel-base alloys. One outstanding programme, dealing with *age-hardening*,[2] led to the discovery of the influence of aluminium and titanium in nickel alloys, the combination which continues, even at the present time, to provide the basis for strengthening and hardening nickel alloys at high temperatures.

Among the topics given closest attention in those early days was the combating of corrosion, by using corrosion-resistant alloys or by electroplating. It was already apparent that alloying with nickel imparted considerable corrosion-resistance to many metals, although a full understanding of its appropriate fields of application had yet to be established. Results of research projects gradually provided a greater understanding of the rôle of nickel-containing materials in that field and several nickel-base alloys were developed, including, in 1931, the first of the series of nickel-chromium alloys to which the trademark Inconel was later applied.

In the middle 'twenties the Mond Nickel Company, then under the Chairmanship of Sir Alfred Mond, embarked upon an appropriate programme of laboratory research, in the hope of finding new outlets for nickel. A fundamental study was made of the constitution, structure and thermal treatment of alloy steels, in relation to their mechanical properties; the results obtained represented a major contribution to metallurgical understanding of the complex reactions involved.[3] At a very early stage the research team in Great Britain also became concerned with the problem of alloys suitable for service in sparking plugs and for electrical-resistance heater elements. This experience in high-temperature nickel-chromium alloys was later to prove invaluable as a basis for development of alloys which made possible outstanding advances in the gas turbine.

Although the research facilities and budget were on a modest scale at the Bayonne laboratory in the early days, bold and imaginative research programmes were organised. For example, a comprehensive study of the structure and characteristics of cast iron was carried out, in spite of the fact that this material had never provided a market for alloying elements. Particular attention was devoted to the problem of combining enhanced strength with machinability, and the studies soon proved that addition of nickel, with suitable adjustment of the carbon and silicon contents, was the answer to the problem.[4] The findings were duly communicated to the industry, and, as a result, foundrymen began to recognise the advantages to be gained by making appropriate alloy additions to their cast irons. First nickel, then nickel-chromium, and later nickel-molybdenum grey cast irons became standard for items in which a combination of good machining qualities and improved mechanical properties is mandatory.

It was found, too, that alloying with nickel and other elements was beneficial in white cast iron used for parts such as metal-working rolls, crushing balls and rolls in mining equipment, and for mill liners and other components. Addition of nickel (2·5–5%) and chromium (1·2–1·7%), produced a white cast iron which showed phenomenal hardness and high resistance to abrasion. To the first material of this type the trademark Ni-Hard[5] was subsequently applied.

There was need also for irons which would give good resistance to corrosion and to oxidation and heat, and there was growing interest in non-magnetic castings.[6] Research led to the discovery of certain high-nickel and nickel-copper cast irons, to which the trademark Ni-Resist[7] has been applied. The nickel content of these cast irons varies from 13·5 to 36%, with copper 0·5–

7·5%, and silicon normally between 1·0 and 2·80%. Where specially high heat-resistance is required the silicon is raised to 5–6%. The applications of these high-alloy irons are extensive, including chemical plant and food-processing equipment, components of plant used in the petroleum industry, power plant, pulp- and paper-making equipment, and precision machinery.

The uses for constructional nickel steels had expanded appreciably since their début, late in the nineteenth century. By the nineteen-twenties several rival or complementary additives had put in an appearance, including chromium, vanadium, molybdenum, and manganese. The rôle of these elements, *vis-à-vis* that of nickel, in low-alloy steels, called for critical investigation. The possibility that one or another of these elements would confer the desired level of properties more economically than use of nickel presented a competitive threat.

Expansion of the use of nickel in steel was furthered by research on the effect of nickel in response to heat-treatment and the relation of heat-treatment and resulting microstructures to properties. Service tests were made to demonstrate the economic and technological advantages of nickel-alloy steels in specific applications. Some major uses resulting from these researches were the adoption of nickel-steel boiler plate for high-pressure steam locomotives and the introduction of nickel-steel forgings for side and main rods, of nickel-steel axles and generator shafts for electric locomotives and of cast nickel-steel frames for locomotives and for passenger-car trucks. The nickel-alloy steels also proved suitable for more severe requirements such as machinery for oil-drilling and pumping equipment.

The Metallurgist comes into his own

During these two decades the automotive industry contributed substantially to the advance in metallurgy of steel; progressive increase in the size of buses, trucks, tractors and off-the-road equipment multiplied the demand for heavy-duty steels, in many of which nickel was essential. Nickel-containing steels were also adopted for many highly stressed parts of aircraft engines.

Further developments during the same period included a group of structural nickel-copper steels which, in the as-rolled condition, had about twice the yield strength of carbon steel, improved resistance to atmospheric corrosion, and excellent welding qualities. It was at that time also that the unique effect of nickel in making steel resistant to the embrittling effect of sub-zero temperatures was defined, a characteristic which was usefully applied in equipment for the de-waxing of oils by the propane method, and in other types of plant operating at low temperatures.

Of particular importance during the nineteen-twenties was the early commercial development of the chromium-nickel stainless steels. Recognition of the advantages of these materials came slowly. Although they gradually found application in various sections of industry, several years went by before they fully came into their own. (Following further advances in the metallurgy of these stainless steels, demand soared rapidly, and in the years to come they were to develop into the largest single outlet for nickel.)

Monel nickel-copper alloy 400 and commercial nickel constituted the main wrought, or mill, products available during the early 'twenties, along with a few modified versions slightly varied in composition to provide a useful combination of good corrosion-resistance, in a variety of environments, and attractive mechanical properties. In fact, Monel alloy 400 pioneered many of the markets now served by stainless steel and represents a major effort on the part of the International Nickel Company to achieve acceptance of a white corrosion-resisting material.

Subsequently, when need arose for stronger nickel-base alloys possessing equally good corrosion-resistance, other elements were added to the nickel-copper base, to produce an *age-hardenable*[8] alloy. The first age-hardening alloy of promise was a nickel-copper base containing about 4–5% of aluminium, developed in 1924. Later it was found that replacement of $1\frac{1}{2}$% of aluminium by about 0·5% of titanium resulted in an alloy which retained the hardening response of the 5% aluminium alloy but exhibited much better hot-workability. This alloy, which showed about a two-fold increase in tensile strength over the basic Monel nickel-copper composition, is currently designated Monel alloy K-500.

It soon became apparent that in order to promote growth of the nickel business it would not suffice merely to mine, refine and market primary nickel, but that it was essential for the producers themselves to make available, both in malleable nickel and in certain of its alloys, a wide range of semi-fabricated shapes, such as sheet, strip, tape, rod and wire. For that purpose the International Nickel Company, after evaluation of various sites, erected a new plant at Huntington, West Virginia,[9] where operations started in 1922. At first only rod, wire and sheet were produced, but during the first ten years of operation extra facilities were provided for the production of highly polished sheet, cold-rolled strip, cold-drawn rod, wire and tubing. In the second decade a machine shop and much new equipment were added,

The Metallurgist comes into his own

and induction melting was installed for production of a range of high-grade nickel alloys.[10]

About the same time the Mond Nickel Company also started to manufacture semi-fabricated products, in the belief that output of such products in malleable nickel would immediately ensure expansion in consumption of the metal. At their new plant in Birmingham, which came to be known as the Globe Works, facilities were provided for melting, hot-rolling, cold-rolling, wire-drawing, and the production of both rolled and cast anodes. However, before long it became evident that it was in the alloys of nickel, rather than in malleable nickel, that a worthwhile and lasting expansion in business could be brought about.

Alongside these developments the old-established firm of Henry Wiggin and Company, of Birmingham, had been a pioneer, in Europe, in the production of nickel silver, nickel-chromium electrical-resistance alloys, cupro-nickel, nickel-clad materials and other nickel-containing products. Following negotiations shortly after World War I, the firm became a subsidiary of Mond Nickel.[11]

It was not long before the production facilities of the Wiggin organisation had expanded to such an extent that it was necessary to purchase adjacent land, and soon afterwards Globe Works were closed down and all nickel and nickel-alloy activities were concentrated in the Wiggin Street plant. The developments sponsored by the firm at that time blazed the trail for new and increased business in nickel alloys, quite apart from the continuing production of nickel anodes.

Because of their excellent resistance to oxidation, coupled with high electrical resistivity and good mechanical properties, the alloys of nickel and chromium

Nickel: An Historical Review

Sir Henry Wiggin, Bart, 1824–1905

The Metallurgist comes into his own

had for many years been in demand as heating elements for various types of domestic equipment. Development of those alloys for industrial uses, such as heat-treatment furnaces and even melting furnaces, was an obvious corollary. This led, in 1927, to the formation, by Henry Wiggin and Company, of a new company called Birmingham Electric Furnaces Ltd., later abbreviated to Birlec.[12]

In the early nineteen-twenties nickel consumption had fallen to so low a figure as to be comparable with that of the closing years of the previous century, but energetic research into new outlets, backed by equally energetic market development brought its reward. Proof of the wisdom of the resolute policy adopted is reflected in the following figures:

World Production of Nickel

1922	1925	1929
24,000,000 *lbs.*	82,000,000 *lbs.*	124,000,000 *lbs.*

An unbalanced situation had been rectified.

(15)

A Time for Expansion

DURING the nineteen-twenties there were certain fundamental and far-reaching changes in nickel mining and refining activities, which set the stage for the spectacular expansion that followed.

The French-owned refineries continued to draw their raw material from New Caledonia. The malaise from which the nickel industry had been suffering hit the French producers hard. It was realised that drastic re-modelling of methods and more economic operation were essential. In particular, there was urgent need to obviate the necessity for importing coke from Australia.[1]

To develop the extensive chromite deposits in New Caledonia, the principal operating company, Sté. Le Chrome, had constructed, at Yaté, a 15,000-kW. hydroelectric installation. Le Nickel purchased from the Yaté plant electric power for the purpose of producing ferro-nickel or nickel 'fonte', by means of electric furnaces.

At the helm of Le Nickel at that period was Maurice Carrier (1862–1927). Joining that organisation as its Secretary-General, late in the previous century, Carrier had become a Director of Le Nickel during the First World War and its Vice-President in 1923.

A Time for Expansion

The other French producer, Calédonia (formerly Hauts Fourneaux de Nouméa), owned by Ballande, which had as a subsidiary the United States Nickel Company, with a refinery at New Brunswick, New Jersey, preferred to retain the old process, using coke. They therefore erected in New Caledonia their own coking plant, fed normally by local coal from the Moindou area, or, failing such supply, by Australian coal.

Economic considerations indicated the wisdom of combining the interests of the two companies and, although keeping their own individualities, Le Nickel and Calédonia merged their mines and plants into a single management company called Calédonickel.[2] The new concern had a five-fold programme, which included re-grouping of the more efficient nickel mines, including those at Thio, and closing down of the less efficient; streamlining the shipping system, obviously a matter of primary importance; centralisation of all smelting in a single plant; improving the quality of the nickel-containing matte for refining abroad; and production of 'fonte' locally in New Caledonia, by means of the electric furnace.

Consequent upon this reorganisation there was an upward surge in the amount of nickel ore produced in New Caledonia, although the grade became progressively leaner.

In the continent of Africa Rustenburg is the only area from which nickel in any commercial quantity has emanated, albeit as a by-product. In the area known as the Bushveld igneous complex in the Transvaal, South Africa there are certain deposits in which nickel-copper-

Nickel: An Historical Review

iron sulphides are associated with ores mined primarily for their content of platinum metals. These platiniferous ores, containing about 0·25% Ni,[3] have been worked since about 1928. The present-day technique is to crush and treat the ore by flotation, and the concentrate is smelted into a bessemer matte containing about 48% Ni and 25% Cu.[4] Part of that matte is refined locally at Rustenburg, into cathode nickel, and the remainder is shipped for electrolytic refining in the U.K. by Johnson, Matthey and Company.

In the United Kingdom, product research and market development work of the Mond Nickel Company had borne fruit and, in anticipation of the results in increased sales of nickel, the refinery at Clydach had been enlarged. Increase in production of pellet nickel over this period can be seen from the following chart:

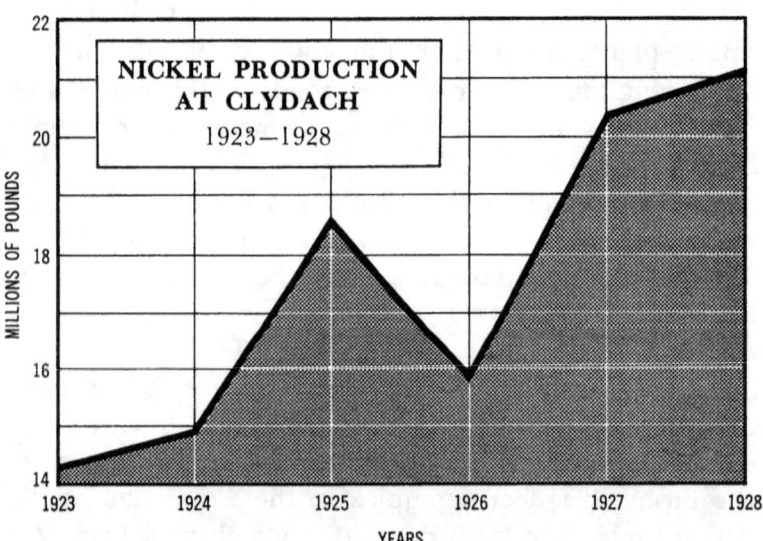

A Time for Expansion

Throughout these years the raw material delivered to Clydach was bessemer matte supplied from Canada and the company was taking steps to relate its expanded mining programme to the growing output of the refinery.

In 1928 a new nickel producer named Falconbridge Nickel Mines Ltd. was incorporated in Canada, to mine nickel deposits in the township of Falconbridge, in the Sudbury area. These sizeable deposits had been drilled during the First World War by the E. J. Longyear Company, of Minneapolis, Minnesota, but lay idle until bought by Falconbridge.[5]

Ownership of the refinery in Norway, previously belonging to Kristiansand Nikkelraffineringsverk Aktieselskap, passed to the Falconbridge Nikkelverk Aktieselskap, a wholly-owned Norwegian subsidiary of Falconbridge Nickel Mines. Although for a little while a small quantity of matte made from Norwegian nickel ore mined locally was also treated at the refinery, in later years the whole of the electrolytic nickel produced at Kristiansand has come from the mines of Falconbridge in Canada.[6]

At Kristiansand the mixed sulphides of copper and nickel, after oxidation to remove most of the sulphur, were treated with dilute sulphuric acid, which brings about preferential dissolution of the copper. The residue was then reduced and employed as anodes in electrolytic baths from which nickel cathodes were produced, using the Hybinette process.

The Port Colborne refinery, located not far from Niagara Falls, where ample hydroelectric power exists, had meanwhile considerably expanded its production of

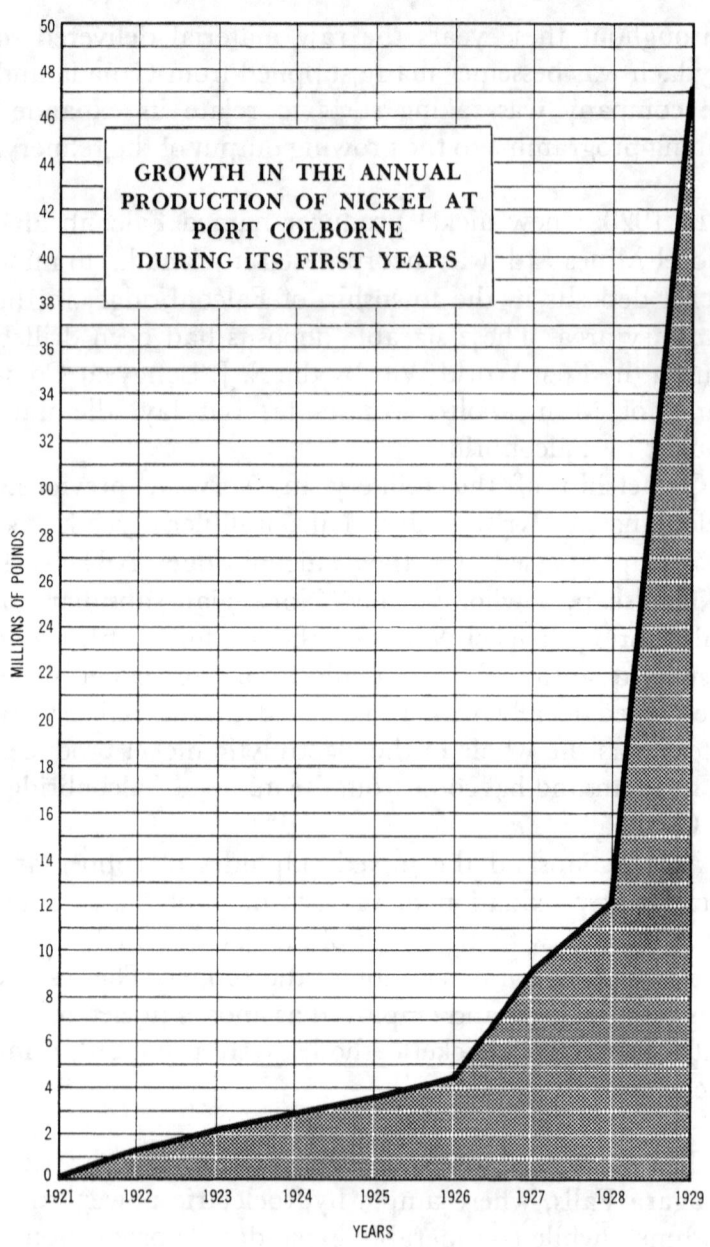

A Time for Expansion

electrolytic nickel. Briefly, the process was as follows. Nickel sulphide, resulting from the normal 'tops-and-bottoms' separation, was roasted to oxide. The resulting nickel-oxide was reduced to metal[7] and poured into moulds. The rough nickel anodes thus cast were electrolysed in tanks containing a solution of nickel sulphate and boric acid, heated to 56°C. (135°F.). Copper was cemented out by nickel powder produced by the reaction of charcoal with nickel oxide. When formed, the nickel cathodes were removed from the tank and washed in warm water, to remove any nickel salts present. Each cathode weighed about 128 lbs., and thirty cathodes could be stacked in each rack.

To supply the promising new markets they were creating for nickel, International Nickel and Mond Nickel had been preparing for increasing mine production in Ontario.

Frood mine, discovered in 1884 by Thomas Frood, was opened in 1899.[8] It was worked from 1900 until 1903 and then closed down, because the ore contained insufficient nickel to make it economically workable at that time. The main portion of the orebody was owned by the International Nickel Company; the other part, the Frood extension, had been bought in part and staked in part by the Mond Nickel Company. Diamond drilling in 1912 on the portion owned by the former company had shown encouraging mineralisation and preparations were again made to mine the property. But drilling operations at Creighton around that time indicated that that mine had sizeable quantities of higher-grade ore, and accordingly in 1915 mining of the Frood by the International Nickel Company was again discontinued.

Nickel: An Historical Review

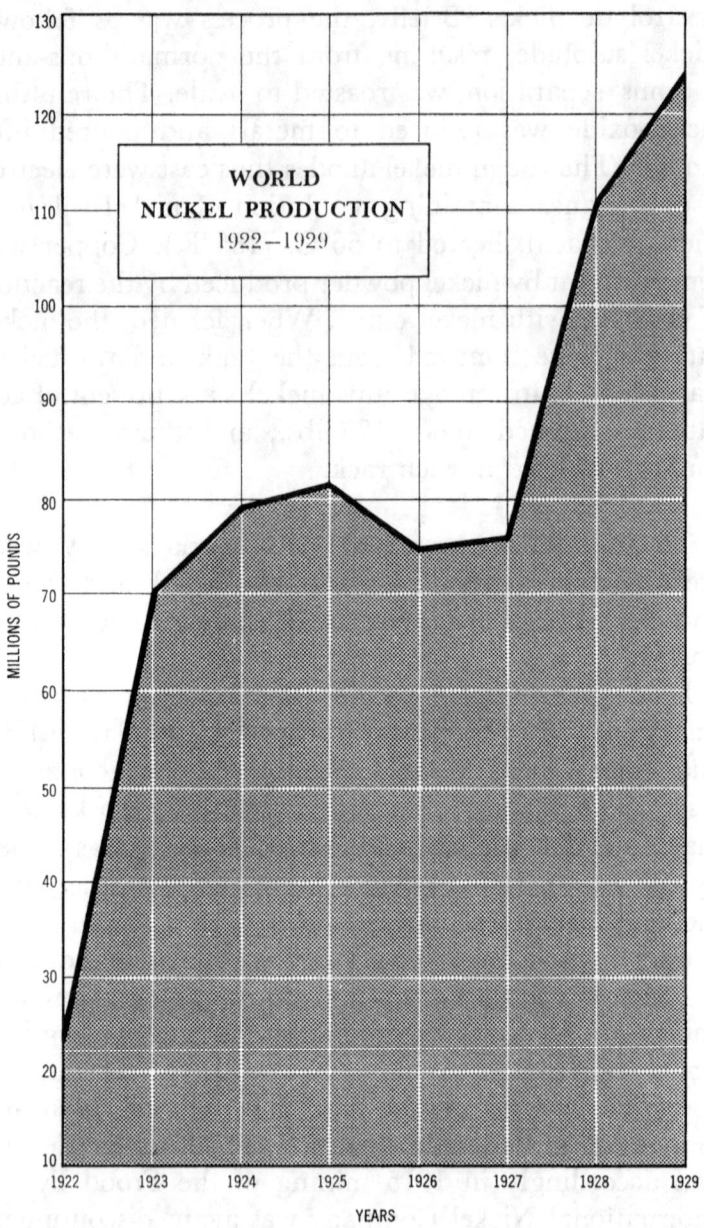

A Time for Expansion

Drilling had been started on the Mond-owned Frood extension in 1916 and had been carried out to just below 1,000 ft.

About ten years later the two companies each decided to embark on an intensive diamond-drilling programme in depth at the Frood mine and, as a result, a hitherto undiscovered orebody of large size was revealed, between the 2,000 and 3,000 ft. levels.

About that time[8] there was again apprehension that the Creighton mine might be approaching exhaustion (though later discoveries removed this fear) and a programme for active development at Frood was launched by International Nickel. From International Nickel's Frood shaft, already down to below 3,000 ft., cross cuts had been driven, and adequate reserves of high-grade ore were assured for many years to come. An outlay of some twenty-five million dollars was envisaged for improvements on the Frood mine, and for the construction of a new concentrating and smelting plant. Moreover, it was planned to draw upon Frood, where copper values were higher in the lower levels, to feed a new copper refinery at Copper Cliff, where electrolytic, instead of blister, copper would be produced.[9]

Figures prepared for Mond Nickel, with regard to its holding of the Frood extension, had confirmed the costliness of further development. As 1928 drew on, talks between the two companies started. The conclusion they reached was that there was only one solution for the economic and sound development of this important orebody: single ownership.

By 1st January, 1929, the two organisations had merged.[10]

(16)

New Growth of the Nickel Industry

IN the early nineteen-thirties the world was in the throes of a slow, though steady, comeback from the situation which had culminated in the financial crash on Wall Street a few years before.

The nickel industry started energetically on the road to recovery. Looking forward, the International Nickel Company, of which the Mond Nickel Company was now a part, actively demonstrated its faith in the future[1] by completing the plant and modernisation programme begun some years before. In June 1933 the Creighton mine was re-opened after having been shut down since August 1932, and production at Frood was increased. At Copper Cliff the rate of treatment at the concentrator was gradually stepped up, and a third reverberatory furnace was brought back into operation; the Coniston smelter was re-opened, with two furnaces under blast, and at the Port Colborne refinery six electrolytic units were started up. During 1933 the output amounted to 47 million lbs. of cathode nickel and nickel in oxide, and sales of nickel in all forms totalled 74 million lbs., an increase of 116% over the previous year.

Prior to 1933 the material processed at Clydach had

New Growth of the Nickel Industry

been bessemer matte containing 35–40% of nickel and 40–45% of copper, but this was unsuitable for direct refining of nickel because of the high copper content; indeed, concurrently with its output of nickel, the Clydach refinery was then annually producing about 78 million lbs. of sulphate of copper. Trials on several types of product arising at various stages in the Orford process showed, however, that more efficient extraction of nickel and higher output could be obtained by using as the raw material a low-copper nickel sulphide ('nickel bottoms'), produced in the course of separating nickel sulphide from the copper-nickel sulphide in the bessemer matte. A changeover was therefore made in 1935, when a 50% mixture of sinter and bottoms was used. This was subsequently abandoned, and from 1937 until after World War II partly-roasted nickel sulphide was the main raw material from which the pellet primary nickel was produced.

As a yardstick of development at Clydach resulting from improvements in materials and equipment, the following figures are significant: over the years 1902 to 1928 annual average production of nickel at that refinery rose gradually from 0·9 to 13 million lbs.; ten years later output was of the order of 45 million lbs. and, in 1939, as a result of much improved plant and process facilities, a record production of 47 million lbs. of nickel was achieved, an increase of 85% over the 1929 figure.

The Germans, too, were making advances with the carbonyl process.[2] As far back as the early nineteen-twenties I.G. Farbenindustrie had been carrying out research on the properties of iron carbonyl, for use in petrol as an anti-knock ingredient. This study led logically to experimental work with other carbonyls, including that of nickel. Badische Anilin- und Soda-Fabrik, then a subsidiary of I.G. Farbenindustrie, had available at Oppau, near Ludwigshafen on the Rhine, a plant which could be adapted for production of nickel *viá* its carbonyl. For other operations at Oppau nitrogen was being extracted from the air in high-pressure chambers, and as at that period some of those towers were idle, the technologists of I.G. worked out a process whereby a good extraction of nickel could be obtained by passing carbon monoxide, under pressure, through a nickel-copper matte of suitable composition. The resulting carbonyls, after separation by fractional distillation, were stored as liquids and the nickel was ultimately recovered as powder, formed by decomposition when the carbonyl was passed into a hot chamber. I.G. Farbenindustrie arranged to purchase, from Mond Nickel, a nickel-copper matte suitable for their process.

In the middle nineteen-thirties I.G. Farbenindustrie built a second plant at Frose-bei-Nachterstedt. The combined output met about one-third of Germany's requirements in primary nickel.

In the early nineteen-thirties the newly-formed Canadian firm, Falconbridge Nickel Mines Ltd., had declared its first dividend. So far that organisation had operated, in Canada, only one blast furnace and two converters, but in 1933 a new concentrator was brought into use, a new sintering plant was built and an extension was made to the original smelter.

Ore from the Falconbridge mines was separated, by a preliminary treatment, into four products: 'fines' for the sinter plant; 'raggings' (below $1\frac{3}{4}$ in.) for converter flux;

New Growth of the Nickel Industry

magnetic coarse ore for blast-furnace feed; and non-magnetic coarse ore for mill feed.[3] From the mining of ore up to the production of bessemer matte, the practice of Falconbridge conformed to standard methods. At that stage all the matte was shipped to Kristiansand in Norway and refined there by the Hybinette electrolytic method.

In the middle 'thirties they discovered, two miles south-west of International Nickel's Levack mine, a concealed nickel-ore deposit, which later came to be called the Hardy mine. To process this ore, the Falconbridge concentrator was further enlarged by adding a second ball mill and other equipment, and the smelter was also extended. A couple of years later Falconbridge expanded further, by acquiring the Mount Nickel Mine. The capacity of the Kristiansand refinery was increased to 14 million lbs. of nickel per annum.

It was in the nineteen-thirties that the Government geologists of Finland discovered a nickeliferous deposit far above the Arctic Circle, in the vicinity of Petsamo. Located near Kolosjoki, it was some 300 miles north of Rovaniemi, the northernmost railhead of the railway which ran up through central Finland to Helsinki. A hundred miles away to the north-east was the harbour of Liinahamari, on the Arctic Ocean, but that port, often icebound, was open for shipping during only a limited period each year.

The Finnish Government granted to the International Nickel organisation the right to prospect for, mine, and treat nickel-containing ores within a concession area which contained the Petsamo deposit. An extensive programme of geological reconnaissance and investigation by diamond drilling and magnetic survey, started

Nickel: An Historical Review

New Growth of the Nickel Industry

soon afterwards, established the presence of sufficient nickel to justify opening a mine and building a smelter. The mining was to be accomplished through an adit, or tunnel, into the orebody as well as by sinking a shaft. Steps were also taken to make possible the production, in Finland, of a nickel-copper bessemer matte.

Geologically the Finnish ore was sulphidic in character, akin to that of Sudbury. Although sufficient ore of suitable grade was proven to justify a substantial sum being spent on equipping the property, the deposit was never appraised as being of the same magnitude as the leading mines in Canada.

By the end of 1938 the mine-development programme at Petsamo had reached the stage of construction of an adit, over 8,580 ft. long, and a vertical shaft, already 680 ft. deep, had been sunk to connect with the adit. Surface buildings, including shops, storehouses and houses, had been built, and the smelter was under construction. A hydroelectric power scheme at Lake Inari, near Janiskoski, had been started, with the object of assuring a continuous and permanent supply of low-cost electric power, and to obviate the need for transporting oil or coal into so remote a spot. It was the intention that the matte produced in Finland should be shipped to Canada for refining, but within a matter of months the Soviet army was to march into Finland and all mining and construction activities in the Petsamo district came to an end for the time being.

In the years prior to World War II remarkable results were realised from the product research and market development activities of the International Nickel

Company and a striking increase in the consumption of nickel was the reward. It was a time of extensive development of new applications and markets for Monel alloy 400. The need for a better metal for handling milk was recognised and the development of the original Inconel nickel-chromium alloy (alloy 600) provided the answer for this market, again paving the way for stainless steel. It soon became apparent that this alloy had other, perhaps more important, attributes. Inconel alloy 600 was to be the solution of many problems in the application of metals for high-temperature service.

All branches of engineering were increasingly persuaded of the benefits obtainable by the use of alloy steels, particularly of such factors as toughness and ductility with higher strength per unit weight, improved fatigue strength, and enhanced resistance to abrasion and corrosion. The nickel-containing stainless steels were playing an increasing part in various industries.

The International Nickel Company's research laboratory for the development of new alloys and products containing nickel were greatly expanded in 1930 and re-located in a new building. In addition, a new research facility was established in 1935, at Kure Beach, near Wilmington, North Carolina, to conduct corrosion tests, on a scale beyond what had been possible at the Bayonne laboratory. The consumption of nickel for plating was substantially increased by the significant development, in collaboration with Harshaw Chemical Company, of anodes capable of dissolving uniformly under a wide range of operating conditions at low anode potentials. These anodes are not subject to the passivity characteristics of other forms of pure nickel when used as anodes. The anode characteristics such as purity, uniform dissolution and absence of sludging (i.e. local disintegration), required to improve the quality and acceptability of nickel plating were determined, and extensive laboratory work established the optimum composition and processing techniques. These improved anodes soon attained widespread popularity and their use has materially helped to raise the standards of electrode-position.

For cast nickel bronze and wrought copper-nickel and copper-nickel-zinc alloys a fairly well established market had already been developed. For example, at that time the invention of zip fasteners afforded an opportunity for manufacturers of nickel silvers to enlarge the market for these alloys in this service to the extent that at one time it was the largest market for nickel silver. Other important applications were found in springs, contact arms and telephone system relays. Ornamental work in architecture offered yet another potential market which was exploited for nickel silver.

The replacement of the reciprocating engine by the steam turbine in marine service brought about an increase in the severity of operating conditions and a need for better condenser tubes. This afforded the opportunity to open up a large new market for cupro-nickel, to replace brass tubes. These copper-nickel alloys were originally the 15% or 20% nickel type; later 70% copper, 30% nickel was introduced. This was subsequently modified, as a result of further research, by the addition of a small amount of iron, to achieve improved resistance to erosion by high-velocity sea water.[4] Large-scale installations were made in the navies of the United States and Great Britain and the same alloys were chosen for such important merchant ships as the *Queen Mary* and the *Queen*

Elizabeth. Sir Winston Churchill later paid tribute to the improved tubing, by saying that 'condenseritis' had been cured.[5]

The nineteen-thirties also witnessed a spectacular development in materials for permanent magnets. While experimenting with ternary alloys of iron, nickel and aluminium, the Japanese metallurgist T. Mishima[6] found materials having coercive forces far superior to those of the cobalt magnet steels. The preferred composition of Mishima's MK alloy was 25% nickel, 12% aluminium, and the balance iron. Later Mishima, and also W. E. Ruder of the General Electric Company, and others added cobalt, producing materials which permitted a lower cooling rate and thus made them practical for use in large sizes. These alloys, and others of related types, revolutionised the permanent-magnet industry.[7]

As a natural consequence of its notable success in building markets for Monel alloy 400 since 1906 and in expanding domestic nickel markets in America since 1922, the International Nickel Company in 1927 tackled also the far more complex problem of developing world markets in the same way. The idea was conceived of establishing bureaux of technical information on nickel, which would collect information from all sources, including the results obtained from the company's own research activities, and disseminate that information, in various languages, in connection with their efforts to perceive problems and needs which could be resolved with overall economy by nickel-containing materials. These activities would be supplemented by technical assistance given by engineers versed in the needs of their respective countries.

The first bureau established was the Centre d'Information du Nickel opened in Paris, with a branch in Brussels, the forerunners of similar centres of information in various parts of the world. Joseph Dhavernas, a graduate of the Ecole Polytechnique and formerly Manager of the Ballande works in New Jersey, was President of the Centre d'Information du Nickel until his retirement in 1950.

Realisation of the need for disseminating information had led the Mond Nickel Company to establish, as a feature of its Research and Development Department in London, a technical information section.

The great and increasing variety of uses for nickel-alloyed materials reflects the efforts of research and development by both International Nickel and Mond. Industrial and engineering problems requiring an improved metal were sought for study and research, and it was by that means that many new materials and new applications were developed. Their technical offices, located in the important industrial centres of the world, were of great assistance, both in regard to presenting problems appropriate for research as well as in providing technical assistance to metal and manufacturing industries.

Whereas at the peak of the First World War the annual consumption of nickel, then largely for armaments, had topped the 100 million lbs. mark, and then, in the early nineteen-twenties, had fallen away to a mere 25 million lbs. a year, by the late nineteen-thirties the demand had risen to no less than 240 million lbs., used almost entirely for industrial purposes.

These striking figures demonstrate beyond doubt the remarkable recovery which the industry had made. Concentration of effort on creation and broadening of

Nickel: An Historical Review

peacetime markets for nickel had met with spectacular success. Conditions thus augured well for still further expansion, but once again this promise was dashed to the ground by world-wide upheaval.

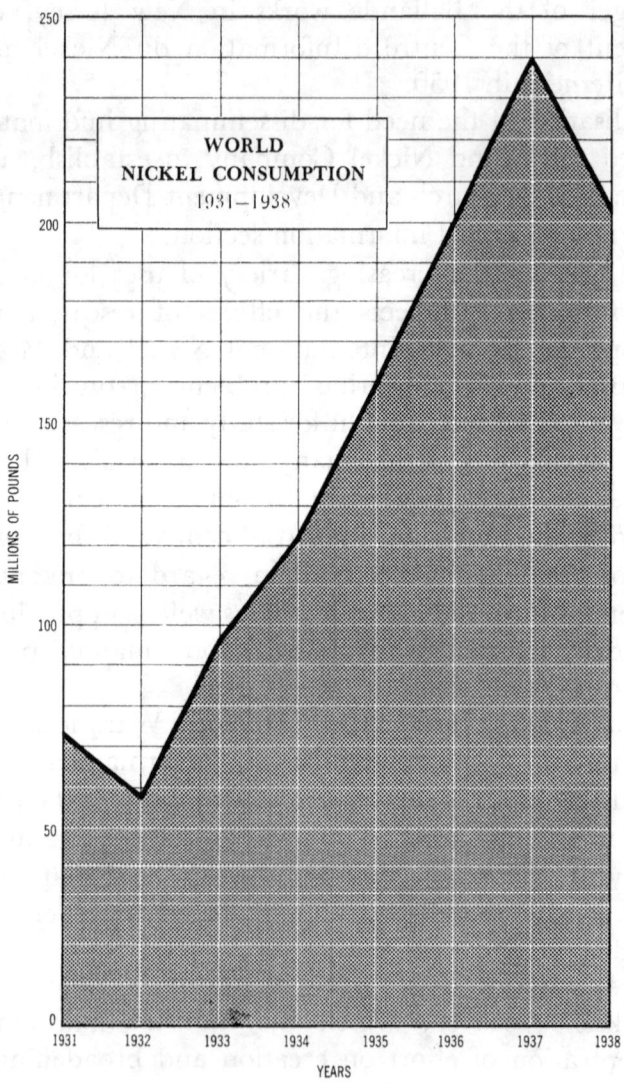

(17)

Nickel in Coinage

IT is computed that no less than 150 million lbs. of nickel have been used in coinage during the past 75 years.

From the earliest days of civilisation the difficulties of trade by barter gave rise to a need for coinage as a token of the value of goods changing hands. In international trading the intrinsic value of coins was a *sine quâ non*, and, quite naturally, gold and silver were ideal, providing a scale of valuation which could be applied without difficulty. Coins made of those metals were, moreover, easy to transport. The subsequent realisation that there was no longer a valid basis for maintaining a close ratio between the actual value of token money and its denominational or face value opened up the whole field of metallic coinage to base metals.

Even with base-metal currencies used for local trading, the idea that the value of coins should approximate their face value remained extraordinarily persistent. When, in 1857, a law was promulgated in the United States authorising replacement of the cumbersome copper 1-cent piece by a smaller 88-12 copper-nickel alloy coin, the added nickel served merely to raise the intrinsic value appropriately. Although the proportion of nickel used was sufficient to change the colour of the copper appreciably, as was pointed out at that time by the Director of the Philadelphia Mint, any advantages of the nickel addition were outweighed by concomitant metallurgical difficulties.

Over one hundred years ago the Swiss authorities decided to use *Argentan,* i.e. nickel silver, as a basis for three pieces, of 5-, 10- and 20-centime denomination respectively. Nickel silver as it is now known, is normally very easily worked, but unfortunately the Swiss authorities, in their anxiety to reconcile the nominal and actual values of the metal coins, decreed that a proportion of silver should be added to the alloy, not appreciating that silver and nickel are miscible to only a very limited extent. The alloy proved to be extremely intractable, and although, with persistence, they produced fairly substantial numbers of the coins between 1850 and 1877, they were finally forced to acknowledge failure.

In choosing a new coinage material, they first resolved to adopt, for all three coins, the 75–25 copper-nickel alloy which had meanwhile been successfully used in Belgium, the United States and Germany. In the case of the 20-centime coin, however, the decision was modified yet again, to satisfy the dominant desire for a material of adequate intrinsic value. Finally, in 1881, the choice for the 20-centime piece settled on pure nickel, which at that time was twice as expensive as cupro-nickel. Although it was the intrinsic value of pure nickel which originally led to its adoption for coinage, the choice was singularly fortunate, and the serviceability of the nickel 20-centime piece has proved so satisfactory that specimens of even the earliest issues are still regularly

Nickel in Coinage

in normal circulation in Switzerland.

Durability is now well recognised as one of the principal virtues of coins made from pure nickel. During manufacture, the pieces acquire a brilliant white colour and clean appearance, which are not marred by the combined effects of wear and corrosive influences during long periods in circulation. Good resistance to corrosive attack is an inherent property of nickel, and it is significant that both technical and economic considerations allow the metal to be used in an unalloyed condition for coinage, in a wide range of denominational values.

In some alloy systems the corrosion-resistance of the alloy is lower than that of its more noble constituent metal. This has given rise to problems in silver coinage when economic conditions have necessitated debasement and the adoption of complex alloy compositions. As long ago as 1914, commenting on researches into the wear characteristics of silver-copper alloys, Sir Thomas Kirke Rose, Chief Assayer to the British Royal Mint, wrote as follows:

'It thus appears that wear in circulation (of silver-copper coinage alloys) is a more complex matter than was formerly believed. The good wearing qualities of copper-nickel are no doubt to be attributed to the fact that they form homogeneous solid solutions. A pure metal, such as nickel, offers still more resistance to chemical attack'.[1]

The high melting point of nickel, 1,453°C. (2,647°F.), is advantageous, from a security aspect, making counterfeiting extremely difficult. Electric furnaces are normally used for melting, and when the metal is molten it is treated, before casting into ingot moulds, with very small additions of manganese and magnesium, so that the required degree of malleability is achieved. Nickel is easily manipulated, with modern metallurgical equipment, into the form of strip, as required for coin manufacture, and it should be noted that, in one instance at least, pure nickel coinage strip has been produced by direct rolling of electrolytic nickel cathodes without intermediate melting.

The ingots are hot-rolled to strip of intermediate thickness, which is then cold-rolled with great accuracy to the finished thickness required. At this stage the material is in a relatively hard condition, eminently suitable for punching-out the coin blanks, but this degree of hardness would be too high for the actual minting operation. Blanks punched out of the hard-rolled strip are therefore softened by annealing.

Nickel coin blanks are bright-annealed in furnaces provided with non-oxidising atmospheres, thus avoiding scale formation. Before minting, the blanks are tumbled in rotating barrels, to produce a clean matt surface. When the nickel blanks so prepared are struck between minting dies, a true and sharp impression is obtained; such is the ductility of the metal that the most elaborate and intricate designs can be accommodated. To facilitate identification by touch in purse or pocket, polygonal-shaped coins have been issued. Yet another distinguishing feature, not infrequently used, is to provide certain coins with a central hole. This confers the additional benefit of making it possible for the coins to be threaded on a cord. To provide a further measure of security, the edges of some coins are milled or indented.

Not unnaturally, in view of the similarity in colour, pure nickel coins have been introduced chiefly in replacement of pieces previously minted in silver alloys.

Nickel in Coinage

The largest pure nickel coin to date is a 20-franc Belgian piece weighing 20 grams, issued in 1931; the smallest nickel coin is the current Netherlands 10-cent piece, which has a weight of only 1·5 grams.

Since 1881, when the first pure nickel coin was issued in Switzerland, no fewer than 45 countries have used this metal, for a total of 134 different coins.[2] Following the favourable experience of Switzerland with pure nickel currency, the authorities of the dual monarchy of Austria-Hungary, when reforming the monetary system in 1892, adopted it for 20- and 10-heller pieces. More than 550 million of these coins were struck.

Between 1902 and 1923 Italy on five occasions selected pure nickel for coinage. In France a pure nickel 25-centime coin was issued in 1903, but it failed to obtain public approval due to its similarity, in size and appearance, to the 1-franc silver piece. In 1913 a perforated 25-centime coin was authorised, and the same law provided also for the issue of pure nickel 10- and 5-centime pieces. However, owing to wartime needs for economy in materials, only about one and a half million of these coins were issued. In 1933 a pure nickel 5-franc piece was put into circulation, but in the following year it was superseded by a larger coin of the same denomination. In the minting programme which accompanied the revaluation of the franc on 1st January, 1960 pure nickel was selected for the new 1-franc piece. In line with France, the Principality of Monaco subsequently issued a pure nickel 1-franc piece of appropriate design.

Before 1914 pure nickel was used in the currencies of the Danish West Indies (1905), Mexico (1906), Montenegro (1906), Germany (1909), Turkey (1911) and

Nickel: An Historical Review

New 1-franc French coin of pure nickel

Greece (1913). A number of pure nickel coins were also struck in 1908 for Zanzibar, but these were not issued.

The political and economic reorganisation following World War I gave rise to many minting programmes and pure nickel coins were successively introduced in the revised currencies of Belgium, Luxembourg, Latvia, Albania, Angola, Morocco, Siam, Canada, Irish Free State, Ecuador, The Vatican State, Iraq, Danzig, Abyssinia, Japan, China, Rumania, Hong Kong, the Basque Republic, Czechoslovakia, the Argentine and Indo-China.

The Canadian 5-cent piece was first issued in pure nickel in 1922, and the famous 'beaver' design was adopted in 1937. Nickel has been used continuously for this coin through to the present day, with the exception of periods during the Second World War and the Korean emergency, when, in order to release nickel for strategic uses, brass or plated steel was temporarily substituted. Since 1945 the largest single use of pure nickel coinage has been for the replacement of the silver rupee, half rupee and quarter rupee throughout the Indian sub-continent.

Nickel in Coinage

As examples of pure nickel coin designs of outstanding artistic merit, the following deserve special mention:

Country	Date of issue	Denomination
Albania	1926	$\frac{1}{2}$ lek
Belgium	1923	2 francs
Canada	1922	5 cents
Czechoslovakia	1938	5 crowns
Danzig	1935	10 gulden
France	1934	5 francs
Germany	1933	1 Reichsmark
Greece	1959	10 drachmae
India	1947	1 rupee
Iraq	1932	10 fils
Irish Free State	1928	3 pence
Italy	1923	2 lire
Japan	1956	50 yen
Netherlands	1950	10 cents
Poland	1929	1 zloty
Switzerland	1881	20 centimes
Turkey	1925	25 piastres
Vatican State	1931	2 lire

Not the least attractive feature of pure nickel coins is their pleasing 'feel' when handled. Although this quality cannot be precisely defined, it is nevertheless a characteristic which lends prestige to a coin. One property of nickel which distinguishes it from any other commonly used materials is its strong magnetic character, and this is naturally of great value in sorting, as well as in the detection of counterfeit coins.

Nickel: An Historical Review

Canada
5 cent, 1922
Beaver

Irish Free State
3d 1928
Wild hare

Germany
1 mark, 1933
German Eagle

Belgium
2 franc, 1923
Allegorical Belgia
wounded but victorious

Poland
1 zloty, 1929
Polish eagle

Czechoslovakia
5 Crown, 1938
Head of Father Hlinka

Vatican State
2 lire, 1931
Good Shepherd carrying
a lamb

France
5 franc, 1934
Head of Liberty

India
1 rupee, 1947
Tiger

Typical Pure Nickel Coins

Nickel in Coinage

Switzerland
20 centime, 1881

Netherlands
10 cent, 1950
Head of Queen Juliana

Albania,
½ lek, 1926
Hercules wrestling with lion

Iraq
10 fils, 1932
Head of King Faisal 1

Italy
2 lire, 1923
Head of King
Victor Emanuel III

Japan
50 yen, 1956
Chrysanthemum

Greece
5 drachma, 1930
Phoenix emerging
from flames

Danzig
10 gulden, 1935
Danzig city hall and star

Turkey
25 piastre, 1925
Oak spray

Typical Pure Nickel Coins

Nickel: An Historical Review

When nickel is used as an addition element in coinage materials its properties are conferred on the alloy to a degree roughly corresponding with the amount of nickel added. Thus, the normal 75-25 cupro-nickel, consisting of three parts copper and one part nickel, has an essentially white appearance, although its colour has a tinge of the copper which is its major constituent.

The use of 75-25-type cupro-nickel for coinage, since nickel was identified, dates from 1860, when it was adopted by Belgium for 20-, 10- and 5-centime pieces. The decision in favour of this alloy followed an exhaustive enquiry by two Commissions, which decided that it combined the merit of simple proportions with ease of melting and fabrication. The melting point of the alloy is approximately 1,200°C. (2,192°F.), and melting can be carried out in relatively simple crucible-type furnaces fired by gas, oil or solid fuel. The example of Belgium was followed five years later by the United States, where, in 1865, a 3-cent coin of 75-25 cupro-nickel was authorised. In the following year the world-renowned 5-cent coin, the so-called 'nickel', was introduced, minted in the same alloy. The 3-cent coin proved inconveniently small, and was demonetised in 1890, but demand for the 5-cent piece increased rapidly; this was due, possibly, to the introduction of slot machines and to the use of the 5-cent coin in buses and subways, also for a drink of beer, a 'five-cent cigar' and many other popular commodities then available for a 'nickel'. By 1958 the total number of 'nickels' which had been issued in the United States exceeded four thousand millions.

There is scarcely a country in the world which, at some time or another, has not had one or more of its denominations in cupro-nickel, and today, in terms of

Nickel in Coinage

monetary value, 75–25 cupro-nickel is undoubtedly the most widely used of all base-metal coinage materials. When it was decided, in 1946, to repay the silver which Britain had borrowed from the United States during the war, the amount required was withdrawn from the Imperial coinage and the coins withdrawn were replaced by issues in 75–25 cupro-nickel.

Copper-nickel alloys of proportions other than the customary 3–1 type have from time to time been employed for coinage: an 80–20 copper-nickel alloy has been used in Czechoslovakia, an 85–15 alloy in Indonesia and a 90–10 alloy by Estonia, whilst in Turkey coins were once issued in an alloy containing only 25% of copper, with 75% of nickel.

Cupro-nickel coinage has gained general acceptance, and in some instances has been received with considerable enthusiasm. For example, in Fiji, in the nineteen-thirties, cupro-nickel pennies and halfpennies were substituted for bronze coins, since the native islanders had an aversion to what they termed 'black money', on account of the colour, size, weight and taste of the bronze coins, which, in the absence of pocket or purse, they normally carried in their mouths.

Under the provisions of the United Kingdom Coinage Act of 1920, the standard fineness of the Imperial silver coinage was reduced from 925 to 500 parts per thousand. To meet these requirements, trials were made with a binary 50–50 silver-copper alloy and a ternary 50–40–10 silver-copper-nickel alloy, but both proved disappointing, due to unsatisfactory resistance to tarnishing and to manufacturing difficulties. After many experiments, a quaternary 50–40–5–5 silver-copper-nickel-zinc alloy was developed in 1927 and was used continuously until

Nickel: An Historical Review

1946 when, as stated above, silver coinage was superseded by issues in 75–25 cupro-nickel. The quaternary silver alloy was adopted for coinage also by Australia, New Zealand, India, Sweden, Colombia, Portugal, Brazil and Bulgaria.

In Mexico quaternary alloys of similar type have been used in recent years, in an effort to maintain a silver-bearing coinage in the face of the falling value of the peso. The compositions formerly used were silver 50, copper 40, nickel 6, zinc 4 and silver 30, copper 50, nickel 10, zinc 10. The present coinage is made from an alloy containing silver 10, copper 70, nickel 10, zinc 10. A quaternary silver alloy containing 10% of nickel has also been used for that purpose in Peru.

In 1929 the Royal Mint in London was commissioned by the Government of Rumania to make 20- and 5-lei coins to replace paper notes, as part of a programme of monetary stabilisation. The Rumanian currency law stipulated that the coins should contain either aluminium or nickel, and, in order to avoid possible confusion with white cupro-nickel coins already in circulation, the Royal Mint decided to use, for the Rumanian pieces, a yellow alloy containing 79% copper, 20% zinc and 1% nickel. This material subsequently came to be known as 'nickel brass', and although once again the addition of nickel was largely fortuitous, the improvement in corrosion- and wear-resistance conferred by that element was soon appreciated.

Nickel-brass coins have since been used in the currencies of Norway, Paraguay, Peru, Guatemala, India, Pakistan, in the Philippines, in Uruguay and in British territories throughout the world. Perhaps the best known nickel-brass coin is the United Kingdom dodecagonal threepenny piece, which aroused great controversy when it was introduced, in 1937, to replace the diminutive silver coin of the same denomination. Since then, however, the public have taken to it well.

A few coins have been issued, notably by Belgium, Nepal, Portugal, El Salvador and Haiti, in a copper-nickel-zinc alloy of nickel silver composition. As already stated, this material, by virtue of its pleasing appearance and good tarnish-resistance, is widely used for ornamental and decorative purposes and it is therefore somewhat surprising that materials of this class have not found wider application in coinage.

Aluminium-bronze coins of Denmark, Iceland and Finland contain 2% of nickel, which serves to improve appearance and durability.

In recent years, for reasons of economy, a few countries have used composite materials for coinage. Usually these have consisted of a central steel core, with outer surfaces covered by nickel or cupro-nickel layers formed by plating or mechanical-bonding techniques. Ordinarily, however, this has been a case of 'needs must'; the straight alloy or pure metal is much to be preferred. More recently one manufacturer has employed powder metallurgy in the production of pure nickel coinage strip. The satisfactory results obtained open new perspectives in the field.

The most popular coinage composition is the alloy of nickel and copper; some 70 countries have coins of that material in circulation, in more than 200 different coins.

(18)

The Continuing Search

THE close of the nineteen-thirties and the first half of the nineteen-forties were spanned by the second world conflict in twenty-five years.

Late in 1939 Russian troops invaded Finland, and the development and construction which International Nickel had been carrying out at Petsamo were stopped. As a result of the occupation of Norway by the Germans, early in 1940, the refinery of Falconbridge at Kristiansand was cut off from its source of raw material and the partly processed and finished stocks of nickel held there became inaccessible to the Allies. The occupation of France by German troops led to a complete shut-down of the refinery of Le Nickel at Le Havre. Nor was Le Nickel free from problems in New Caledonia, where the uncertainty and unsettlement in South-East Asia led to a paucity of personnel at the mines. The difficulty of finding adequate wartime fuel supplies also had to be faced, because Australia could no longer supply coal for coking, and coal and coke had therefore to be brought all the way from the North American continent to this island in the South Seas.

Since World War II was a contest of machines as well

The Continuing Search

H.M. King George VI being shown the Clydach refinery by D. Owen Evans, Chief Executive of Mond Nickel

as men,[1] an ample and sustained supply of nickel was important. The superior qualities inherent in the various types of nickel-bearing steels and in the many non-ferrous nickel alloys developed for peacetime uses were the very properties sought by manufacturers of war equipment.

With the disruption elsewhere, the nickel resources of Canada assumed top significance.[2] To augment ore output, shaft-sinking at the Garson mine was expedited and a new underground shaft was started at the Creighton mine. Removal of ores from the Frood-Stobie open-pit had been started prior to the outbreak of hostilities, but with the wartime necessity for producing

Nickel: An Historical Review

Frood-Stobie open-pit mine

greatly increased quantities of nickel, the projected scale of operations was more than trebled in a short period of time. To meet emergency requirements, an ever-increasing percentage of ore was produced from open-pit, as well as from underground, workings. Additional refining facilities were installed at Port Colborne, to match the stepped-up mining, milling and smelting programme, and improvements were made in the refining technique. Research led to development of a new nickel-chloride/nickel-sulphate electrolyte and this proved to be so advantageous that complete changeover to that type of solution was made. These additional facilities made possible very substantially increased output, and provided the refining capacity needed for

The Continuing Search

the treatment of Falconbridge matte, which International Nickel undertook to process when the Falconbridge refinery in Norway was occupied by the Germans.

After the refinery at Le Havre fell into German hands, arrangements were made by the French nickel producers to switch all their nickel matte from New Caledonia to North America for refining. That matte was supplied to the Metals Reserve Company, a United States Government agency, under agreements to which the Canadian and Australian Governments and Le Nickel were parties. International Nickel installed, at their Huntington plant, the facilities requisite to refine the matte for the Metals Reserve Company. The matte was shipped half-way around the world from New Caledonia, through the Panama Canal, and was unloaded variously at New York, Buffalo and Philadelphia.

The amount of nickel available to the Axis powers during the war was much more severely restricted. After they had driven the Russians out of Finland, the Germans made good the damage done at Petsamo during the Russo-Finnish fighting. The mine was restored to working order, and the hydroelectric plant was completed. The annual output of matte from that plant, containing about 10,000 metric tons of nickel, was shipped to Germany for refining. Additional ore from Petsamo, beyond the capacity of the smelting facilities there, and concentrates from another Finnish deposit at Nivala, were also shipped to Germany. According to figures made available when hostilities were over, Germany's annual nickel production at the peak of the struggle was only a little over 20 million lbs.[3]

The war had indeed been a time of test. Nickel-production facilities had been strained to the utmost. In order to conserve nickel for applications in which it was necessary, the industry had had to adopt the policy of encouraging the use of materials of lower nickel content, or even, in some cases, of nickel-free substitutes. Technical consultant services were placed at the disposal of users, to assist in solving problems which arose as a result of such changes in practice.

During the war years International Nickel was able to make available to the Allied countries not less than 1,500 million lbs. of nickel, 1,800 million lbs. of copper, and over 1·8 million ounces of platinum-group metals. The tonnage of ore mined by that company alone during the war years was equal to its own output and that of its predecessors during the preceding 54 years of their existence.

Once again, following a world conflict, the demand for nickel fell off. Production had to be adjusted, new markets had to be created and developed, and old applications re-established. This time, however, due to the vigour with which the industry had built up civilian uses for nickel during the nineteen-twenties and nineteen-thirties, the drop was not a disaster. Compared with a decline of 80% in world production from the peak of 105 million lbs. in 1916 to 18 million lbs. in 1921, there was a drop of only 33% from a peak in 1943 of 341 million lbs. to a trough of 227 million lbs. in 1946.

Immediately peace was declared, there was acceleration by the industry of research, development and engineering sales activities in co-operation with nickel consumers.

But the lull was short. With the outbreak of hostilities in Korea, in 1950, demand for nickel again rose sharply.

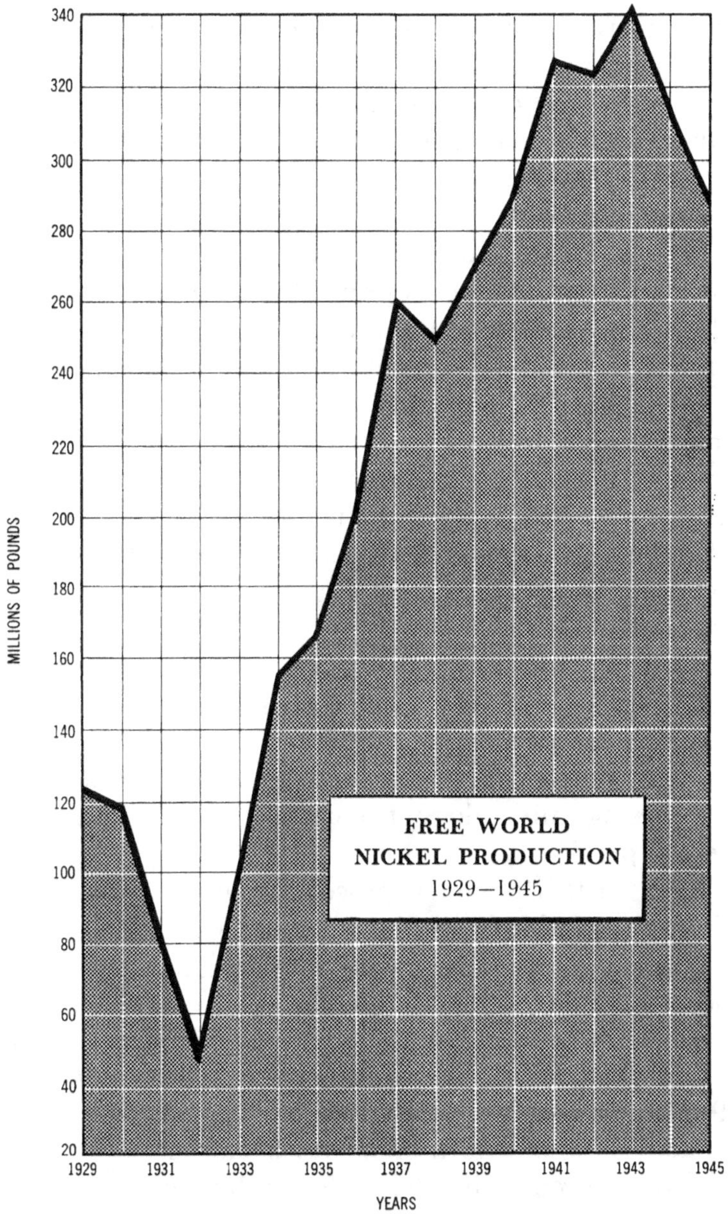
340
320
300
280
260
240
220
200
180
160
140
120
100
80
60
40
20
MILLIONS OF POUNDS
FREE WORLD
NICKEL PRODUCTION
1929–1945
1929
1931
1933
1935
1937
1939
1941
1943
1945
YEARS

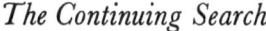

Once more the major part of the output of nickel was allocated to military production, and civilian consumption had to be cut back. Moreover, when the war in Korea came to an end, return to full availability of nickel for civilian use did not come at once, for the armistice in Korea was not the conclusion of a conflict in the usual sense. Hostilities ceased, but defence build-up continued on a large scale. Added to the heavy demands which this imposed on the available supply of nickel, the United States Government, in order to augment its supply, sharply stepped up its recently inaugurated programme of stockpiling materials for possible future defence needs, and this programme extended to nickel. As a result, there was not enough excess nickel to satisfy all civilian demands in full and its use for such purposes continued to be allocated.

With the ever-growing uses and increasing consumption of nickel, the past two decades have witnessed the development of a number of new or improved methods for extracting nickel from ores of lower grade than, and of differing mineralogy from, those which had been treated previously.

Early in this period a process invented by Professor M. H. Caron of Delft, Holland, involving the ammoniacal leaching of lateritic ores,[4] was developed and applied to the ores found in the vicinity of Nicaro in Cuba. The plant built by the United States Government during World War II, to treat those ores, was re-opened in 1952 and was subsequently expanded to a rated annual capacity of about 50 million lbs. of nickel.

Another process, involving the leaching of nickel from lateritic ores with sulphuric acid, the precipitation of the

The Continuing Search

nickel from solution by hydrogen sulphide, and the treating of the resulting sulphide slurry (developed at a later date) was to have been used by Freeport Nickel Company in its projected operations at Moa Bay in Cuba. The intention was to ship the slurry to Louisiana in the United States for final refining, with a planned annual capacity of the order of 50 million lbs. of nickel, and production was scheduled to commence in 1960. As the nickel would have been in powdered form, it was proposed to market it as briquettes.

These Cuban mines and plants were confiscated in 1960 by the revolutionary régime in that country. It is reported that the plants at Nicaro and Moa Bay are operating on a partial basis and that their products are being shipped to Communist controlled countries.

During the late nineteen-forties Professor F. A. Forward,[5] Head of the Department of Metallurgy at the University of British Columbia, invented a hydrometallurgical method for the dissolution of the sulphides of nickel, cobalt and copper by pressure-leaching in ammoniacal solutions. That process was developed by Sherritt Gordon Mines, and applied to its nickel-sulphide deposits in the Lynn Lake area of Manitoba. Refining takes place at Fort Saskatchewan in Alberta. Sherritt Gordon's new plants for the production of nickel from the Lynn Lake deposits came into production in the middle nineteen-fifties; they have an annual capacity of approximately 25 million lbs. of nickel, in the form of powder and briquettes.

Yet another process was one invented by René Perrin, President of Société d'Electro-Chimie, d'Electro-Métallurgie et des Aciéries Electriques d'Ugine in France, for the production of ferro-nickel from lateritic ores. This

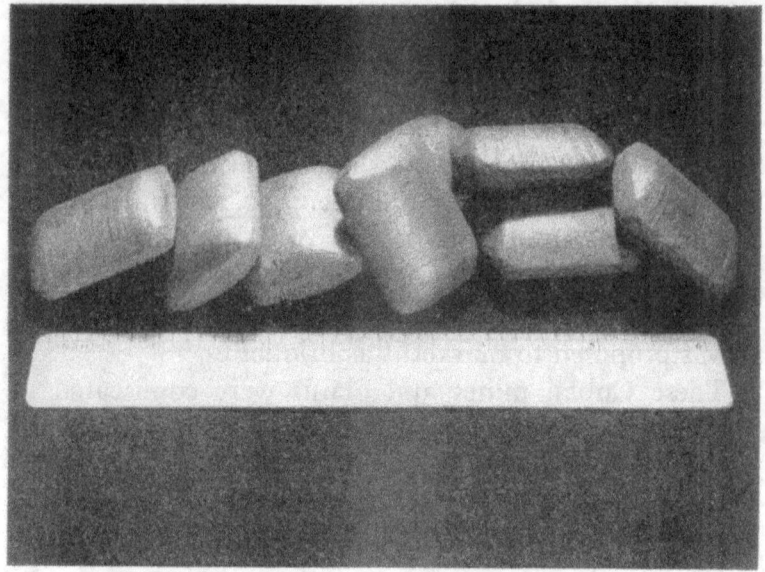

Briquettes from Sherritt Gordon's refinery in Alberta
(Each briquette is 1½″ in length)

pyro-metallurgical process was applied in the United States, by the Hanna Mining Company, to a nickel deposit at Riddle, Oregon, for the production of ferronickel. Output exceeds 20 million lbs. of nickel content per annum.[6]

The developments just described involved the opening of orebodies not previously worked, although in almost all cases it had been known for a considerable period that the deposits existed. Far-reaching metallurgical improvements were introduced also in existing operations.

In 1948 International Nickel, for example, after years of research, made a complete changeover from the Orford 'tops-and-bottoms' process, which had been a mainstay of its operations for nearly sixty years, to a

The Continuing Search

The open-pit mine of the Hanna Mining Company's nickel mine in Riddle, Oregon
Courtesy: The Hanna Mining Company

radically new method providing greatly improved separation of copper and nickel.[7] It involves a technique of slowly cooling the matte, with formation of sizeable crystals of nickel sulphide (low in copper content) and of copper sulphide (low in nickel content), which are readily separable by flotation. Metallic crystals containing the precious metals are also formed and these are readily recoverable by magnetic separation.

They also introduced fundamentally new mining methods, which made possible the treatment of ore appreciably lower in grade than had previously been economically processed. An improvement introduced at the Creighton mine early in the nineteen-fifties was 'induced-caving'. This lower-cost, bulk-mining method is an adaptation of a technique by which great masses of ore are induced to cave and disintegrate by their own weight. At the Frood section of the Frood-Stobie mine yet another low-cost bulk-mining procedure was introduced. This method, known as 'blasthole' mining, differs from the 'induced-caving' method in that explosives are used to break up the ore. The newest method, 'undercut-and-fill', was also worked out in the Frood section of the Frood-Stobie mine. It has brought impressive improvements in efficiency, safety and costs as compared with 'square-set' methods, which it is expected to replace, especially for mining at deep horizons.

Expansion was certainly the keynote of the 'fifties as far as the nickel industry throughout the world was concerned. There were many cases of increased production in addition to those turning on the introduction of new metallurgical processes already mentioned.

Confronted with the exhaustion of its open pit surface ores, as a consequence of greatly accelerated mining during World War II, the International Nickel Company embarked during the war on a major expansion of its underground mining capacity. This huge undertaking, scheduled over ten years, was driven to conclusion with the utmost dispatch and was accompanied by the introduction of far-reaching improvements in mining and metallurgical methods. As a result of this long and very costly programme the company increased its annual production rate of ore from underground mines to over 15,000,000 tons a year, as compared with a historical prior peak rate of some 6,000,000 tons.

Falconbridge very substantially expanded their facilities in Canada and Norway. Several new orebodies were brought into production. Additions were made to

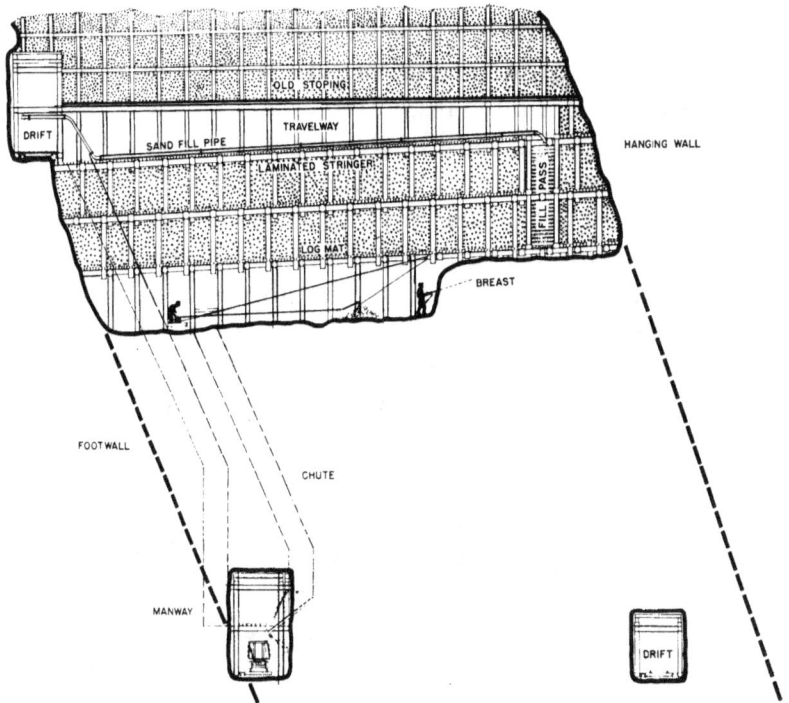

'Undercut and Fill' Method of Mining

In this method the ore is mined in successive layers or cuts, progressing from the top down. The miners work under the protection of a timber structure called a mat. This consists of a roof of logs placed on top of two continuous timber beams. As the mining face advances underneath the mat, posts are installed to support the beams. When the cut is completed another mat is built on the floor of the cut and the opening is filled with waterborne sand. Mining is then resumed on the cut below

smelting, concentrating and refining facilities. All these programmes, completed towards the end of the nineteen-fifties, increased the annual capacity of Falconbridge from about 35 million to 70 million lbs. of nickel.[8]

During this period Le Nickel erected, in New Caledonia, an electric smelting plant for the production of ferronickel, improved other facilities there, and increased the capacity of their refinery in France. As a result, at the end of the period Le Nickel is reported to have had an annual capacity to produce ferro-nickel of a nickel content of 30 million lbs., and nickel in rondelle or cube form of the order of 25 million lbs.

Although for a considerable number of years Japan has been a substantial consumer of primary nickel, the country does not possess any known economic nickel-ore deposits. With Government restrictions preventing importation of nickel processed abroad, during the nineteen-fifties Japanese companies commenced production, from New Caledonian ores, of primary nickel in the form of cathodes, nickel pig and ferro-nickel, and in 1961 their production exceeded 45 million lbs. nickel content. Costs of production, however, have been very high, and as a consequence primary nickel is being sold in Japan at substantially higher prices than those prevailing in world markets generally.

Prior to 1939 the only nickel deposits worked in the Soviet Union were oxide ores. In 1944, following her war with Finland, Russia annexed the portion of northern Finland which encompassed the Petsamo nickel mine.[9] Other deposits of nickel-sulphide ore have been found in Russia at Monchegorsk in the Kola Peninsula, and at Norilsk in Siberia. These new sources have resulted in increased production. Recent total U.S.S.R. production has been estimated by the U.S. Bureau of Mines at 166 million lbs. nickel content.

Since mines are a wasting asset, search for new sources of nickel is an ever-present problem. Improved means of transportation and communication, and scientific mineral detection now enable modern prospectors, with their new tools, to explore vast, heretofore inaccessible, areas.

In 1951 a major advance in the science of exploration was achieved with the development of aerial geophysical

The Continuing Search

Le Nickel plant at Doniambo, New Caledonia
The electric foundry is in the right centre of this aerial photograph
Courtesy: S. A. Le Nickel

prospecting.[10] It was pioneered, for metallic ore deposits, by International Nickel, and was applied to its exploration of the Canadian Shield in northern Manitoba, which had been under way since 1946. In 1956 a large new nickel-sulphide orebody was proved and named the Thompson mine. This important new source of nickel had been found entirely by scientific means; there was no showing on the surface. Five years of strenuous effort converted the waste land where that orebody was discovered into a fully integrated nickel operation, near the site of the thriving new town of Thompson, Manitoba, which came into being along with the mining development.

At the dedication ceremony of this project the Premier of Manitoba referred to the grant, some three hundred years earlier, of a charter to the 'Company of Adventurers Trading into Hudson's Bay', for developing the fur trade

Nickel: An Historical Review

Tractor trains, such as this one, were used during the winter to haul supplies and equipment to International Nickel's new mining site in Northern Manitoba

there. Commenting on the fact that 'a lump of ore has replaced the pelt as a symbol of richness and the potential of this great region', he paid tribute to the 'Mining Adventurers' of today.

With its new facilities in Manitoba, and improved facilities in Ontario and in the United Kingdom, International Nickel now has a combined total annual production capacity of 400 million lbs. of nickel.

In the course of 1957, with increased production, the stringency in supply of nickel for civilian uses disappeared. The extraordinary demands for defence purposes and stockpiling had indeed impeded the creation and development of civilian markets, but some of these

The Continuing Search

potential markets were already known. A vigorous search for new and expanded uses for nickel and nickel-containing products could once again be set in motion.

Existing facilities are susceptible of expansion, the search for new sources of nickel continues, and research is leading to improved techniques for winning nickel from its ores. The prospect for nickel is one of plentiful supply for the years ahead.

The many uses of the metal could well form the subject of a separate book, but it may be of interest here to make a brief survey of some of the fields in which nickel is today offering the greatest potential in furthering progress and adding to the amenities of life.

The desire for progress is a constant challenge to the metallurgist, who must search untiringly for materials capable of matching-up to the increasingly severe requirements imposed by modern life. Search among nickel steels and high-nickel alloys has proved singularly rewarding.

The nickel-chromium stainless steels and certain nickel alloys form the backbone of a group of materials which offer excellent resistance to wet and dry corrosion, combined with good fabricating qualities and high strength. Such materials are extensively used in the chemical industry, in laundry, textile and dyeing machinery, in dairy and food-processing plant and, not least important, in the home, for food-handling equipment, hardware and a host of other items in everyday use.

Architecture is of growing interest for nickel. Nickel-containing stainless steels are durable, non-corrodible, and easily maintained in good condition; their usefulness for curtain-wall construction, as well as for interior

Nickel: An Historical Review

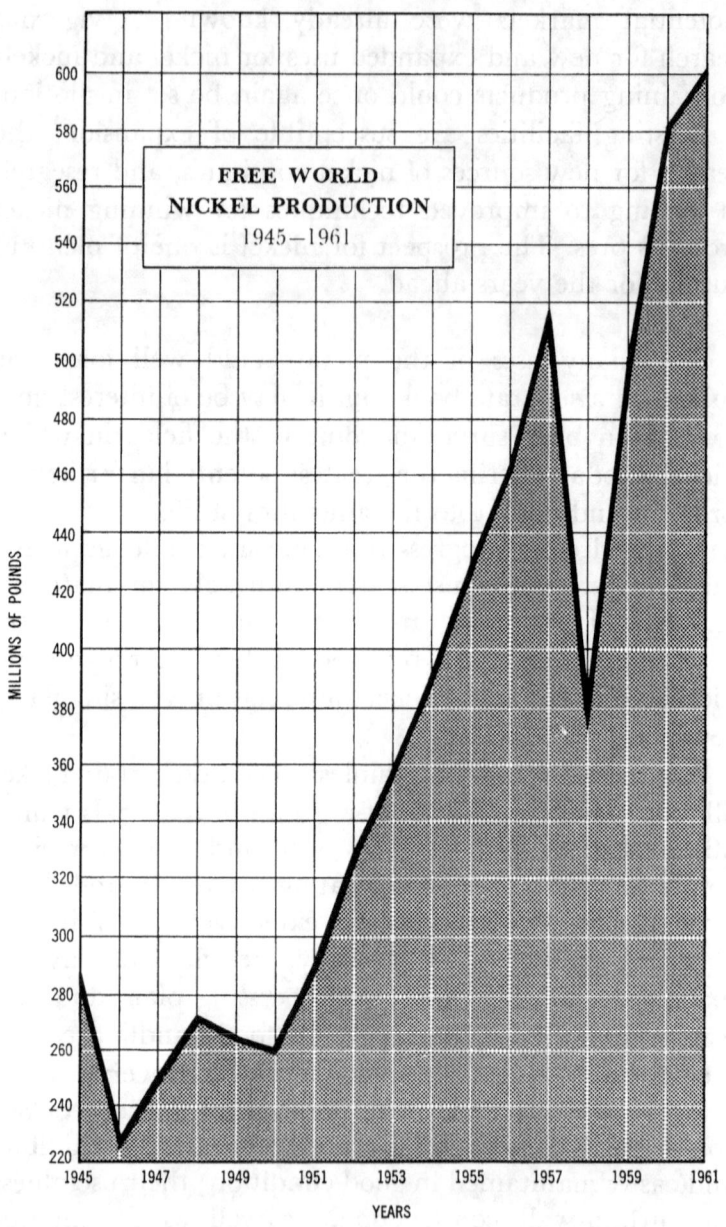

purposes, is being increasingly realised. The aesthetic appeal of the imposing buildings using this type of construction is self-evident. The nickel silvers find application for internal decorative items, affording an ideal combination of workability and attractive appearance.

Developments in cryogenic engineering have received considerable impetus from nickel-containing steels, which retain good mechanical properties, particularly high impact strength, at sub-zero temperatures, and are thus suitable for plant operating low-temperature processes in the oil, chemical and petrochemical industries.

Very recently there has been developed a series of maraging steels[11] of dramatically high strength, containing approximately 12–30% nickel, which promise to have a wide application in vessels operating at high pressure and in other applications where an unusually high combination of strength and toughness are required.

With the unfettered growth of productive industry, and the endeavour to lessen human toil in every walk of life, there is an insatiable need for increased supplies of power, and thus a constant call for more generating capacity. Operating temperatures and pressures have already risen to a spectacular extent, and are likely to rise still higher. Here nickel-containing materials are most valuable for superheater tubes, steam piping and turbine components. Exemplifying this trend mention may be made of the Eddystone Supercritical Unit, in which a variety of alloys of high nickel content have been used for such purposes.

For rotors and rotor shafts for steam turbines and electric generators, for blading, and sometimes for the

Nickel-containing stainless steel ensures the permanence and beauty of the exterior of Thyssen Haus in Düsseldorf
Courtesy: Deutsche Edelstahl Werke A.G.

The Continuing Search

inner casing of the turbine itself, nickel-containing materials are being used, and for steam condensers (particularly in locations where cooling is by means of salt or brackish water) copper-nickel alloys containing 10–30% of nickel are standard on both land and sea.

In the realm of nuclear energy extensive use is being made of nickel stainless steels and nickel-base alloys, to overcome the corrosion and other problems associated with the generation of power in gas-cooled or liquid-cooled reactors.

The Telstar communications satellite made use of nickel in ways which illustrate the versatility of the metal in meeting specific and unique requirements. Nickel cadmium batteries stored the energy from the solar cells. The use of nickel in these batteries took advantage of its electrochemical properties, strength, toughness, ease of fabrication, electrical conductivity and corrosion-resistance. Nickel as the cathode material in the travelling wave tube utilised its special electrochemical properties, strength and low volatility at red heat, which are the same properties that account for its use in radio and TV receiving tubes.

It has been possible to mention only a few of the significant happenings bearing on nickel during this recent span of years, the new and expanded facilities for the production of nickel, the continuing search for new nickel deposits, and some of the new uses for the metal. Finally, however, as one interesting facet of this story which the future historian will be able to report, the book closes with a chapter on the part played by nickel in helping to make possible man's most dramatic achievement in recent times; his ability to travel at fantastic speeds in air and outer space.

(19)

Mach I and Beyond[1]

DURING the twentieth century man has achieved amazing developments in air travel, with increasing range, speed, reliability and economy. This has been the result of a most productive combination of science and engineering, including the development and use of materials that have permitted translation of advanced design concepts into practical aerial flight. Nickel has played an important rôle in this progress.

Air travel had been the sole prerogative of birds and an occasional balloonist until, in 1896, as the culmination of more than nine years' work, an American named S. P. Langley, Secretary of the Smithsonian Institution, developed an unmanned '25-lb. model of steel, hickory and silk' which, under its own *steam* power, flew for 4,200 ft., more than three-quarters of a mile.[2] That achievement so aroused the imagination of President McKinley of the United States that, at the outbreak of the Spanish-American war, Langley was officially given the assignment of developing a 'flying machine' as a weapon of war.

Not long afterwards two brothers, Orville and Wilbur

Wright, likewise started to wrestle with the problems of aerial flight. On 17th December, 1903 they made history[3] in a biplane described as 'a stick and string boxed kite', achieving man's first powered flight. On that day four flights took place at Kitty Hawk, North Carolina, the longest lasting 59 seconds and covering a distance of 852 ft.; the air speed attained was about 31 m.p.h., against a 20-m.p.h. wind.

Wright's power unit consisted of an internal-combustion, piston-type, 4-cylinder, water-cooled engine which was momentarily capable of developing 16 h.p., though for most of its time its power barely equalled that of twelve languid horses. It has not been possible to verify the statement that the crankshaft of the original Wright engine was machined from a solid piece of nickel-steel armour plate. It is, however, a certainty that in the later Wright engines nickel steel was used for the crankshafts.

The discovery, by A. Wilm,[4] in about 1908, of a means of strengthening an aluminium-base alloy by an *age-hardening* heat-treatment made it practical to use this light metal, in the form of an alloy called duralumin, in aircraft structures. This gave the aircraft designers a lightweight material with which they could build stronger and more efficient aircraft and achieve increased air speeds. A noteworthy application of duralumin was for the structure of the Zeppelin and other rigid airships.

In 1919 P. D. Merica and his colleagues, at the Bureau of Standards, working on duralumin, postulated that the hardening responsible for the superior properties of duralumin was due to the precipitation of minute particles consisting of compounds of aluminum with one of the alloying elements present.[5] This explanation of the nature of the phenomenon turned an empirical process into a metallurgical science, and provided the groundwork for the application of the same principle to many other alloy systems.

While nickel was not a component of the original duralumin alloy, it came into use around 1921 in aluminium alloys required for highly stressed engine parts. Metallurgists in Great Britain developed a series of alloys containing nickel, copper and magnesium, which could be strengthened by age-hardening. Among these, one containing about 2% of nickel, with 4% copper and 1·5% magnesium, was outstanding, and has been known since then as 'Y' alloy.[6] The most important feature of these alloys was retention of strength and hardness at elevated temperatures, a property that led to their use for pistons, cylinder heads and other components that had to be strong when they were hot. Other alloys were developed further by Rolls-Royce in their R.R. series and marketed by the firm of High Duty Alloys. Similar compositions were introduced by aluminium-alloy producers for the engine builders in the United States and other countries. A further development for pistons, in the United States, was a low-expansion aluminium-silicon alloy containing up to $2\frac{1}{2}\%$ nickel. Nickel is still being used as a component of vital aluminium-alloy parts that must remain strong at elevated temperatures.

Under the momentum of developments of World War I, nickel-containing materials helped to make possible flights of longer duration and at higher altitudes. Increasing use was made by aero-engine designers of steels containing nickel (about 3%), chromium, and later molybdenum, selected for gears, crankshafts and

Mach I and Beyond

other highly stressed components.

Following World War I advances in the speed capabilities of aeroplanes were measured and stimulated by the Schneider Trophy contests. Engines built in Italy, England and the United States powered winning aircraft in these events. In the late 'twenties several dependable *air-cooled* radial engines were developed. Of these the Wright 'Whirlwind' (225 h.p.) was the best known, having been the power unit in Lindbergh's Spirit of St. Louis and other transoceanic planes of the day; it was an important factor in the growing civil aviation industry. In turn came the larger Pratt and Whitney 'Wasp' (450 h.p.) and the Wright 'Cyclone' (525 h.p.), the size used in many military and transport aeroplanes of that period.

In England the *liquid-cooled* engine had been brought to a high state of perfection. A well-known example is the Rolls-Royce 'Merlin' (1,500 h.p.), which later, in World War II, powered the 'Hurricane' and the 'Spitfire' during the Battle of Britain. The steadily rising performance of the engines developed in the period between the two wars was in no small measure due to the availability of nickel-alloy steels and other nickel-containing materials: which were put to good use by the engine designers.

The use of higher compression, along with leaded (anti-knock) fuels, brought about a need for valve materials less subject to corrosive attack at high temperatures. This requirement was satisfied by the development of nickel-chromium steels for valves and nickel-chromium as protective coatings for the critical surfaces. Typical of the exhaust-valve steels favoured in Great Britain for long-term service at temperatures as high as 760 °C. (1,400 °F.) was, in the case of the Merlin,

KE 965 (14% nickel), which conformed to Air Ministry Specification DTD 49B. In the United States a similar iron-base alloy (19% nickel), developed by Universal Cyclops for the same purpose, could withstand operating temperatures of 700°C. (1,300°F.). One of the outstanding exhaust-valve materials in use today is an alloy containing about 70% nickel. The development of such alloys, able to retain their hardness and resist the corrosive effects of exhaust gases at high temperatures, was an important contribution to the next stages in the evolution of aircraft engine power.

As an aircraft rises to higher altitudes there is a progressive falling-off in power, due to reduced density of the air and hence less oxygen, but, by utilising an idea which originated with Rateau in France, such power as would otherwise be lost can be preserved by the use of a supercharger, which compresses the air being fed into the engine. The supercharger can be driven off the engine, by gearing, or by a small turbine in the exhaust stream. During the nineteen-twenties an exhaust-driven turbo-supercharger was being developed in the United States, by S. A. Moss of the General Electric Company. As temperatures of the exhaust stream which drove the supercharger ranged from 650 to 815°C. (1,200°–1,500°F.), and as the turbine rotor rotated at speeds varying from 20,000 to 30,000 r.p.m., a metallurgical problem of no mean magnitude arose. In the early turbo-superchargers the alloys used for the highly stressed turbine parts were the nickel-chromium exhaust-valve alloys previously mentioned, and these were followed by sundry cast cobalt-base alloys.

Later, for improved turbo-superchargers, certain nickel-chromium *precipitation-hardening* alloys containing

Mach I and Beyond

aluminium and titanium were successfully introduced. These latter alloys were based on the precipitation-hardening mechanism utilised about 1929 by the International Nickel Company in nickel-chromium-iron alloys.[7] Around the same time important work was done in France, by S.A. Commentry Fourchambault et Decazeville (Imphy), on nickel-chromium alloys susceptible to thermal hardening.[8]

The highest development of piston engines, in a period which overlapped the introduction of the aircraft gas turbine or turbo-jet engine, made further use of the energy of the piston-engine exhaust in what the manufacturers, Curtiss-Wright, called a turbo-compound engine. This was achieved by making the high-velocity exhaust gases drive small gas turbines, each placed in the exhaust gas stream from a group of cylinders. These turbines transmitted their energy, by fluid coupling, to the crankshaft of the engine and thus added about 20% extra power for driving the propeller. The hubs and rotors of these turbines required materials having the same temperature capabilities as components of jet engines and benefited from development of alloys used for superchargers and gas turbines. These turbo compound engines reached a high stage of engineering development and commercial use in the early 'fifties, in large transatlantic and transcontinental propeller-driven aircraft.

Despite a tenfold increase in piston-type aero-engine power during some 35 years of development, by the time the Second World War came to a close a ceiling was being reached in the power which could be transmitted through a propeller, at aircraft velocities approaching the speed of sound. Important as had been the embodiment of multi-stage superchargers in the power unit,

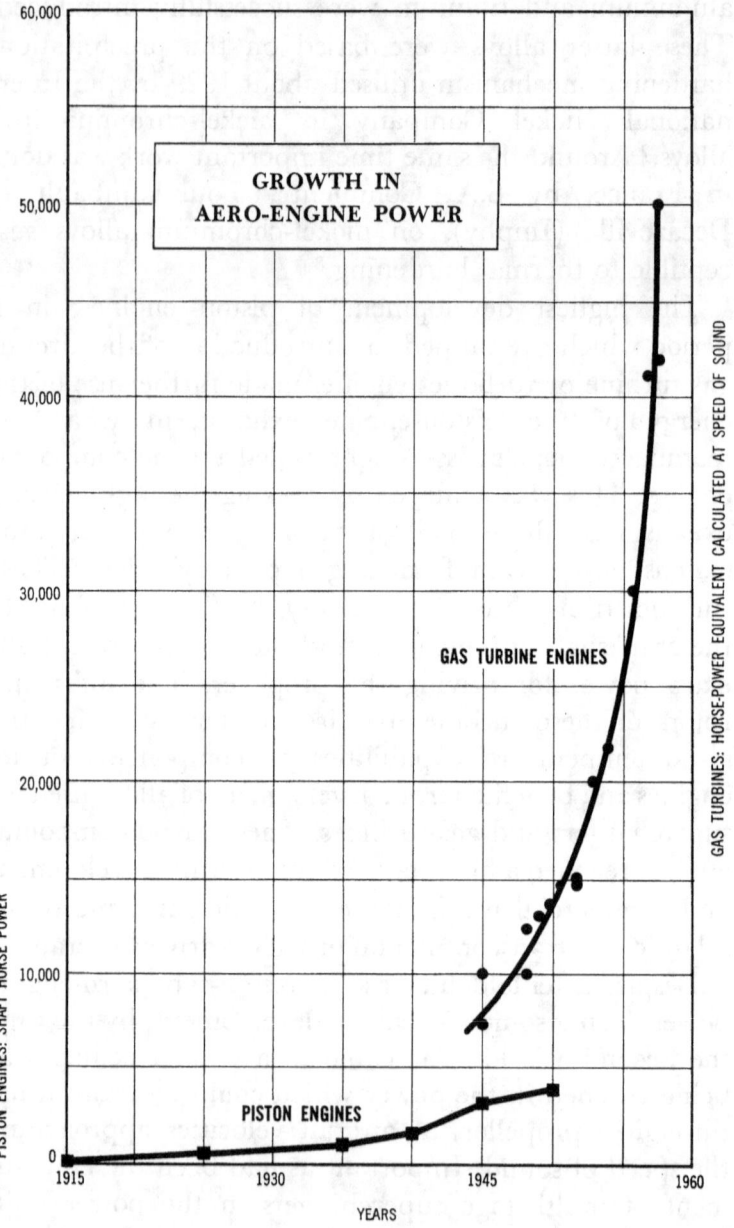

Mach I and Beyond

coupled with the use of high-octane fuel and with other aids utilised by the aero-engine designer, a fundamentally different principle of propulsion was essential if speeds in the air approaching, or exceeding, that of sound were to be attained. The solution to the problem was found in the gas turbine. Its power curve, as shown on the right of the diagram opposite, brings out the revolutionary rate of increase in power which was to result, in the subsequent 15 years, from the changeover from the piston-type engine to the aircraft gas turbine, or jet engine.

The research on nickel alloys that solved the materials problems encountered in the evolution of piston engines, e.g. exhaust valves, superchargers and exhaust-driven turbines, provided an invaluable base for the further development of the alloys that helped make the jet age possible.

The concept of the use of this form of prime mover goes back as far as Hero of Alexandria (150 B.C.), to whom is attributed the first approximation to a turbine.[9] He designed a spherical vessel, supplied with steam through the supports which carried its bearings, and these rotated through the reaction produced by expulsion of this steam from jets tangential to the axis of rotation.

The basic idea persisted through the ages, and in the present century, even before World War I, there was sporadic interest in Europe in the application of the jet-engine principle to propulsion of aircraft. Later the English engineer, Frank Whittle, after countless disappointments, evolved a power unit embodying principles which improved the efficiency of the air compressor and of the gas turbine. Although Whittle chose the gas turbine as being, at that period, the most practicable mode of aircraft propulsion, he considered several other concepts.[10]

The gas turbine could, however, become a practical

proposition only if it were possible to develop alloys capable of accommodating the combination of high stresses and high temperatures encountered by the turbine blades and other critical components of jet engines. Alloys to be used for these purposes had to be resistant to progressive deformation under constant stress ('creep'), and also be capable of withstanding high stresses for prolonged periods before they eventually failed by progression of creep into actual rupture.

The physical phenomenon of creep was already well recognised.[11] The subject had received attention in several countries, in connection with high-pressure, high-temperature steam-power plant and piston-engine superchargers. Thus, when metallurgists came to study materials suitable for use in aircraft gas turbines the need for provision of resistance to creep and to stress was fully appreciated. Although many problems remained to be solved, this metallurgical background was of vital importance in the early days of gas-turbine development.

The disc and blades of Whittle's first turbine (1937) were of Firth-Vickers' Stayblade, a heat-resistant titanium-modified chromium-nickel steel (8·5% nickel). An alternative alloy, Rex 78, produced by the same firm, contained 18% nickel, with molybdenum, copper and titanium; it set what at that time was a high standard of creep-resistance. However, although these alloys, then the best available, were used for the first few of the Whittle jets, it was realised that, if adequate life and further advance in engine performance were to be achieved, materials having a higher level of resistance to creep and rupture must be developed. In England this challenge was met as a result of work carried out by the Mond Nickel Company, with the encouragement of the Air Ministry. A detailed study of world literature on the properties of all the then-known high-temperature alloys, together with consideration of results of work already carried out in England, the United States, France, Germany and elsewhere, and long experience with the characteristics of nickel-chromium alloys as shown in electrical-resistance materials, indicated conclusively the potential usefulness of oxidation-resistant nickel-chromium-base alloys strengthened by addition of hardener elements, to produce the required combination of properties. This work gave rise to a series of remarkable nickel-chromium alloys, which are patented in a number of countries throughout the world.[12] These alloys, manufactured and marketed by Henry Wiggin and Company, under the trademark 'Nimonic', are based on the principles of age-hardening by means of aluminium and titanium, supplemented, as required, by other hardener elements acting by a different mechanism.[13] Similar age-hardening principles were utilised in the U.S.A., in the age hardenable Inconel nickel-chromium series developed by the International Nickel Company at their Huntington works.

The first use of the Nimonic nickel-chromium alloys in Whittle's engines was Nimonic alloy 75 (then numbered 750) (75% Ni) sheet, and Nimonic alloy 80 (at that time 800) bar in the W. 2. B. turbojet, first made experimentally by the Rover Company and later superseded by the Rolls-Royce 'Welland' (1,700 lbs. thrust) centrifugal-flow type of design, followed by the 'Derwent' (3,500 lbs. thrust). At the same time Metropolitan Vickers were developing an axial-flow turbine which incorporated, experimentally, Nimonic alloy 75 forgings and sheet. In his own story of the jet engine,[10] Whittle refers to the research which led to the development of this series of alloys.[14]

In the United States a Government Committee had been appointed at the beginning of 1941 to enquire into the basic problems of jet propulsion in the air. In July 1941 Westinghouse, Allis-Chalmers and General Electric were each told to go ahead with a detailed study of an engine of the type each preferred, on the basis of which contracts were to be awarded. The urgency occasioned by the Japanese attack on Pearl Harbor later in that year resulted in the Westinghouse 'Yankee 19A', an axial-flow gas turbine designed for a thrust of 1,200 lbs. Westinghouse also produced a prototype of their 'J.30-WE20' axial-flow gas turbine, which was approved for production a few years later. The axial-flow gas turbine, which consists of an inlet diffuser, an axial-flow compressor and combustion chambers arranged annularly to drive one or more rows of turbine blades, is a design predominant today.

The General Electric Company, who had in the meantime received blue prints of Whittle's W. 2. B. engine, together with a prototype of that unit, used the Whittle engine in the first of their 'I' series, and the company also developed a turbine of their own design, the 'I. 40', which had a thrust of 4,000 lbs. That model was the first aircraft gas turbine to enter quantity production in the United States.

The nickel alloys used in these first U.S. jet engines were a natural adaptation of similar alloys which had already reached a high stage of development for use in piston-engine turbo-superchargers. For example, the early General Electric gas turbines used Haynes Stellite's Hastelloy alloy B (60% nickel) for the blades,

Mach I and Beyond

and Timken 16–25–6 (25% nickel) alloy for the turbine disc. Hastelloy alloy B had the advantage of being capable of being forged to size and to close tolerances, while providing high strength properties that were adequate for those early engines. These were followed by a number of age-hardening nickel-chromium alloys containing aluminium and titanium. The development of these alloys had taken place in the late nineteen-thirties, using Inconel alloy 600 (75% nickel) as a base. This was followed in the early nineteen-forties by the production of a series of alloys, including Inconel alloy X-750 (formerly designated Inconel 'X' alloy) which was destined to play such an important rôle in the evolution of air and space travel.

Meanwhile the Germans too had been working on jet propulsion. The prototype gas turbine in that country was designed by P. von Ohain and used in the first jet plane flight made by Heinkel in 1939. The Italians had flown their jet-propelled Caproni-Campini aeroplane in 1940. Its engine consisted of an ordinary reciprocating engine driving a many-bladed fan of small diameter, within a closed air duct. By burning additional fuel within the duct behind the fan, additional thrust was obtained. It thus differed from the jet propulsion obtained from a normal gas turbine.[15]

In the years immediately preceding World War II German metallurgical firms had been giving a good deal of attention to the problem of heat-resisting alloys. One of the best known age-hardenable iron-base alloys developed at this time was Krupp's Tinidur alloy, containing about 30% nickel and 15% chromium, together with titanium. When the Second World War broke out, further metallurgical developments in Germany had been strongly

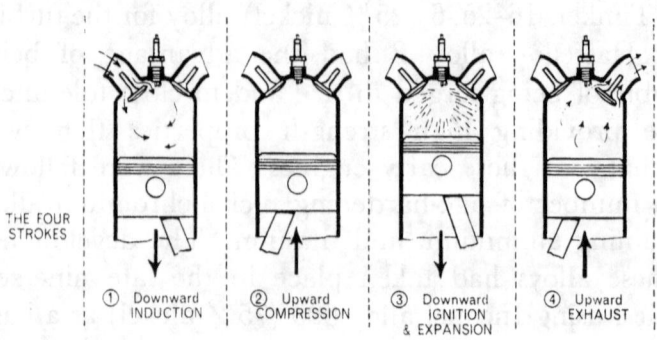

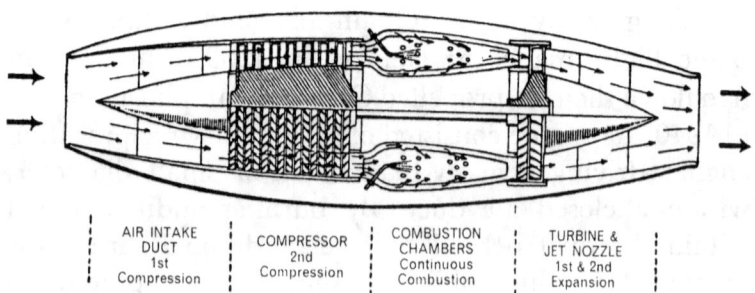

Schematic drawing showing a comparison of Rotating and Reciprocating Power Units

In the upper series of diagrams the four intermittent strokes of an orthodox reciprocating engine are approximately aligned with the four continuous functions of a turbine-jet unit

Courtesy: Iliffe Books Ltd.

Mach I and Beyond

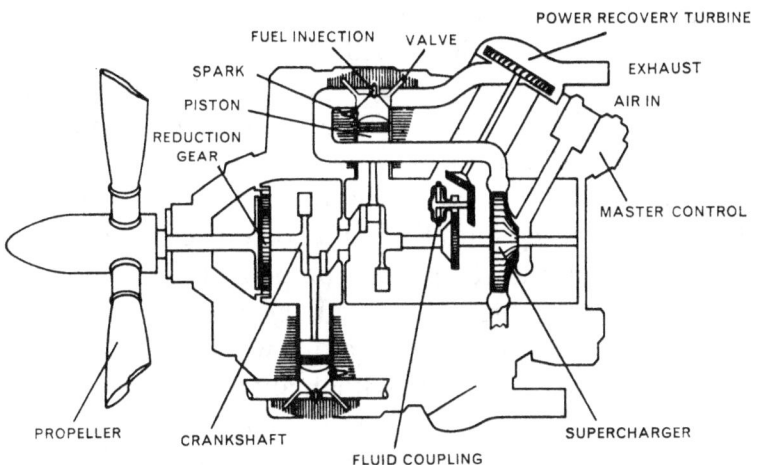

Schematic drawing of a Curtiss-Wright Turbo Compound Engine

The output of a reciprocating system is enhanced by multiple exhaust-gas turbines

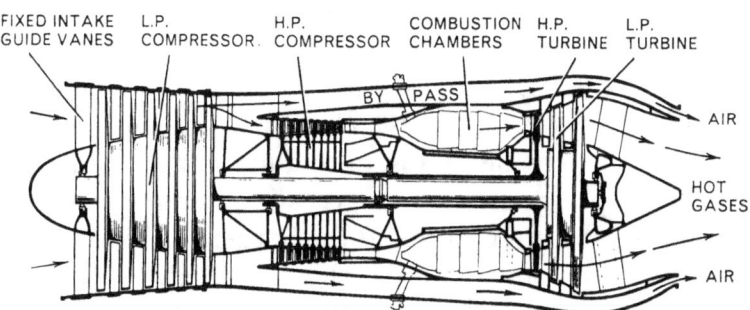

Schematic drawing of a Rolls-Royce 'Conway' Engine

First of the by-pass or 'fan' type engines which dominate the aeroplane gas-turbine field today

influenced by the shortage of nickel. One noteworthy nickel-free material developed in those conditions by Krupp was Cromadur alloy which contained a high proportion of manganese (17–19%), added as a substitute for nickel. Gas-turbine development in Germany was thus naturally retarded by the shortage of essential elements including nickel[16] and a good deal of ingenuity was shown in the design of components, e.g. hollow turbine blades, which permitted the use of greatly inferior materials, although service life was much curtailed. However, two jet engines with manganese-silicon steel blades (Junkers 004 and B.M.W. 003) were in active service use at the end of the war. Both were axial-flow turbojets.

The story of experience in all the countries concerned with production of gas turbines thus demonstrates the unique contribution which nickel-base high-temperature alloys have made in this field. Most of these alloys have depended for their properties on age-hardening resulting from the presence of aluminium and titanium in suitable proportions; the sum of these two elements is frequently referred to as the 'hardener content'. Increasing amounts of these elements, and appropriate adjustments of the titanium-to-aluminium ratio, have provided progressively stronger alloys, and it has been found possible to supplement the hardening effect of precipitated compounds and achieve a higher 'temperature capability' by the addition of alloying elements that stiffen the matrix surrounding the dispersed age-hardening particles. Niobium (columbium), molybdenum and tungsten achieve a stiffening effect by increasing strain in the lattice in which they are present as solute elements. Other elements, such as cobalt, are frequently added to nickel-base alloys of high hardener content, to improve hot-workability during manufacture as well as to enhance high-temperature strength.

The ability to withstand high stresses without rupture has become a measure of quality of alloys designed for use at high temperatures. This so-called 'temperature capability', as used in the present context, is defined as the maximum temperature at which an alloy will withstand a stress of 9 tons per sq. in. (20,000 p.s.i.) for 100 hours without rupture. Progress in terms of 'temperature capability' parallels progress in performance of jet engines.

A striking example of steady rise in 'temperature capability' is to be found in the Nimonic series of wrought nickel-chromium alloys.[17] The most recently developed member of the group, Nimonic alloy 115 (a nickel-base alloy containing chromium and cobalt in association with a balanced proportion of hardener elements), has a 'temperature capability' of 960°C. (1,760°F.). An American alloy of no less outstanding performance is Special Metal's Udimet 700 alloy, also containing a high percentage of nickel. With cast nickel-base alloys, such as IN 100 or Nimocast alloy PK 24, a 'temperature capability' as high as 1,010°C. (1,850°F.) can be realised.[18]

In producing high-temperature nickel-base alloys there are limitations on the hardener content that can be introduced to achieve higher 'temperature capabilities' without encountering serious production difficulties. These limits have been broadened by the introduction of new processing techniques. By melting under a vacuum or in an inert atmosphere such as argon, higher hardener contents can be accommodated;

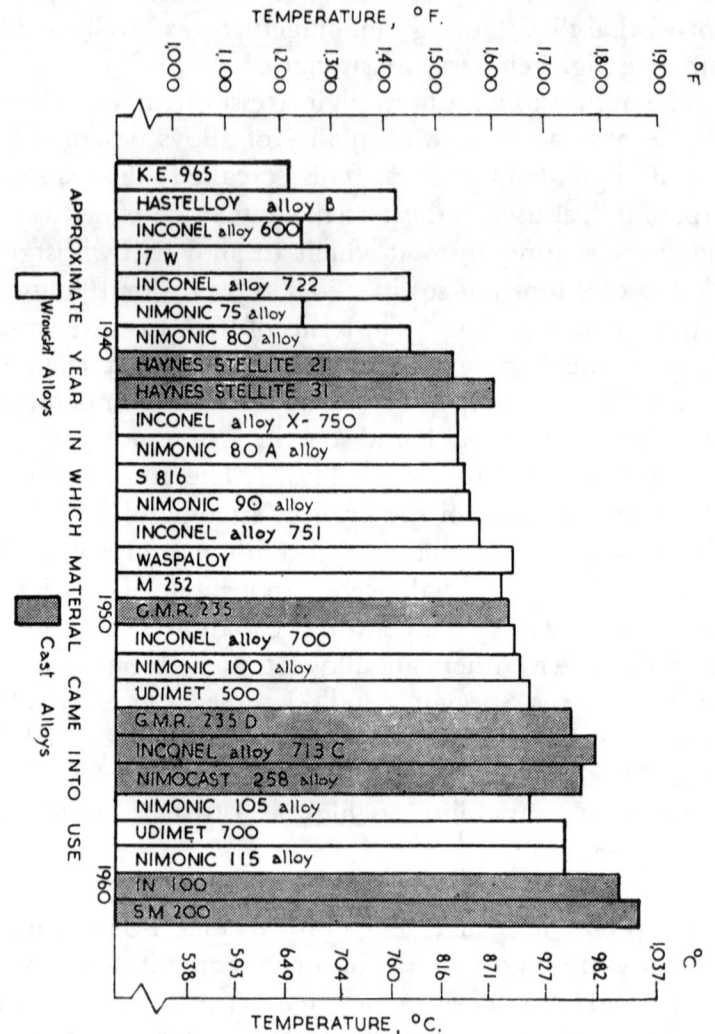

Nickel-containing aero-engine alloys

Temperature at which rupture occurs in 100 hours at stress of 9 tons per sq. in. (20,000 p.s.i.)

Rolls Royce Conway Gas-Turbine Engine

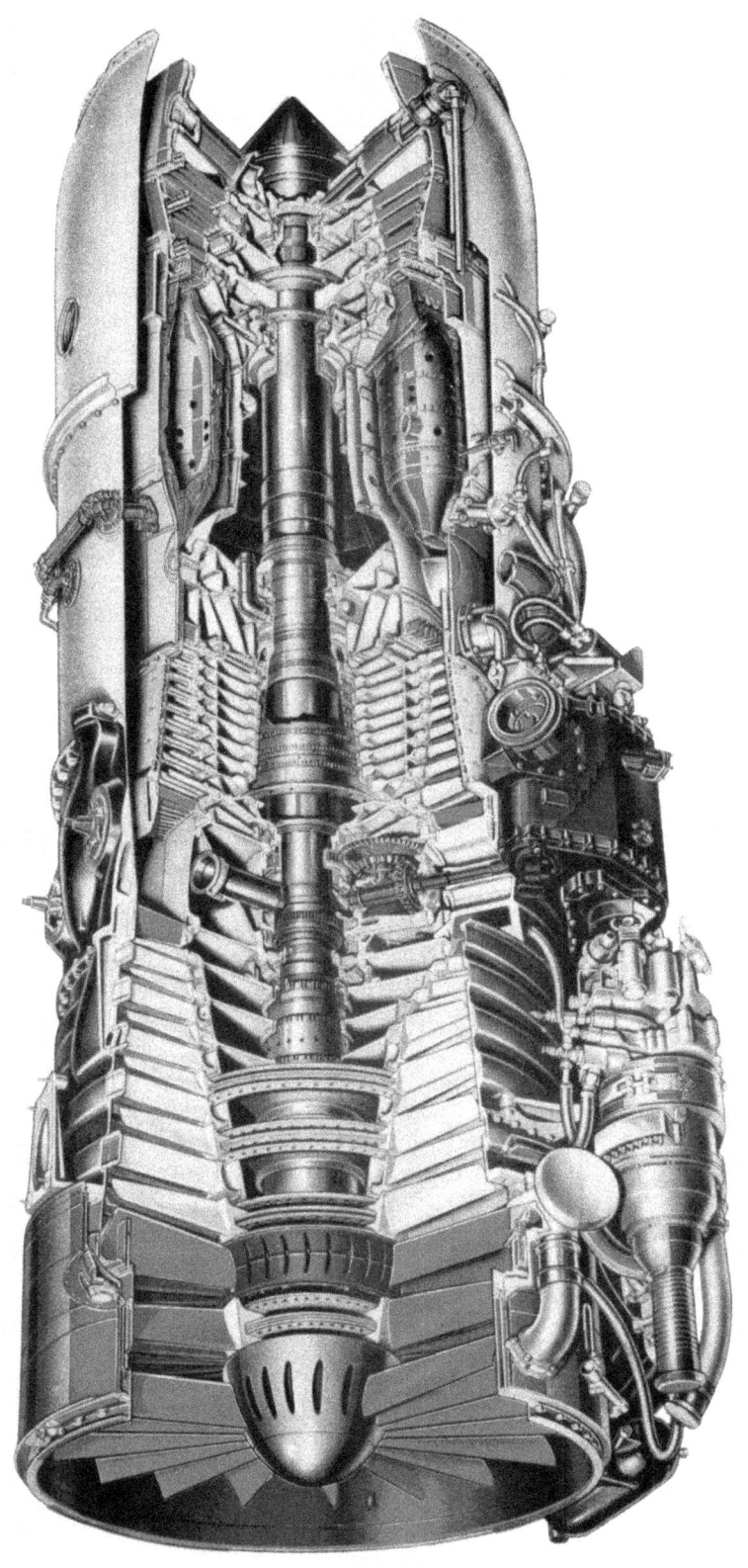

Components made from nickel-containing materials are coloured red

Courtesy: Rolls Royce Ltd.

Mach I and Beyond

contributions have been made also by new deoxidation and pouring techniques. In breaking down the ingots, extrusion and improved press-forging processes have offered many advantages that have permitted the processing of superior alloys of high hardener content.

Alloys to be used for parts that need only be cast to shape can, of course, be made with a higher hardener content, and consequently with a higher 'temperature capability' than those which have to be hot- or cold-worked. The use of the alloys in a cast form, requiring very little further processing to final shape, has been greatly aided by the revival and perfection of the so-called 'lost-wax' casting process used over 400 years ago by Benvenuto Cellini for the manufacture of jewellery and other metallic works of art. Use of the techniques mentioned has made possible a steady advance in 'temperature capabilities' of both wrought and cast alloys.

The jet engine has made spectacular advances in terms of performance capabilities, reliability and economy of operation. An outstanding development was the introduction of the fan-type engine, of which the first production unit was the Rolls-Royce 'Conway'. This engine has already reached an overhaul life of 4,800 hours. This species of engine known as the by-pass jet or turbofan incorporates an air by-pass duct situated down stream of the low-pressure compressor which by-passes a proportion of the airflow past the high pressure compressor through to a mixer zone where the by-passed air is mixed with the hot exhaust gases. This results in a reduced jet stream velocity and greater engine efficiency.

In the United States comparable progress is found in the Pratt and Witney 'Turbofan'. This unit is an axial-flow engine in which the first row of the compressor are designed oversize, to move a large mass of air. These fan blades sweep air round the outside of the engine casing, so that it flows in with the slip stream of the exhaust gases from the tail pipe. Other engines make use of the 'aft fan', in which the by-pass is effected by a radial extension of the turbine blades.

The fan-type engines, which have lower fuel consumption and higher thrust than earlier designs are used predominantly in the new large jet air transports.

The extent to which nickel-containing engineering materials are used in a modern four-engine jet airliner is indicated by the fact that a typical model contains no less than about 2,600 lbs. of nickel. Each of the four jet engines contains about 600 lbs. of nickel in the form of alloys. In addition to the 2,400 lbs. of nickel in the engines there are 200 lbs. in steels used for structural components of the aircraft.

To go far beyond the present ceilings in 'temperature capabilities' of either wrought or cast alloys will require employment of new techniques and work on new alloy systems based on higher-melting-point metals. Among the new approaches is the production of alloys from metal powders, either mechanically mixed or pre-alloyed, and possibly in admixture with finely divided inert particles.

In addition to meeting specifications for nickel-base alloys in respect of creep life and other properties, the metallurgist has been faced with the problem of ensuring, during production, the close metallurgical control needed to give the greatest possible uniformity, heat-by-heat, in order that the performance of components, such as turbine blades, may be predicted with reasonable certainty. Without such uniformity, fluctuation in service life of components can seriously affect maintenance costs.

Mach I and Beyond

Looking ahead to the future of aircraft powered by jet engines, it is reasonably likely that in the not-distant future supersonic airliners could be flying the Atlantic (or equivalent distances) in two hours or less, cruising possibly at 75,000 ft. and at a speed of 1,500 – 2,000 m.p.h. (between Mach 2·5 and Mach 3).

Already representing an advanced stage of development in the U.K. is the vertical-take-off aeroplane, as exemplified by the Hawker P. 1127 and as distinct from the helicopter. For vertical-take-off aircraft gas turbines are a *sine quâ non*, and nickel thus will play an important rôle in further developments in this direction.

The introduction of the jet engine was required to permit a substantial advance in the speed capabilities over those established by the most advanced piston-engine-powered aircraft. Similarly, another mode of propulsion was needed to extend the limits of speed achievable with jet-engine power, and reach into space where the oxygen needed to support combustion is not available. This has brought about the extended use of rocket power for space vehicles and, in a more limited way, for manned aircraft, such as the X-15 research aircraft.[19] As was the case with piston engines, and later with jet engines, the availability of nickel alloys having the required performance characteristics has contributed in a very significant way to the development of rocket propulsion.

As an introduction to a discussion of rocket power, the principal characteristics that distinguish the three kinds of aircraft propulsion should be noted. Piston-type aeroplane engines turn a propeller which gives the thrust to drive the plane. In turbo-prop planes the propellers are driven by gas turbines instead of piston engines. In a turbo-jet engine the reaction to the exhaust resulting from the combustion of air and fuel furnishes the thrust to drive the plane. In both piston engines and jet engines the fuel is carried on the plane and the oxygen necessary for combustion is obtained from the atmosphere through which the plane flies. A rocket engine obtains its thrust from the combustion of fuel and an oxidiser, both of which are carried in the vehicle. Consequently rocket engines can operate in an environment containing no oxygen (air) to support combustion of the fuel.

The earliest recorded use of the reaction principle in rocketry was in China, in the eleventh century. This was a *solid-propellant* rocket somewhat similar to the skyrocket of current fireworks displays. The 'bazooka' used in World War II represents a development of the solid-propellant rocket. This same type of thrust propels many of the small missiles and is the source of propulsion for the large Polaris missile with which submarines are equipped, and for the Minuteman Intercontinental Ballistic Missiles. A solid-propellant rocket motor consists of a case filled with solid propellant chemicals (a mixture of fuel and oxidiser) which burn at high pressure on their exposed surfaces, to provide hot reaction gases for expulsion through a nozzle.

It was on 16th March, 1926 that the first *liquid-propellant* rocket, which R. H. Goddard had designed and built, was launched. Petrol was the fuel, liquid oxygen the oxidiser. The development of this type of power plant has advanced through many stages of increased thrust, improved design, higher performance and simplification. Such engines which use liquid chemicals (fuel and oxidiser), which are fed under pressure (by pump or

Mach I and Beyond

pneumatically) from separate storage tanks, into thrust chambers, where they are burned and expelled through a nozzle at high velocities, to impart a propulsive force. The highest specific impulse attainable in liquid-propellant engines is higher than the maximum attainable in solid-propellant motors. Specific impulse—pounds of thrust per pound of propellant burned per second—is used to indicate the performance of rocket motors and engines. The Germans were the first to develop a high-thrust engine (56,000 lbs.) of this type: it burned alcohol and liquid oxygen, and was used in their V-2 rocket missile.

The liquid-propellant rocket engine was further developed by Rocketdyne, a Division of North American Aviation, for the Redstone missile. Their engine developed about 50% more thrust than the V-2, at about the same engine weight. The Redstone's double-walled thrust chamber, made of welded steel, similar in construction to that of the V-2, is cooled by circulation of the fuel. The injector is made of high-nickel steels and alloys. The next important step was the development of the engines for the Navaho booster, made by Rocketdyne. It was in these engines that the thrust chamber made of seamless nickel tubing and a high-temperature gas system for driving the turbines for the pumps were developed. These engines were further perfected, and powered the Thor, Jupiter and Atlas missiles, as well as the first stage of most of the U.S.A. satellites and space-probe launchers. Their thrust chambers were made of as many as 300 formed seamless nickel tubes, which were clustered, reinforced with bands, and brazed together. In the Atlas missile there are three thrust chambers, one for each engine. By 1963 over 500 of these engine-thrust chambers had participated in successful missile launchings.

A similar engine was developed by Rolls-Royce under licence agreement with Rocketdyne. This engine was developed to power Britain's Blue Streak rocket, originally designed as a missile and is now planned for the first stage of the launch vehicle for Europe's space programme.

Stainless steel (10% nickel) seamless tubes are used in the thrust chambers of the Titan missile's rocket engine made by Aerojet.

The Saturn is the high-thrust rocket designed as the weight lifter for satellite stations and space ships. The first stage of the 1,500,000-lb. thrust Saturn C-1 is made up of a cluster of eight of the most advanced and simplified H-1 Rocketdyne engines. In a later model of the Saturn the first stage will produce five times the thrust using five F-1 Rocketdyne 1,500,000-lb. thrust single engines. The thrust chambers are currently made of thin formed seamless tubes of an alloy of very high nickel content.

The next step towards higher specific impulse in accomplishing greater thrust is the liquid-oxygen/liquid-hydrogen engine coming into production, which presents the problem of much higher temperatures.

The thrust chambers of all of these rockets are made of tubes through which the fuel flows on its way to the injector. The cooling provided by the fuel flow prevents local melting of the thrust chamber where the extremely hot products of combustion are contained and directed. For the thrust chambers nickel or high-nickel alloys have been selected, due to the irresistance to corrosion and erosion, strength at high temperatures, and good fabricating and brazing qualities.

F-1 Rocketdyne rocket engine

The tubes, brazed and banded together, are of a high-nickel alloy

Courtesy: North American Aviation, Rocketdyne Division

Nickel: An Historical Review

It is interesting to note that much of the experience with alloys developed in the early days of turbo-superchargers and used for highly stressed turbine parts and exhaust valves has found similar application to the turbines and turbine shafts of the pumps for liquid-propellent rocket engines. High-nickel steels and alloys have played a major rôle in the development of compact, light-weight turbines of high efficiency, developing as much as 60,000 h.p.

As the speed of travel in the earth's atmosphere or of re-entry into it from outer space increases, the designer of aircraft and spacecraft structures encounters a new problem of kinetic heating. In a grossly over-simplified way, this can be likened to frictional heating of the surfaces, especially the leading edges of the aircraft, as it passes through the air at high speed. Although this heating effect increases with speed, it decreases to an even greater extent with altitude, so that it presents no problem in outer space beyond the limits of the earth's atmosphere. The problem reappears, however, upon re-entry into the earth's atmosphere from outer space. The temperatures that can be generated on the surfaces of aircraft operating at supersonic speeds within the earth's atmosphere are beyond limits acceptable for use of such conventional aircraft structure materials as aluminium alloys and even titanium. This barrier to progress has been referred to as the 'thermal thicket'. Operational temperatures have been raised considerably by the use of nickel-base alloys for manned rocket-propelled aircraft structures such as the X-15, which is sheathed with Inconel alloy X-750. Nickel alloys were used extensively in the early manned rocket planes such as the Bell X-2 United States research plane

Mach I and Beyond

X-15 Rocket Plane — *Courtesy: North American Aviation*

which had an airframe structure made entirely of Monel age-hardened alloy K-500 (65% nickel) except for the wings, which were made of stainless steel containing about 10% nickel. As early as 1956 this aircraft set a new speed record for manned aircraft of 2,094 m.p.h. or Mach 2·93.

The advanced record-breaking research rocket plane X-15 is powered by a 57,000-lb. thrust liquid-ammonia/liquid-oxygen engine built by Reaction Motors, a division of Thiokol. The thrust chamber is made of seamless tubing of 10% nickel stainless steel and is coated with a ceramic material. The injector head and fuel manifolds are of uncoated Inconel alloy X-750 (75% nickel)[19] produced by the International Nickel Company. Of the extensive information obtained from the flights of this aeroplane, one of the most important is that of the high-temperature structural integrity of the aircraft at different speeds and in varying positions upon re-entering the earth's denser atmosphere from the fringes of outer space. The current models were designed for temperatures up to 650°C. (1,200°F.), which has been reached on several flights. While the sheathing must withstand, on the outside, a temperature of 650°C. (1,200°F.), on the inside, only a little distance away, it is subjected to the ultra-low temperature of liquid oxygen, namely −184°C. (−300°F.). The solution to the problems of heat flow to internal parts of the X-15 will be useful in the design of advanced aeroplanes and space vehicles.

The first United States manned space capsule to orbit the earth made use of nickel alloys, principally in the 'shingles' covering the outer cylindrical surfaces, which were made of General Electric's René 41 (55% nickel),

WORLD RECORD SPEEDS

1906-1939

ALL AIRCRAFT ON THIS CHART WERE POWERED BY RECIPROCATING PETROL ENGINES. THESE ENGINES CONTAINED MANY PARTS MADE OF NICKEL-ALLOY STEELS

1939 MESSERSCHMITT Bf 109 R (GERMANY) 469·22 m.p.h.
1939 HEINKEL HE-112U (GERMANY) 463·92 m.p.h.
1934 MACCHI M.C.72 (ITALY) 440·68 m.p.h.
1933 MACCHI M.C.72 (ITALY) 423·82 m.p.h.
1931 SUPERMARINE S.6.B. (GREAT BRITAIN) 406·99 m.p.h.
1929 SUPERMARINE S.6 (GREAT BRITAIN) 357·7 m.p.h.
1928 MACCHI M-52 bis (ITALY) 318·62 m.p.h.
1927 MACCHI M52 (ITALY) 297·82 m.p.h.
1924 BERNARD-FERBOIS V2 (FRANCE) 278·48 m.p.h.
1923 CURTISS R2C-1 (U.S.A.) 266·58 m.p.h.
1923 CURTISS R-6 (U.S.A.) 236·59 m.p.h.
1923 NIEUPORT-DELAGE (FRANCE) 233·01 m.p.h.
1922 CURTISS R-6 (U.S.A.) 222·9 m.p.h.
1921 NIEUPORT-DELAGE (FRANCE) 205·2 m.p.h.
1920 NIEUPORT-DELAGE (FRANCE) 194·5 m.p.h.
1913 DEPERDUSSIN (FRANCE) 126·7 m.p.h.
1912 DEPERDUSSIN (FRANCE) 108·2 m.p.h.
1911 NIEUPORT (FRANCE) 82·73 m.p.h.
1910 BLERIOT XII (FRANCE) 68·2 m.p.h.
1909 BLERIOT XI (FRANCE) 47·84 m.p.h.
1909 CURTISS "GOLDEN FLYER" (U.S.A.) 43·38 m.p.h.
1907 VOISIN BIPLANE (FRANCE) 32·75 m.p.h.
1906 SANTOS-DUMONT No. 14 bis (FRANCE) 25·66 m.p.h.
WILBUR WRIGHT (U.S.A.) 31 m.p.h. 1903

Mach I and Beyond

to withstand the effects of exposure to elevated temperature, dynamic and acoustical effects, and fatigue.

Speed is relative. For example, a man riding in an automobile is not moving in relation to the seat in which he is sitting, but when related to a point outside the vehicle, his speed is that of the automobile. Similarly, throughout man's life on this earth, he may have been stationary at a point at the equator while travelling over 1,000 m.p.h. around the axis of the earth, which in turn was travelling at an average speed of 66,600 m.p.h. in its orbit around the sun. Within his own capacity, when a man runs one mile in 4 minutes, he averages 15 m.p.h. Man's top sustained speed, until the advent of the steam locomotive, was about 40 m.p.h., on horseback.

By the end of the nineteenth century steam locomotive speeds had increased to over 100 m.p.h. At the end of the Second World War propeller-aeroplane speeds approached 500 m.p.h. and jet aeroplanes flew at about 600 m.p.h. Since then jet-engined aeroplane speeds have exceeded 1,600 m.p.h. and a manned rocket research plane has exceeded 4,000 m.p.h. The records of achievement of higher and higher speeds attained in level flight by rocket research craft are listed below.

Speed in excess of Mach No.	Aeroplane	Pilot	Date
1·0	X-1 Bell	Yeager	Oct. 1947
2·0	D-558-II Douglas	Crossfield	Nov. 1953
2·9	X-2 Bell	Everest	July 1956
3·1	X-15 North American	Walker	Aug. 1960
4·4	,, ,, ,,	White	Mar. 1961
5·2	,, ,, ,,	,,	June 1961
6·0	,, ,, ,,	,,	Nov. 1961

While these recorded speeds are accurately determined by electronic devices, fuel capacity limits the 'power-on' period to a few minutes. This does not permit rocket-type aircraft to meet the official speed-record requirements for conventional aeroplanes, which are based on average runs in opposite directions.

In space capsules estimated speeds in excess of 18,000 m.p.h. have been attained. The speed of sound was first achieved by man in flight on 14th October, 1947, and was a technological milestone. Speed required to escape the gravitational effect of the earth is 25,000 m.p.h. (7 miles per second); speed to escape the solar system, 384 miles per second; and within the limits of our current knowledge, the speed of light, 186,300 miles per second, would seem to be the ultimate.

This spectacular advance, at various stages in aircraft development, is due not only to the engineer but also, in no small measure, to metallurgical progress. Metals have been the 'tools' without which the 'job' could not have been done. The principles of age-hardening have been of paramount importance. In the early days the principles of precipitation-hardening, first applied to duralumin, made possible a major advance in aircraft construction. Application of the same principles to nickel-base alloys has been equally important in jet engines and space vehicles. Through just such increased technological understanding reduced to practical application man is overcoming his personal limitations. Such then is the pattern of the future.

Per ardua ad astra

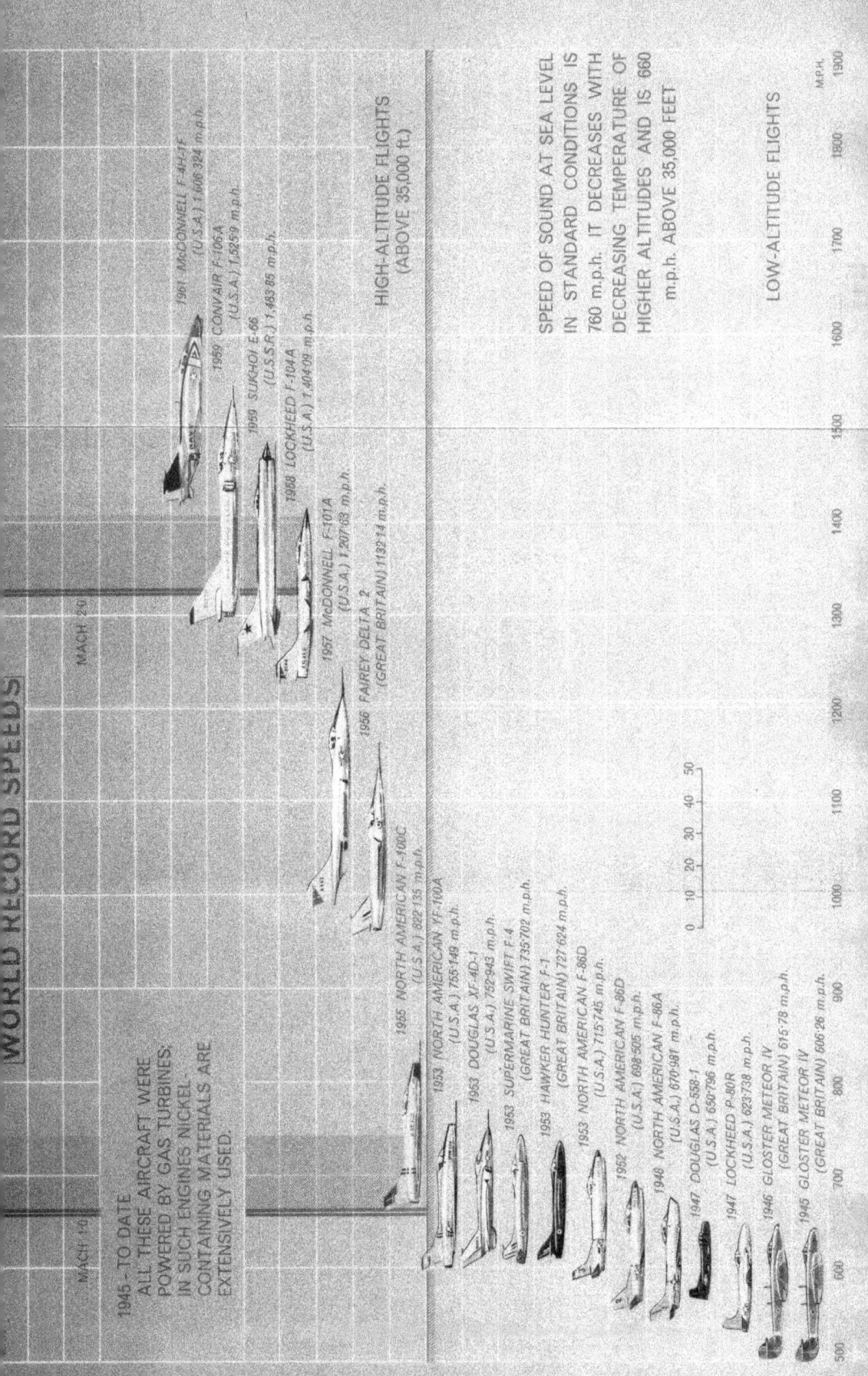

Notes

CHAPTER I

1. A British billion denotes a million millions (1,000,000,000,000). This method is also used in Germany. In the U.S. and France a billion denotes a thousand million (1,000,000,000). A metric ton contains 2,204·6 lbs.

2. Mason, B. *Principles of Geochemistry*. 2nd ed. New York: Wiley, 1958.

   For details of the mode of formation of typical nickel orebodies the reader is referred to Chapter 7, Note 13.

3. Laevastu, T. *and* Thompson, T. G. *Jnl. Conseil Exploration de la Mer*, 1958, **21,** 125–143.

4. The number of microgram atoms per kilogram, when multiplied by the atomic weight of the element concerned, e.g., Ni = 58·69, gives the concentration, by weight, of that element in micrograms per kilogram. 1 microgram per kilogram equals one part per thousand million.

5. Nickel in trace amounts is likewise present in marine organisms. Laevastu and Thompson say that the plankton which they sampled had twice as much nickel as was present in the higher marine plants, and that its nickel content was ten times that of the fish and molluscs which they examined. It has been suggested that this concentration of nickel is evidence that the element has some function in the growth or metabolism of plankton.

Nickel: An Historical Review

Plankton is a generic term covering all unattached living creatures in the sea, including many hundreds of species of both plants and animals, some of the latter being quite sizeable, e.g., some tropical jellyfish, which can be several feet across.

[6] The Downwind Expedition, which formed part of the International Geophysical Year programme of 1959, confirmed the existence of these nodules.
Menard, H. W. *and* Shipek, C. J. *Nature*, 1958, **182**, 1156–1158.

[7] When light emitted by a source such as a star passes through the slit of an optical instrument called a spectrograph the component wavelengths in that beam of light are bent, or refracted, forming images of the slit, and these images appear as lines on a photographic plate. Each element present in the star gives rise to its own characteristic lines, which are collectively referred to as its *spectrum* and, by measuring the positions and densities of those lines in the photograph, the quantity of each particular element present can be computed.

The principal constituents of the sun are:

Element	*Volume, %*	*Element*	*Volume, %*
Hydrogen	81·76	Carbon	0·003
Helium	18·17	Sulphur	0·003
Oxygen	0·030	Iron	0·0008
Magnesium	0·020	Calcium	0·0003
Nitrogen	0·010	Nickel	0·0002
Silicon	0·006		

The sun is, in fact, a gigantic nuclear power house. Its temperature at the centre is around 13,000,000°C. (23,500,000°F.), a fantastic degree of heat which is caused by the continuous conversion, through nuclear processes, of hydrogen into helium.

An atom consists of a number of negative electrical units called *electrons*, which revolve around a positive electrical nucleus. When *electrons* are freed from their orbit the rest of

Notes

the atom is said to be *ionized* but, as such, is unstable, and, as quickly as circumstances permit, the *electrons* are recaptured. The nickel observed spectrographically in the solar *corona* is in a highly ionized state, as Ni XIII and Ni XV.

[8] Bruun, A. F., Langer, E. *and* Pauly, H. *Deep-sea Research*, 1955, **2**, 230–246.
Fredriksson, K. *Nature*, 1956, **177**, 32–33.
Private communication from J. Green, Space and Information Systems Division, North American Aviation, Inc.
Green, J. *Geological Exploration of the Moon*. Columbia University (in preparation).

CHAPTER 2

[1] Braidwood, R. J., Burke, J. E. *and* Nachtrieb, N. H. *Jnl. Chem. Education*, 1951, **28**, 87–96.

[2] British Association. *Report of the 96th Meeting, Glasgow*, 1928. London: the Association, 1929. Sumerian Copper. *Report of the Committee*, pp. 437–441.
Marshall, J. H. *Mohenjo-Daro and the Indus Civilization, being an Official Account of Archaeological Excavations carried out by the Government of India*, 1922–1927, vol. 2, 486–488. London: Probsthain, 1931.

[3] Dr. Masumi Chikashige was Emeritus Professor of Kyoto Imperial University, Tokyo.
Cheng, C. F. *and* Schwitter, C. M. *Amer. Jnl. Archaeology*, 1957, **61**, 351–365.

[4] Numismatic specialists may care to consult
Flight, W. *Numismatic Chronicle* (New Series), 1868, **8**, 305–308.
Gardner, P. *The Coins of the Greek and Scythic Kings of Bactria*

Nickel: An Historical Review

and India in the British Museum. London: British Museum, 1884.

Tarn, W. W. *The Greeks in Bactria and India*. 2nd ed. Cambridge University Press, 1951.

Narain, A. K. *The Indo-Greeks*. Oxford University Press, 1957.

[5] The method of X-ray fluorescence analysis involves no damage to the object assayed. The procedure consists of exposing the surface of a specimen, such as a coin, to an intense incident beam of X-rays, which is absorbed by the surface layers of the specimen. In consequence, the specimen emits secondary X-rays of separate wave lengths characteristic of the elements present, the respective intensities of the rays being dependent upon the concentration of those elements. The secondary radiation is dispersed into a spectrum by means of a diffracting crystal, and the intensity of each wavelength is measured by suitable means. In general, the accuracy of the method can be adjusted to suit the analysis in hand, although in the analysis of coins the accuracy is reduced by the relief of the surface presented to the X-ray beam. In such cases the accuracy of the non-destructive method is probably equivalent to that of the chemical method which employs dimethylglyoxime.

[6] Assays of Bactrian coins and particulars of known nickel-ore occurrences in China, India and the Middle East are given by Cheng, C. F. *and* Schwitter, C. M. (see note [3] above).

[7] Cammann, S. V. R. *Amer. Jnl. Archaeology*, 1958, **62**, 409–414.

[8] Schwitter, C. M. *Amer. Jnl. Archaeology*, 1962, **66**, 87–92.
Cammann, S. V. R. *Amer. Jnl. Archaeology*, 1962, **66**, 92–94.

[9] J. Needham (author of *Science and Civilisation in China*; Cambridge University Press, 1954) has pointed out that *t'ung* and *thung* are simply different forms of romanisation.

Notes

Both indicate that the word should be pronounced *toong* and not *doong*, which would be indicated by *tung*, as the *t*, even though unaspirated, never quite becomes a *d*. For that reason the spelling *thung* has been adopted throughout this book. Eighteenth-century transcribers, to cite Bonnin (note [10], below), wrote the word *petong* and *pehtong*. Other variations are *paaktong* and *packtong*. G. von Engeström, the eminent Swedish chemist, no doubt fell into a scribal error when he spelled it *pak-fong* or *packfong*, as it has so often been misquoted since. Nowadays, if the official romanisation of the People's Republic of China were to be used, the word would be written *baitong*. (All these variations result from attempts to translate Chinese into phonetic English.)

[10] Bonnin, A. *Tutenag and Paktong*. Oxford University Press, 1924.
Du Halde, J. B. *The General History of China, containing a Geographical . . . and Physical Description of the Empire of China, Chinese Tartary, Corea and Thibet* . . . London, 1736.

CHAPTER 3

[1] Zimmer, G. F. *Jnl. Iron and Steel Inst.*, 1916, **94,** 306–356.

[2] Rickard, T. A. *Jnl. Roy. Anthropological Inst.*, 1941, **71,** 55–56.

[3] Paneth, F. A. *Meteorites* in *Encyclopaedia Britannica*, vol. 15, 336–341. London: Encyclopaedia Britannica, 1956.

[4] Tuček, K. *Časopsis Národního Musea, Praha*, 1947, **116,** 1–11.

[5] Nininger, H. H. *Our Stone Pelted Planet*. Boston: Houghton, 1933.

[6] Stone, G. C. *Glossary of the Construction, Decoration and Use of Arms and Armor*, p. 384. Portland, Maine: Southworth Press, 1934.

[7] *Nature*, 1935, **135,** 39.

[8] Heide, F. *Kleine Meteoritenkunde*. Berlin: Springer, 1957.

[9] Graham, R. P. *Canadian Geographical Jnl.*, 1949, **39,** 222–227.

[10] Comprehensive catalogues of all the meteorites of which records are available have been compiled, and from those sources the following data on geographical distribution have been prepared:

Inventory of Meteorites

Territory	Seen to Fall	Found	Total	Doubtful	Paired *	Gross Total
Europe	278	52	330	91	4	425
Asia	204	45	249	24	7	280
Africa	52	34	86	7	1	94
N. America	112	543	655	13	15	683
S. America	22	60	82	6	16	104
Australasia	13	83	96	4	9	109
Miscellaneous	2	2	4	3	—	7
	683	819	1,502	148	52	1,702

* The paired falls are those pairs or groups of falls which are probably identical and have therefore been counted as only one.

Prior, G. T. *Catalogue of Meteorites*, 2nd ed. by M. H. Hey. London: British Museum, 1953.
Brown, H. *Bibliography on Meteorites*. Chicago: University of Chicago Press, 1953.
Mason, B. *Meteorites*, New York: Wiley, 1962.
Moore, C. *Research on Meteorites*, New York: Wiley, 1962.

Notes

[11] Divisions II and III of the classification adopted for meteorites relate to types other than irons, i.e. stony irons and stones. The meteoritic stony irons contain a very high proportion of nickel-iron, through which the stony matter is distributed in crystals or grains. The meteoritic stones consist mainly of silicates of magnesium and iron with some calcium, with only minor amounts of nickel-iron, but nearly always some. E. L. Krinov (note [12] below), quoting A. G. Vinogradov, gives the average for stony meteorites as Ni $1\cdot10\%$, Fe $15\cdot5\%$, but that includes the iron in the silicates. The nickel-iron in four selected Russian meteorites (stony meteorites) ranged from $5\cdot3\%$ to $22\cdot6\%$.

Among the meteorites seen to fall, by far the greater number are stony meteorites. They differ in their composition and structure from nearly all known terrestrial rocks and can be distinguished, except in rare instances, from these by the presence of metallic nickel, though sometimes in only low percentages. Moreover, over 90% of the stones are characterised by the presence of very remarkable small *chondrules*, mostly spherical in shape, but sometimes oval or cylindrical, quite unlike anything ever found in terrestrial rocks. The

Widmanstätten Structure in Meteorites
Courtesy: The Minerological Society

Nickel: An Historical Review

meteorites containing *chondrules* are *chondrites;* those with no *chondrules* are *achondrites.*

The nickel in meteorites is present as nickel-iron alloys which in their meteoritic form are called *kamacite*, from the Greek word καμαξ, a pole or stake, and *taenite* from the Greek word ταινία, a narrow band or fillet. These two irons are inter-grown, each having a regular crystalline pattern based on octahedral or cubic forms and this structure can, in some meteorites, be demonstrated elegantly by etching a polished face of the iron. The patterns revealed are called Widmanstätten figures. This curious Widmanstätten structure is clearly seen in the illustration which appears on previous page.

[12] Krinov, E. L. (*Principles of Meteorites.*) Moscow: Gostekhizdat, 1955. English translation. Oxford: Pergamon Press, 1960.

CHAPTER 4

[1] Agricola, G. *De Re Metallica*. Basle: 1556. English translation by H. C. Hoover *and* L. H. Hoover. New York: Dover Publications, 1950.

[2] The root *Nick* stems from the Beowulf saga, about A.D. 1000, in which the word *nicor* appears. It denoted a sea monster associated with devastation. Out of that root grew *niker, nyker, neck, necker, nicker* and other variants, depending on the language or dialect.

In Central Europe the word *nickel* was used as early as 1329 to apply to hussies or strumpets who had earned (*ernickelt*) this or that; to small and ugly horses; to a disability of goats; to the sound *nickt* made when a saw or knife tip was clicked; to a spintop; to a hill or mountain; and finally, in an adjectival sense, it was associated with the Devil, implying bewitched, illusory, spurious, false, or even stubborn.

There is also an amusing legend of an encounter between 'Old Nick' and St. Dunstan (A.D. 909–988). The story is

Notes

Stanza from MS. of the Beowulf saga (*c.* A.D. 1000), showing origin of the root *nick* from *nicor*
Courtesy: The Trustees of the British Museum

that one day when, in his palace at Mayfield, in Sussex, he was working at his metalcraft, 'Old Nick' appeared to tempt him. The Saint's sturdy reply was to heat his metal-working tongs in the fire and with them seize his adversary by the nose. When the Devil wrenched himself free he leapt at one bound to Tunbridge Wells and buried his nose in the cool and bubbling spring at the foot of the Pantiles, thereby 'imparting to the water its chalybeate qualities', for which it is still famous.

Another word denoting a demon, mischievous sprite or gremlin was *Kobold*, which Mathesius, a cleric of Nürnberg, suggests may have taken its name from *Cabul* (cf. I *Kings*, IX) in Galilee, a mining district which was offered by Solomon to Hiram, King of Tyre, who refused it, saying that it was 'well-named *Cabul*, as Joshua had christened it'.

By the sixteenth century, according to Lazarus Ercker, Chief Superintendent of the Mines of the Holy Roman Empire and the Kingdom of Bohemia, the word *Cobalt* had come into use as a general term signifying impure or hard-to-refine material. Mathesius did not hesitate to associate *Cobelt* with the black devil, remarking 'whether or not the Devil and his hellish crew gave their name to *Cobelt* or *Kobelt*, nevertheless *Cobelt* is a poisonous and injurious metal'.

Thus, both *Nick* and *Kobold* had impolite connotations, but it remains for some future student of semantics to discover why the root *Nick* rather than *Kobold* was applied by the superstitious Saxon miners to troublesome ores. The whole history of nickel might indeed have been altered had they dubbed this recalcitrant ore *Kupfer Kobelt*.

Those wishing to make a further study of the subject should refer to:
Beowulf. Cotton MS Vitellius A XV. British Museum.
Biringuccio, A. *The Pirotechnia of Vannoccio Biringuccio*, translated from the Italian. New York: Amer. Inst. of Min. & Met. Engrs., 1942.
Ercker, L. *Lazarus Ercker's Treatise on Ores and Assaying*, translated from the German edition of 1580. Chicago: University of Chicago Press, 1951.
Grimm, J. *and* Grimm, W. *Deutsches Wörterbuch*, vol. 7, col. 733–735. Leipzig: 1854–1961.
Murray, J. et al. *A New English Dictionary on Historical Principles*, vol. 6, part 2. Oxford: Clarendon Press, 1888– .
Brewer, E. C. *Dictionary of Phrase and Fable*. London: Cassell, 1952.
Morral, F. R. *Wire and Wire Products*, 1957, **32**, 300–303, 334–335.

[3] The search which brought to light the unique information contained in these archives was made possible by the kind co-operation of the then Rektor of the Freiberg Berg-

Notes

akademie, Prof. Dr. Ing. O. Oelsner, by whose courtesy permission to publish has been granted, and of the Librarian and Archivist, Direktor Schellhas.

[4] *Kupfer Nickel* (with several variants) is spelt in each case in the manner in which the words are given in the original document quoted. The preferred spelling is *Kupfer Nickel*.

[5] Hjärne, U. *En Kort Anledning till Åtskillige Malm och Bergarters/ Mineraliers Wäxters/och Jordslags/samt flera sällsamma Tings efterspöriande och angifvande*. Stockholm: 1694.

[6] Wallerius, J. G. *Mineralogie oder Mineralreich*. Berlin: 1750.

[7] Brandt, G. *Acta Lit. Scient. Sveciae*, 1735, **4,** 1–12; *Acta Soc. Reg. Scient. Upsaliensis*, 1742, 33–41.

[8] Cronstedt, A. F. *Kongl. Svenska Vetenskaps Acad. Handl.*, 1751, **12,** 287–292.

Professor Hägg, of Uppsala University, kindly examined, for the purpose of this book, Cronstedt's original manuscript of the paper he read on 2nd November, 1751, in the Swedish Royal Academy of Sciences in Stockholm. He found that before acceptance of that manuscript, the Academy submitted it to two of its members, who endorsed on it a recommendation of which an English translation reads:

'These beautiful new observations deserve to be communicated in the Transactions of the Royal Academy of Sciences.

      (Signed)   G. Brandt   (Signed)   Scheffer.'

[9] The usual meaning of *colcothar* is the brownish-red oxide of iron which remains after ferrous sulphate is heated.

[10] *Op. cit.*, note [8] above, 1754, **15,** 38–45.

Professor Hägg also searched all Cronstedt's archives in the Royal Library in Stockholm and in the Library of the Swedish Royal Academy of Sciences, including the many

Nickel: An Historical Review

manuscripts and various letters he wrote between 1751 and 1754 to scientists interested in chemistry and in mineralogy. In none of these is there any clue why Cronstedt took three years, i.e. until 1754, to select *Nickel* as the name for the new semi-metal he had isolated.

[11] Cronstedt, A. F. *An Essay towards a System of Mineralogy*, translated from the Swedish with notes by G. von Engeström. London: E. & C. Dilly, 1770.

Proof that the Erzgebirge district in Saxony was still the principal source of supply of *Kupfer Nickel* around the period when Cronstedt was carrying out his investigations exists in a 1746 German publication, from which this translation has been made:

'In this country *Cobalt* is mostly mined in Schneeberg, but some is found in Johann-Georgenstadt and Annaberg, and even a little at Marienberg. The Schneeberg *cobalt* mines are in part 120 to 130 fathoms (Lächter) deep; the surface mines are not good, but the deeper ones break better; parts break into quartz, usually of a very pretty colour, and parts into *Kupfer Nickel*, brown in colour, and then also parts into shale.'

Zimmermann, C. F. *Ober-Sächsische Berg-Academie* . . . Dresden: F. Hekel, 1746.

CHAPTER 5

[1] Cronstedt, A. F. *Kongl. Svenska Vetenskaps Acad. Handl.*, 1751, **12,** 287–292; 1754, **15,** 38–45.

[2] Bergman, T., *Praeses and* Arvidsson, J. A. *Respondent. Dissertatio Chemica de Niccolo.* Uppsala: Typis Edmannianis, 1775.

[3] Scheffer, H. T. *Chemiske Föreläsningar Rörande Salter, Jordarter, Vatten, Fetmor, Metaller och Färgning, Samlade, i Ordning Stälde och med Anmärkningar Utgifne.* Uppsala: 1775. (Preface only

Notes

signed 'T. Bergman'. Text contains comments and tables by Bergman.)

4. Fourcroy, A. F. de. *Elements of Natural History and of Chemistry*, translated by W. Nicholson. London: Robinson, 1782.

5. Bredberg, B. G. *Jnl. Prakt. Chem.*, 1851, **53**, 242–248; **54**, 79–83.

6. The chemical symbols of all the elements are given in the Periodic Table, appearing on p. 302. There are now 102 known elements.

7. Proust, J. L. *Jnl. Chem. Phys.*, 1807, **3**, 410–451. *Neues Allgem. Jnl. Chem.*, 1804, **2**, 53–60 (translated from *Jnl. Phys. Chim. Hist.*, 1803, **57**, 169–173).

8. Richter, J. B. *Neues Allgem. Jnl. Chem.*, 1804, **2**, 61–72; 1804, **3**, 244–276, 444–446; 1805, **5**, 699–702.

9. Thénard, L. J. *Ann. Chim.*, 1804, **50**, 117–133.

CHAPTER 6

1. Libavius, A. *De Natura Metallorum*. Frankfurt: 1597.

2. Du Halde, J. B. *The General History of China, containing a Geographical . . . and Physical Description of the Empire of China, Chinese Tartary, Corea, and Thibet . . .* London: 1736.

3. Bonnin, A. *Tutenag and Paktong*. Oxford University Press, 1924.

4. Engeström, G. von. *Kongl. Vetenskaps Acad. Handl.*, 1776, **37**, 35–38.
   Hepar sulphuris was the alchemist's name for a compound of sulphur and an alkaline metal.

⁵ Watson, R. *Chemical Essays*, 2nd ed., vol. 4, pp. 1–84. Cambridge: 1786.

⁶ Fyfe, A. *Edinburgh Phil. Jnl.*, 1822, **7,** 69–71.

⁷ Thomason, E. *Memoirs*. London: 1845.

⁸ Keferstein, C. et al. *Schweiggers Jnl. Chem. Phys.*, 1823, **39,** 17–37.

⁹ Erdmann, O. L. *Schweiggers Jnl. Chem. Phys.*, 1826, **48,** 129–139; postcript by Schweigger, 139–152.

¹⁰ The first people in Germany to produce, about 1823–24, a locally-made version of *pai-thung* were J. C. Hochheim, of Leipzig, J. R. von Gersdorff of Reichenau, near Schneeberg (Chief Assay Master to the Imperial Mint in Vienna, where he also had a factory) and E. A. Geitner, a highly-skilled manufacturer in Schneeberg. Geitner called the alloy *Argentan;* von Gersdorff used the name *Alpakka*.

Neumann, B. *Zeitsch. angew. Chem.*, 1903, **16,** 225–232.
Gersdorff, J. R. von. *Ann. Phys. Chem.*, 1826, **8,** 103–106.

¹¹ The Askin story is based on a private communication sent on 14th December, 1878, to Henry Wiggin by H. W. Keates of the smelting firm of Newton, Keates and Company. Apparently, in 1824, Keates had been asked to go to Mexico as manager of a smelting plant, but he declined the offer and, knowing that a great number of mules were used there, he suggested that Askin, who was a veterinary surgeon, would be the man for the job.

As stated in the text, Askin decided first to study technique on the Continent because 'he was fast becoming disgusted with the difficulties and drudgeries of his own profession and particularly with having to combat the ignorance and prejudices of grooms and coachmen, whose influence with their masters, almost as ignorant as themselves, had so

Notes

wearied him of the whole business'. He was in a mind to avail himself of any chance of quitting the veterinary profession and taking up some job more in harmony with his powers and inclinations, and had determined to see whether, among the multifarious metal industries in Birmingham, he could find something to do.

Keates, who since his boyhood had been familiar with pottery *speiss*, commonly known as *nickel*, was the first to introduce this material to Askin. This *nickel* was at that time being used in small quantities in an alloy for 'mill brass' bearings for the gudgeons and axles of machinery.

[12] Barker, S. *History of the Manufacture of Nickel and Cobalt.* Birmingham: J. Upton, 1865.

[13] Before long an unbelievably large number of trade names (some of which were the registered trademarks of the makers) had been coined for this alloy; these are set out in the table below. Actually it was not until the present century that these copper-nickel-zinc alloys came to be known as nickel silver, but that designation has been included in this list for the sake of completeness.

Trade Names for Nickel Silver

Albata	Argyrine
Alfenide	Argyrolith
Alpaca	Bismuth brass
Alpakka	Bismuth bronze
Ambrac	Blanca
Argent allemand	British plate
Argent neuf	Carbondale silver
Argentan	China silver
Argentine	Chromax bronze
Argozie	Colorado silver
Argozoil	Craig gold
Arguzoid	

(*continued on next page*)

Nickel: An Historical Review

Trade Names for Nickel Silver—continued

Electroplate	Ruolz alloy
Electrum	Semi-argent
German silver	Silverine
Iridium argyroide	Silverite
Keene's alloy	Spoon metal
Lutecin	Sterlin
Maillechort	Sterline
Markus alloy	Stuffing-box alloy
Merry's metal blanc	Suhl white copper
Merry's plate	Swedish nickel
Neogen	Toucas metal
Neusilber	Tuc tur
Nevada silver	Tungsten brass
New silver	Victor metal
Nickel bronze	Virginia silver
Nickel oreide	Weiss Kupfer
Nickel silver	Wessels silver
Nickeline	White Argentan
Platinoid	White copper
Pope's island metal	White metal
Potosi silver	White solder
Prata teutonica	Wolfram brass
Queen's metal	

[14] Lathrop, W. G. *The Brass Industry in the United States.* Mount Carmel, Conn.: priv. print, 1926.

CHAPTER 7

[1] The Werner collection of minerals, at Freiberg, in Saxony, contains every known mineral found in the Erzgebirge area. Abraham Gottlieb Werner (1749–1817) was Professor of Mineralogy and Mining at the Mining Academy in Freiberg.

Important mining centres were at Aue and Joachimstal; the names of some of the mines were Weisser Hirsch, Gesellschafter Zug, Sieben Schleen, Adam Heber, Wolfgangmaasen, Alter Türke, Priester and Beustschacht. Other

Notes

nickeliferous deposits in the Erzgebirge, from which mineral specimens in the collection were obtained, were the Himmelsfürst, Segen Gottes, Erbstollen, Daniel, Adolphus, Fabian and Catharina Fundgrube.
Beck, R. *Die Lehre von den Erzlagerstätten.* Berlin: Borntraeger, 1901.
Charleton, A. G. *Jnl. Soc. Arts*, 1895, **43,** 609–661.

[2] Lacroix, A. *Minéralogie de la France et de ses Colonies*, vol. 2. Paris: Baudry *et* Béranger, 1893–1913.

[3] Barlow, A. E. *Canada Geological Survey*. Report No. 961, 1907, 166.

[4] Garnier, J. *Annales des Mines*, 1867, **12,** Sér. 6, 1–92, especially 84 and 85.

[5] A description of the wet method of extraction used at that time is given by Roberts-Austen, W. C., *An Introduction to the Study of Metallurgy*. London: Griffin, 1891.
See also Chapter 8.

[6] Heurteau, E. *Annales des Mines*, 1876, **9,** Sér. 7, 232–373.

[7] Garland, J. *Trans. Instn. Min. and Met.*, 1893–1894, **2,** 121–134, especially 131; disc. 134–148.

[8] Thompson, J. F. *and* Beasley, N. *For the Years to Come: a Story of International Nickel of Canada.* New York: Putnam, 1960.

[9] Robert Means Thompson and John Fairfield Thompson, each of whom became Chairman of the International Nickel Company, were not related in any way.

[10] In 1883 the name of The Orford Nickel and Copper Company was changed to The Orford Copper and Sulphur Company.

[11] The Orford Copper Company was incorporated in 1887, after W. E. C. Eustis and R. M. Thompson had decided to separate. Thompson kept the smelter. Eustis kept the mine

Nickel: An Historical Review

at Capelton, but in 1888 changed the name of the Company from The Orford Copper and Sulphur Company to The Eustis Mining Company.

[12] Canada, Royal Commission on the Mineral Resources of Ontario and Measures for their Development. *Report.* Toronto: 1890.

[13] Nickel-ore deposits fall into two classes, sulphide and lateritic. In the Sudbury district of Ontario, for example, the nickel-bearing sulphide minerals were concentrated when the rocks in which they occur were at depths of a few thousand or many thousand feet below the then-existing surface of the earth.

Several thousand million years ago the earth already had its basic shape and size and as a whole may have been heating-up instead of cooling-down. In sweeping through some of the heaviest concentrations of cosmic débris, the mass which was to become the earth had gathered up a wide variety of elements from which, aeons later, its rocks were to be formed. Deep down in the crust of the earth, due, perhaps, to heat resulting from the breakdown of radioactive elements, a mass of molten rock had formed. This mass existed under a great pressure, and eventually was forced towards the earth's surface, along a channel of weakness in the earth's crust. Where the molten rock came into contact with the underside of a thick layer of sedimentary and volcanic rock it spread out laterally, to form a large lens-shaped mass known as the nickel intrusive. At that stage the intrusive may have been nearly horizontal, but there is evidence to suggest that it was somewhat basin-shaped.

As the molten material began to cool it separated into two main layers. In the heavier bottom layer, dispersed through the rock-forming materials, were sulphur and small amounts of nickel, copper, iron and cobalt, together with trace quantities of gold, silver and platinum. Over countless ages the molten material slowly cooled and the rock constituents began to crystallise. The crystals grew until they touched each other, rejecting, in this process, some of the metal

Notes

elements and sulphur, and these, still in molten form, filled the spaces between the crystals. Finally, within this molten liquid, a combination of temperature, pressure, and concentration of elements created the conditions in which the sulphur combined with the other elements; first with copper, then with nickel, and lastly with iron, until all the sulphur was used up. The sulphide liquids trickled downward between the rock crystals, some forming pools on the floor of the intrusion and some being trapped as droplets above the pools. With time the nickel intrusive collapsed towards the underlying place whence it had initially been ejected, thereby forming a more pronouncedly basin-shaped structure. Subsequent erosion exposed the intrusive.

The molten sulphides finally crystallised, as minerals containing various combinations of copper sulphide, nickel sulphide and iron sulphide. In some such manner the nickel-bearing sulphide deposits were formed in the unique elliptical area known as the Sudbury Basin in Canada.

In the oxide type of ore, commonly known as lateritic, the nickel has been concentrated by rock-weathering related to the present, or a former, erosion surface of the earth. When rocks are exposed to the atmosphere at the earth's surface they are gradually decomposed. The continued chemical and mechanical action of air, water, heat, and cold breaks them down into soil or clay. If the rocks contain nickel the weathering process may act to concentrate their nickel content to such a degree that the resulting deposits can be mined as nickel ore. Essentially, nickel is taken into solution in the groundwater and re-deposited at greater depth, producing a zone where the nickel content is abnormally high.

The type of weathering that tends to separate nickel from silicon and associated elements, and produce nickel deposits, is the same as that which, acting on rock of another type, would produce aluminium ore (bauxite). The process is called lateritic weathering, the term deriving from the Latin word for brick earth; hence the generic term 'lateritic nickel ores' for the oxide nickel deposits of New Caledonia, Cuba, and elsewhere.

Nickel: An Historical Review

CHAPTER 8

[1] There are records of the production, in Germany, of the cobalt-containing blue pigment during the first half of the sixteenth century. Blaufarbenwerke in Schneeberg appear to have been the first in the field, but the growing popularity of the material later led to its manufacture in several other districts. The many names by which the pigment was known included *Smalt, Zaffer, Safflor* and *Eschel*.

[2] McDonald, D. *Percival Norton Johnson; the Biography of a Pioneer Metallurgist*. London: Johnson, Matthey & Co., 1951.

[3] Edward White Benson the chemist was the father of Edward White Benson who was Archbishop of Canterbury (1883–1898). The grandfather of the archbishop had squandered a handsome fortune, and his son Edward White Benson the elder was forced to set up as a chemical manufacturer in Birmingham. It was there that the archbishop was born, in 1829.

[4] Roberts-Austen, W. C. *An Introduction to the Study of Metallurgy*. London: Griffin, 1891.

[5] Glasser, E. *Annales des Mines*, 1903, **4**, Sér. 10, 363–392, 397–536.
Canada, Royal Ontario Nickel Commission. *Report*, pp. 247, 251. Toronto: 1917.

[6] The following information is available on wages paid to miners working in New Caledonia in the early eighteen-eighties: Englishmen were paid from 6 f. to 9 f. ($1.20 to $1.80) per day and the Kanakas received their board and 20 f. ($4) per month. The best workmen were the convicts freed from the French penal settlement on that island; they earned from 5 f. to 6 f. ($1 to $1.20) per day.
Mineral Industry, 1893, **2**, 475–480.

Notes

[7] Wharton, J. *Memorandum concerning small Money and Nickel Alloy Coinage, with Illustrations and Descriptions of existing Nickel Alloy Coins* (Camden, nr. Philadelphia: American Nickel Works), 1877.

[8] Ulke, T. *Mineral Industry*, 1894, **3**, 459–468.

[9] Thompson, R. M. *Mineral Industry*, 1892, **1**, 357–358.

[10] The use of *sal enixum*, or borax, as a flux was in common use as far back as 1838. It is mentioned in British Patents Nos. 7909 and 8232 (1838), granted to Job Cutler.

[11] Thompson, J. F. *and* Beasley, N. *For the Years to Come: a Story of International Nickel of Canada*, p. 89. New York: Putnam, 1960.

[12] Loc cit.[9]

[13] Bartlett, C. C. United States Patent 499,314, 1893.

[14] Engeström, G. *von*. *Kongl. Vetenskaps Acad. Handl.*, 1776, **37**, 35–38. *Hepar sulphuris* was the alchemist's name for a compound of sulphur and an alkaline metal.

[15] Thompson, R. M. United States Patent 489,881, 1892.

[16] Thomson, J. L. United States Patent 489,882, 1892.

[17] Thompson, R. M. United States Patents 489,574–6, 1892.

[18] Donnan, F. G. *Ludwig Mond, F.R.S., 1839–1909*. London: Institute of Chemistry, 1939.

[19] Cohen, J. M. *The Life of Ludwig Mond*. London: Methuen, 1956.

[20] Mond, L. *Jnl. Soc. Chem. Ind.*, 1895, **14**, 945–946.

[21] The pilot plant for production of nickel viâ the carbonyl, built at the Smethwick works of Henry Wiggin and Company,

near Birmingham, was known locally as the 'soap 'ole' because at one time it had been proposed to manufacture soap there. For years afterwards the black wooden shed that housed the nickel carbonyl pilot plant was known as 'The Mond shed'.

[22] Emmens, S. H. *Mineral Industry*, 1892, **1,** 352–356.

[23] Roberts-Austen, W. C. *Proc. Instn. Civil Engrs.*, 1899, **135,** 29–44; disc. 45–53.

[24] It was to Henry Gardner that the Presidency of the International Nickel Company was offered when that company was incorporated in 1902, but he declined the offer.

[25] U.S. Bureau of Mines, *Materials Survey: Nickel*, 1950. Washington: Govt. Print. Office, 1952.

CHAPTER 9

[1] Faraday records that 'my education was of the most ordinary description, consisting of little more than the rudiments of reading, writing and arithmetic at a common day-school'. In 1804 he started life as an errand boy to Mr. George Riebau, a bookseller and bookbinder in London, to whom he became apprenticed soon afterwards. Faraday says 'whilst an apprentice I loved to read the scientific books which were under my hands and, amongst them, delighted in Marcet's *Conversations in Chemistry*, and the electrical treatises in the *Encyclopaedia Britannica*. His leaning towards a scientific career was prompted by the article on 'Electricity' in an encyclopaedia which he was employed to bind. He proved his zeal to increase his knowledge of scientific subjects by paying, out of his own meagre resources, the fees for lectures in natural philosophy.

When about 17, just before completion of his apprenticeship, he started a correspondence with a friend, Benjamin

Notes

Abbot, a confidential clerk in London, who had enjoyed greater educational advantages than had been available to Faraday. It was in a letter to him that Faraday alluded, for the first time, to nickel. At a later date (1845) an entry in Faraday's diary records that he was obtaining nickel from Askin.
Faraday, M. *Experimental Researches in Electricity*. London: Taylor, 1839–1855. *Faraday's Diary, being the Various Philosophical Notes of Experimental Investigations*, 1820–1862. London: Bell, 1932–1936.

[2] Sporadically, small quantities of nickel-copper ore were mined from the deposit in Inveraray, in Argyllshire, but a survey in recent times proved that the occurrence was of no economic significance.

[3] The names mentioned below are among the many who made significant contributions to steel development during the nineteenth century.

In Great Britain there were W. C. Roberts-Austen, R. A. Hadfield, J. Whitworth, E. Vickers, H. C. Sorby, W. Jessop, John Brown, Charles Cammell, and William Beardmore; in America J. Fritz, A. Holley, A. Carnegie, C. Schwab, H. C. Frick and H. Phipps; in France E. and P. Martin, J. Holtzer and J. Schneider; in Germany Friedrich, father of Alfred, Krupp; and in Sweden G. and F. Goransson.

[4] Some years later Sir Henry Bessemer related the story of some experiments which he had made in 1842. While working with a material known as 'silver bronze' he had observed that an addition of nickel toughened the alloy and 'rendered it less liable to chip at the edge'. This observation led him to try the effect of nickel in iron, and so successful were the results which he obtained that he conceived the idea that nickel steel might prove valuable for ordnance. However, he was informed by the then Minister of War that 'steel was wholly inapplicable to the manufacture of ordnance', and his records were consigned to a box in the lumber room!
Wiggin, H. A. *Jnl. Iron and Steel Inst.*, 1895, **48**, 164–209.

Nickel: An Historical Review

[5] Riley's name is always linked with the discovery of nickel steel because he made the first systematic series of practical tests and published his results for all the world to read. (*Jnl. Iron and Steel Inst.*, 1889, **35,** 45–55; disc. 56–67.)

As will be seen from the table opposite, the nickel content of the steels which he used in his experiments varied from 1% to 49·4%, spread over twelve separate samples. Explaining the table, Riley pointed out that the carbon content of 0·22% in heat No. 6 was low enough to make the material comparable with plain carbon steel, which, after annealing, would give an elastic limit of 16 tons per sq. in. (35,840 p.s.i.) and a breaking strain of 30 tons per sq. in. (67,200 p.s.i.). The addition of 4·7% nickel had thus raised the elastic limit from 16 to 28 tons per sq. in. (35,840 to 62,720 p.s.i.) and the breaking strain from 30 to 40·6 tons per sq. in. (67,200 to 90,944 p.s.i.), without appreciably lowering elongation or contraction of area. With 3% of nickel and with the carbon raised to 0·35%, somewhat similar results were obtained, as shown by heat No. 3. In heats Nos. 2 and 5 extreme hardness was obtained, due partly to the higher carbon contents (0·90% and 0·85%) and partly to the presence of nickel.

With carbon lowered to 0·5%, hardness was intensified by increasing the nickel to 10%, as proved by heat No. 9. Hardness was found to rise as the nickel content approximated to 20%, but larger amounts tended to make the steel softer and more ductile, and even to neutralise the influence of carbon, as was shown by heat No. 11, which contained 0·82% carbon and 25% nickel.

Remarkable properties were also obtained by Riley with the steel containing 25% nickel. In the annealed condition, heat No. 11 showed outstanding ductility, up to 40% elongation before fracture, and in the unannealed state this steel had a high breaking strain and a reasonably good elastic limit.

[6] *Engineer*, 1892, **74,** 147 and 396.

Notes

RILEY'S TESTS OF STEEL WITH VARYING CONTENTS OF NICKEL.[5]

Mark	Composition per Cent.			Tensile Tests as Cast				Tensile Tests as Cast and Annealed				Tensile Tests as Rolled				Tensile Tests as Rolled and Annealed			
						Extension per cent. in.				Extension per cent. in.				Extension per cent. in.				Extension per cent. in.	
	Ni.	C.	Mn.	E.L.	B.S.	8 in.	4 in.	C.A.	E.L.	B.S.	8 in.	4 in.	C.A.	E.L.	B.S.	8 in.	4 in.	C.A.	E.L.	B.S.	8 in.	4 in.	C.A.
	Per cent.	Per cent.	Per cent.	Tons.	Tons.			Per cent.	Tons.	Tons.			Per cent.	Tons.	Tons.			Per cent.	Tons.	Tons.			Per cent.
1	1·0	·42	·58	Test-piece defective.					27·3	54·6	...	1·5	9·5	32·1	57·6	...	11·0	24·0	30·1	55·1	...	18·7	45·0
2	2·0	·90	·50	Too hard to machine with musket-steel.									Makes a fine tool tempered at dull red in boiling water.										
3	3·0	·35	·57	19·8	34·9	2·5	5·6	24·0	34·9	...	2·5	9·0	31·4	51·0	...	20·3	37·0	28·0	48·5	...	20·3	42·0
4	3·0	·60	·26	...	...	...	...	...	...	...	...	29·4	51·5	9·0	10·1	9·0	30·3	42·9	7·5	9·0	12·0		
5	4·0	·85	·50	Too hard to machine with musket-steel.									Makes a fine tool tempered at dull red in boiling water.										
6	4·7	·22	·23	...	...	...	...	...	...	...	...	25·1	40·5	17·75	23·4	42·0	28·0	40·6	20·0	25·0	44·8		
7	5·0	·30	·30	...	...	...	...	...	...	...	...	30·0	46·4	10·0	12·5	22·5	28·0	42·6	15·0	17·5	18·5*		
8	5·0	·50	·34	...	...	...	...	...	...	...	...	31·1	52·0	14·0	15·6	14·0	32·5	46·8	13·5	14·0	17·0		
9	10·0	·50	·50	Too hard to machine.					Makes a good cutting tool when tempered in cold air-blast.														
10	25·0	·27	·85	...	...	...	...	...	...	...	...	38·2	51·4	10·5	11·7	...	12·75	45·8	29·0	30·0	28·6		
11	25·0	·82	·52	...	...	...	...	...	...	...	...	22·0	47·6	43·5	47·6	60·0	15·1	42·1	40·0	45·3	43·6		
12	49·4	·35	·57	...	...	...	...	...	...	...	...	20·5	37·4	12·0	12·0	24·0	21·0	37·0	...	20·0	29·0		

E.L. = Elastic limit.   B.S. = Breaking strain.   C.A. = Contraction of area.
*Average reduced by one piece, giving low result.

283

CHAPTER 10

[1] Phillips, W. M. *Amer. Electroplaters' Soc. Monthly Rev.*, 1933, **20,** 28–35.

[2] Berzelius, J. J. *and* Hisinger, W. *Gehlens Jnl.*, 1803, **1,** 147.

[3] Brugnatelli, L. *Jnl. Phys.*, 1806, **62,** 298–318.

[4] Among the scientists who contributed to the progress of electrodeposition were Volta (1745–1827), Wollaston (1766–1826), Humphry Davy (1778–1821), Grotthus (1785–1822) and Daniell (1790–1845).

[5] Two principles fundamental to electrodeposition were formulated by Faraday:
 (i) Weight of metal deposited is proportional to the quantity of current passed.
 (ii) For a similar quantity of current, the weight of metal deposited is proportional to its chemical equivalent.

These new ideas of Faraday naturally needed new and lucid terms to explain them. He was still probing in his mind for words that would differentiate a positive electrode from a negative one. *Eisode* and *exode* might do. Other proposals, e.g. *zeteisode* and *zetexode*, even *eastode* and *westode; oriode* and *occiode: anatalode* and *dysiode*, were postulated. (*Zetodes* or *stechions*, i.e. things that go, or seek to go, opposite ways, were later named *ions*.) None of these words, however, satisfied so meticulous a man as Faraday, and he sought advice from various scientific friends. One of them, the Reverend William Whewell, D.D., a don (and later Master) of Trinity College, Cambridge, and also a Fellow of the Royal Society, was particularly helpful. Many were the terms discussed, and ultimately the decision was given in favour of *anodes* ($'ανα$ = upwards; $όδός$ = way) and *cathodes* ($κατα$ = downwards; $όδός$ = way). These, said Whewell, were good Greek words, and thus were *anode* (a way up) and *cathode* (a way down) born. But if Faraday did

Notes

not like that pair of words, Whewell gave several alternatives. They included *voltode* and *galvanode; alphode* and *betode:* see p. 286.

[6] Bird, G. *Phil. Trans.*, 1837, **127,** 37–45.

[7] Shore, J. British Patent 8407, 1840.

[8] Ruolz-Montchal, H.-C. *de.* French Patent 10,472, 1841. Ruolz-Montchal, H.-C. *de. Comptes Rend.*, 1841, **13,** 998–1021.

[9] Böttger, R. *Jnl. Prakt. Chem.*, 1843, **30,** 267–271.

[10] A. C. Becquerel, who later became Professor of Physics at the Musée d'Histoire Naturelle in Paris, had announced in 1831 that he had found it possible, using solutions of many elements (including manganese, iron, arsenic, copper, silver, gold and platinum) quickly to precipitate, on the negative wire, a certain quantity of reduced metal. He qualified his statement, however, by remarking that nickel, cobalt, titanium, uranium and chromium showed no noticeable trace of reduction.

[11] Charleton, A. G. *Jnl. Soc. Arts.*, 1895, **43,** 647–661.

[12] Woodbury, D. O. *A Measure for Greatness: A Short Biography of Edward Weston.* New York: McGraw-Hill, 1949.

[13] Langbein, G. E. L. *Vollständiges Handbuch der Galvanischen Metallniederschläge.* Leipzig: 1886; 2nd ed. 1889.

[14] Hampton, T. *The Nickel Plate Road.* Cleveland and New York: World Publishing Company, 1947.

[15] Wharton, J. *Memorandum concerning small Money and Nickel Alloy Coinage, with Illustrations and Descriptions of existing Nickel Alloy Coins.* (Camden, nr. Philadelphia: American Nickel Works), 1877.

Nickel: An Historical Review

Faraday to Whewell—24th April 1834

Whewell to Faraday—25th April 1834

Faraday to Whewell—3rd May 1834

Whewell to Faraday—6th May 1834

Courtesy: The Master and Fellows of Trinity College, Cambridge

Notes

[16] The use of nickel in coinage is of such importance that a whole Chapter (17) has been devoted to it.

[17] Vereinigte Deutsche Nickelwerke A.G. *Private Communication*, 1959.

[18] Fleitmann, T. German Patent 6365, 1878.

[19] Roos, P. F. *van*. *Intern. Conf. f. Hygiene u. Demographie*, 6*th*, Vienna, 1887, pp. 144–149.

[20] Dear Mr. Colby, (see original, p. 288)

Yours of 9/22 to my Phil. office reaches me here, with copy of your letter to Landis and Hampton which seems to me judicious.

I sent to International Nickel Co. the answer to my letter to Secy. Shaw, which answer you have no doubt seen. As Shaw is away from Washington (probably electioneering) there is apparently little or no chance of any one taking up in his absence the question of material for Panama coins. Probably I may be able to do something after Oct. 6.

My recollection concerning the first production of malleable nickel by myself is that I had experimented successfully in 1871 and 1872; that I made in 1872 and the early part of 1873 the articles of malleable nickel which were exhibited at Vienna in 1873; that Dr. Fleitmann seeing those articles there was moved to try for a good working method, and found it in the addition of magnesium to the fluid nickel, thus removing the oxygen, which I had done by Carbon. This reduction of the Nickel Oxide more perfectly than had been practiced, and the demonstration that nickel thus freed from oxide is malleable, is the substance of my work in that line.

Yours truly,
Joseph Wharton

[21] Percy, J. *Metallurgy: Iron and Steel*. London: Murray, 1864.

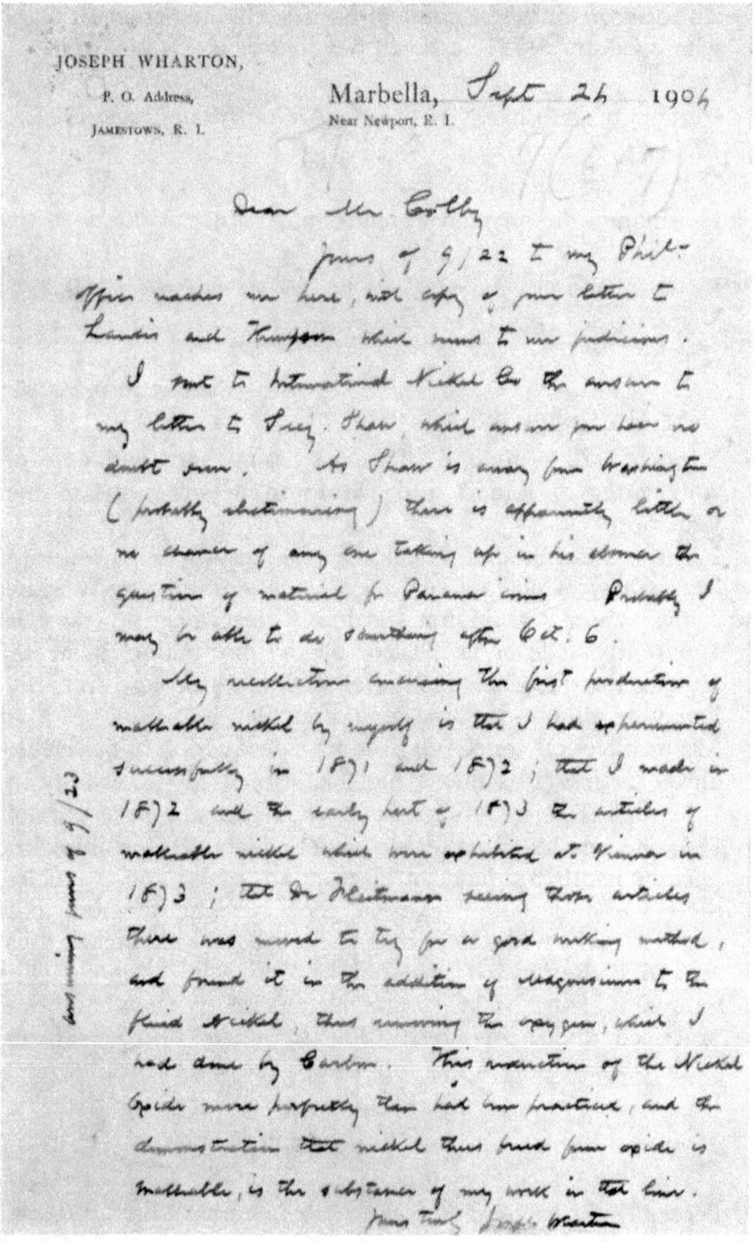

JOSEPH WHARTON,
P. O. Address,
JAMESTOWN, R. I.

Marbella, Sept 24 1904
Near Newport, R. I.

Dear Mr Colby

Yours of 9/22 to my Phila
Office reaches me here, with copy of your letter to
Hawkins and Thompson which seems to me judicious.

I sent to International Nickel Co. the answer to
my letter to Secy. Shaw which answer you have no
doubt seen. As Shaw is away from Washington
(probably electioneering) there is apparently little or
no chance of any one taking up in his absence the
question of material for Panama coins. Probably I
may be able to do something after Oct. 6.

My recollections concerning the first production of
malleable nickel by myself is that I had experimented
successfully in 1871 and 1872; that I made in
1872 and the early part of 1873 the articles of
malleable nickel which were exhibited at Vienna in
1873; that Dr Fleitmann seeing those articles
there was moved to try for a good working method,
and found it in the addition of magnesium to the
fluid Nickel, thus removing the oxygen, which I
had done by Carbon. This reduction of the Nickel
Oxide more perfectly than had been practised, and the
demonstration that nickel thus freed from oxide is
malleable, is the substance of my work in that line.

Yours truly Joseph Wharton

[left margin: answered 9/23]

Notes

[22] Gautier, F. *Congrès. Intern. Mines Métallurgie.* Paris: 1889.

[23] Rudeloff, M. *Verh. Ver. Beförderung Gewerbefleisses*, 1896, 65–84.

[24] Hadfield, R. A. *Instn. Civil Engrs. Proc.*, 1899, **138,** 1–12; disc. 12–16.

[25] Guillaume, C. E. *Arch. Sci. Phys. Nat.*, 1898, **5,** No. 4, 255, 305.

[26] Burgess, C. F. *and* Aston, J. *Univ. Wisconsin Bull.*, 1910, No. 346, 37–80; *Met. Chem. Engg.*, 1910, **8,** 23–26.

[27] Lindeck, S. *Rept. of 62nd Meeting of Brit. Assoc., Edinburgh,* 1892, pp. 139–156. London: Murray, 1893.

[28] Marsh, A. L. United States Patent 811,859, 1906.

[29] Edison, T. A. British Patents 20960, 1900; 2490, 1901.

CHAPTER 11

[1] Browne, D. H. *Jnl. Soc. Chem. Ind.*, 1911, **30,** 248–250.

[2] Wharton, J. *Memorandum concerning small Money and Nickel Alloy Coinage, with Illustrations and Descriptions of existing Nickel Alloy Coins.* (Camden, nr. Philadelphia: American Nickel Works), 1877.

[3] Thompson, R. M. United States Patents 489,574–6, 489,881–2, 1892; British Patent 499, 1893; Canadian Patent 44,723, 1893.

Nickel: An Historical Review

[4] It is a lasting testimony to the technical genius of Carl Langer, who was many years ahead of his time, that until recently no major departure was made from his intricate and ingenious design of the full-scale plant in Clydach.

[5] To meet this dividend Ludwig Mond drew on his own resources to the extent of £14,554. To quote from the report presented to the Board: 'he has been disappointed that the company has taken longer to reach a dividend-paying stage than he had any reason to anticipate'.

[6] Ludwig Mond's nephew, the late Robert Mathias, used to tell of an evening when the guests at dinner included such notables as Lord Avebury, Sir William Crookes, Sir James Dewar, Sir John Brunner, Sir Andrew Noble and Mr. Westinghouse from America.

[7] R. M. Thompson became first President of the American Olympic Association and Chairman of the American Committee for the Olympic Games held in Stockholm and Paris. He found an outlet for his attachment to naval affairs as a leading officer of the Society of Naval Architects and Marine Engineers, of the Navy League, and of the Military Order of the Loyal Legion. First in his affection was the United States Naval Academy. He was organiser and first President of the Naval Academy Alumni Association and was the moving spirit in founding the Navy Auxiliary Athletic Association.

[8] *The Times*, 1905, 22nd August, 8–9.

[9] Canada, Royal Ontario Nickel Commission. *Report*, p. 59, Toronto: 1917.
Op. cit. Appendix, p. 118.

[10] Thompson, J. F. *Private Communication.*

[11] *Mineral Industry*, 1908, **17**, 670–671.

Notes

[12] Merica, P. D. *Chem. and Met. Engg.*, 1921, **24,** 291–294; *Railway Engg. and Maintenance*, 1937, **33,** 28–32.

[13] An impressive list of the honours bestowed on Ludwig Mond by numerous universities and learned societies, as well as particulars of his munificent gifts to science and learning, is to be found in the Ludwig Mond Memorial Lecture given by Professor F. G. Donnan, C.B.E., D.Sc., F.R.S., on the centenary of Mond's birth.
Donnan, F. G. *Ludwig Mond, F.R.S.*, 1839–1909. London: Institute of Chemistry, 1939.

[14] Progressively Alfred Mond was made a Baronet, a Privy Councillor, and a Peer, under the title of Baron Melchett of Landford in the County of Southampton. Twice he was a Minister of the British Crown. Like his father before him, he was elected a Fellow of the Royal Society.

[15] Hybinette, N. V. United States Patents 579,111, 1897; 805,555, 1905; 805,969, 1905.

[16] In 1910 the North American Lead Company was sold to the Dominion Nickel Copper Company.

CHAPTER 12

[1] Canada, Royal Ontario Nickel Commission. *Report*, p. xxix. Toronto: 1917.

[2] *Op. cit.* 1.

[3] Stanley, R. C. *Nickel Past and Present.* Paper presented at the Second Empire Mining and Metallurgical Congress, Toronto, Canada, 1927.

Nickel: An Historical Review

[4] Rondelles are small cylinders 1·1 inches in diameter by 0·80 inch.

[5] Coleman, A. P. *Canada Dept. Mines, Mines Branch Bull.*, 1913, No. 170, 115, 164–167.

[6] Merica, P. D. *Chem. and Met. Engg.*, 1921, **24,** 17–21.

[7] Wünsch, H. *Das Nickel in der Weltwirtschaft unter besonderer Berücksichtigung Deutschlands.* Dissertation, Cologne University, 1925.

[8] Jaeger, K. *Die deutschen Reichsmünzen seit 1871.* Basel: Münzen, Medaillen A.G., 1948.

CHAPTER 13

[1] Mond, R. *Jnl. Soc. Chem. Ind.*, 1936, **55**, 181T–186T.

[2] Parkes, O. *British Battleships.* London: Seeley Service, 1957.
The formula by which the tonnage of armour has been calculated is as follows:

Battleships—1st and 2nd line
  Gross weight × 0·78 = light displacement.
  Light displacement × 0·26 = tonnage of armour.

Battle Cruisers—1st line
  Gross weight × 0·72 = light displacement.
  Light displacement × 0·22 = tonnage of armour.

[3] International Nickel Co., Inc. *Nickel Steels and other Nickel Alloys in Bridge Construction.* 1954.

[4] Boussingault, J. B. J. *Ann. Chim. Phys.*, 1878, **15,** Sér. 5, 91–126.

Notes

[5] Hadfield, R. A. *Jnl. Iron and Steel Inst.*, 1892, No. 2, 49–175.

[6] Guillet, L. *Rev. Métallurgie*, 1906, **3,** 332–354.

[7] Maurer, E. *and* Strauss, B. German Patents 304,126 and 304,159, 1912. *See also Zeitsch. angew. Chemie*, 1914, **27,** 633–645.

[8] Brearley, H. United States Patent 1,197,256, 1916.

[9] Haynes, E. *Proc. Engg. Soc. Western Pennsylvania*, 1920, **35,** 467–474.

[10] Krainer, H. *Tech. Mitt. Krupp*, 1962, **20,** 165–179.

[11] In 1954 the name of Société Anonyme de Commentry Fourchambault et Decazeville, at Imphy, was changed to Société Métallurgique d'Imphy.

[12] Elmen, G. W. *and* Arnold, H. D. *Jnl. Franklin Inst.*, 1923, **195,** 621–632; 1928, **206,** 317–338.

[13] Randall, W. F. *Jnl. Instn. Elect. Engrs.*, 1937, **80,** 647–658; disc. 658–667.

CHAPTER 14

[1] Merica, P. D. *Nickel and its Alloys*. Washington: 1921. (National Bureau of Standards Circular No. 100; 2nd ed. 1924; *see also* No. 485, 1950, and No. 592, 1958.)
A summary of the physical properties of nickel, culled from Circular No. 592, appears as Appendix II, p. 304–307.

[2] *Age-hardening* (also referred to as *precipitation-hardening*) is a process causing structural change which may occur gradually in some metals and alloys at atmospheric temperature

(natural ageing), or more rapidly at higher temperature (artificial ageing). The effects are caused by precipitation of minute particles of minor phases, from a super-saturated solid solution. Ageing is usually preceded by solution treatment, which comprises heating at a high temperature at which the constituents of the alloy are mutually dissolved. After this treatment the alloy is rapidly cooled, in order to retain the constituents in solution. Subsequently, re-heating at a lower temperature, or, in the case of some alloys, storage at normal temperature, causes precipitation of particles of the hardening phase.

[3] Griffiths, W. T. *et al*. *2nd Report of the Alloy Steels Research Committee*, Special Report No. 24, Sect. VII, pp. 343–367, 369–390. London: Iron and Steel Inst., 1939.

[4] Wickenden, T. H. *and* Vanick, J. S. *Trans. Amer. Foundrymen's Assoc.*, 1925, **33,** 347–408; disc. 409–430.
Everest, A. B. *et al*. *Jnl. Iron and Steel Inst.*, 1927, **116,** 185–213; disc. 214–216.

[5] Vanick, J. S. *Trans. Amer. Inst. Min. Met. Engrs.*, 1933, **105,** 53–76.

[6] Dawson, S. E. *Foundry Trade Jnl.*, 1924, **29,** 439–444; disc. **30,** 18.

[7] Merica, P. D. *and* Vanick, J. S. *Trans. Amer. Soc. for Steel Treating*, 1930, **18,** 923–940; disc. 940–942.

[8] Mudge, W. A. *and* Merica, P. D. *Trans. Amer. Inst. Min. Met. Engrs.*, 1935, **117,** 265–276; disc. 276–278.

[9] Wotherspoon, W. L. *Trans. Amer. Soc. Mech. Engrs.*, 1922, **44,** 975–1003.

[10] *Canadian Mining Jnl.*, 1937, **58,** 716.

Notes

[11] Wiggin, Henry, & Co., Ltd. *History of Henry Wiggin & Company Ltd.*, 1835–1935. *Centenary Publication*. Priv. print., n.d.

[12] Although, a quarter of a century later, Birlec became part of Associated Electrical Industries, Limited, it had meanwhile made a valuable contribution to the general expansion programme of the Wiggin organisation.

CHAPTER 15

[1] Dhavernas, J. *Histoire du Nickel*. Paris: Centre d'Information du Nickel, 1955.

[2] Calédonia contributed substantial additional ore reserves, including those of Société Minière Calédonienne and those of the Nickel Corporation. Although Le Nickel had the larger smelting and refining capacity, they closed down their smelter at Thio and used instead the smelter of Calédonia at Nouméa.

[3] In the Rustenburg ores only a small proportion of the precious metal occurs as native platinum. Most of the platinum metals exist as the sulphide minerals *cooperite* (PtAs) and *braggite* ((Pt, Pd, Ni) S) and the arsenide *sperrylite* ($PtAs_2$).
Wagner, P. A. *The Platinum Deposits and Mines of South Africa*, pp. 97–98; 118–119. London: Oliver & Boyd, 1929.

[4] Institution of Metallurgists. *Platinum Metals Exhibition*. London: the Institution, 1953.

[5] These deposits were indicated around 1901 by Thomas Edison's dip-needle surveys and originally staked by him. He proposed to enter the field of nickel mining in order to secure a supply of nickel for his newly invented storage battery, but

after spending a good deal of time and money drilling he allowed the claims to revert to the Crown.
Canada, Royal Ontario Nickel Commission. *Report*, pp. 94, 185–187; Appendix, pp. 144–157. Toronto: 1917.

[6] *Canadian Mining Jnl.*, 1959, **80,** No. 6, 103–230.

[7] Peek, R. L. *Engg. and Mining World*, 1930, **1,** 632-638.

[8] Thompson, J. F. *and* Beasley, N. *For the Years to Come: a Story of International Nickel of Canada.* New York: Putnam, 1960.

[9] The Ontario Refining Company Limited was formed, on 1st April, 1929, to construct and operate an electrolytic copper refinery at Copper Cliff. Associated in this project were The American Metal Company of Canada Limited; The Consolidated Mining and Smelting Company of Canada Limited; Ventures Limited; and The International Nickel Company of Canada Limited, which owned 42%, as did The American Metal Company of Canada Limited. In June 1935 The Ontario Refining Company Limited became a wholly-owned subsidiary of The International Nickel Company of Canada Limited.
Mineral Industry, 1926, **35,** 475.

[10] For well-nigh thirty years the Mond Nickel Company had been run more or less as a family concern, although the shares had been widely held by the public at large. With the consolidation of the two companies the executive was reorganised, and D. Owen Evans, a former Mond Nickel Director, became chief executive of that company in the United Kingdom.

David Owen Evans, a Welshman and a barrister, represented, in the House of Commons, his home county of Cardiganshire. His legal mind, suave manner, and natural flair for negotiation had brought him to the forefront at the time of the merger between the two companies, and there

Notes

is little doubt that he played a great part in combining, in one team, men of various nationalities and of differing technical skill, talent and temperament. He died in 1945. The Parliamentary Dissolution Honours List in June of that year contained the announcement that a Knighthood had been conferred on him, but he did not live to receive the accolade.

CHAPTER 16

[1] International Nickel Co. of Canada, Ltd. *President's Address to Shareholders*. Toronto, Ont., 28th March, 1933.

[2] *Carbonyl Nickel and Carbonyl Iron Powders, their Production and Properties*. B.I.O.S. Final Report No. 1575. London: H.M. Stationery Office.

[3] Gronningsater, A. *et al. Canadian Min. and Met. Bull.*, 1934, No. 264, 219–233, 234–250.
See also *Canadian Mining Jnl.*, 1959, **80,** No. 6, 103–230.

[4] Bailey, G. L. *Jnl. Inst. Metals*, 1951, **79**, 243–292.

[5] *The Times*, 28th February, 1940.

[6] Mishima, T. British Patents 392,656–8, 1932.

[7] General Electric Co. *Alnico: a new powerful Magnet Alloy*. c. 1936.

CHAPTER 17

[1] Great Britain, Royal Mint. *Annual Report*, 1923.

Nickel: An Historical Review

[2] Figures based on *A Century of Nickel Coinage* dated September 1955, but including Japanese issue (one coin) in 1956, and Greek (one coin), French (one coin), and Monaco (one coin) issues authorised in 1958.

Feely, E. F. *Numismatist*, 1956, **69,** 269–273; 1958, **71,** 811–815.

CHAPTER 18

[1] International Nickel Co. of Canada, Ltd. *Robert C. Stanley... Address to Shareholders.* Toronto, Ont., 29th April, 1941.

[2] In a private memorandum written by the late King George VI after his two conversations with President Roosevelt in June 1939, the following note appears:

'F.D.R.'s ideas in case of war:
Credits. U.S.A. will want nickel from Canada.
They will buy our surplus rubber.'

Wheeler-Bennett, J. W. *King George VI; his Life and Reign*, p. 392. London: Macmillan, 1958.

[3] *I.G. Farbenindustrie—Oppau Works, Ludwigshafen.* (*Report on Nickel and Iron Powder Plants.*)

Nord Deutsche Affinerie, Hamburg. (*Report on the Treatment of Nickel-Copper Ores and Residues.*)

B.I.O.S. Final Report No. 263. London: H.M. Stationery Office, 1946.

[4] Caron, M. H. United States Patent 1,487,145, 1924.

Notes

[5] Forward, F. A. *Trans. Canadian Inst. Min. and Met.*, 1953, **56,** 363–370.

In 1962 the Institution of Mining and Metallurgy awarded its Gold Medal to Professor F. A. Forward, 'in recognition of his contributions to the development of metallurgical processes, particularly that of pressure leaching'.

[6] Coleman, E. E. *and* Vedensky, D. N. *Production of Ferronickel at Riddle, Oregon:* in *Extractive Metallurgy of Copper, Nickel and Cobalt,* edited by Paul Queneau, pp. 263–285, disc. 285–286. New York: Interscience, 1961.

[7] Sproule, K. *et al.* *Treatment of Nickel-Copper Matte* in *Extractive Metallurgy of Copper, Nickel and Cobalt,* edited by Paul Queneau, pp. 33–52, disc. pp. 52–54. New York: Interscience, 1961.

[8] *Canadian Mining Jnl.,* 1959, **81,** No. 6, 105–130.

[9] Churchill, W. S. *The Second World War,* vol. 5, p. 353. London: Cassell, 1948–1954.

[10] By means of geophysical prospecting, Sherritt Gordon had been able to map out its Lynn Lake deposit in a remote area in northern Manitoba, mostly swamp and drift-covered.

[11] The maraging steels are characterised by high toughness at high strength levels. Their properties are developed by transformation of austenite to martensite followed by controlled ageing of the martensite (maraging).

CHAPTER 19

[1] The Mach number represents the ratio of the velocity of an object to the velocity of sound in the medium in which it is travelling. Mach I is 760 m.p.h. at sea level, in standard conditions of pressure, temperature, and humidity. This speed decreases, with the lower temperatures prevailing at high

altitudes, to 660 m.p.h. The designation 'Mach' is derived from the name of the Austrian scientist who discovered the phenomenon of the shock wave which exists when an object reaches the speed of sound.

[2] Veal, C. B. *Trans. S.A.E.*, 1959, **44**, No. 4, 145–153.

[3] Gough, H. J. *Jnl. Roy. Aero. Soc.*, 1938, **42**, 922–1032.
Fedden, R., *op. cit.*, 1955, **59**, 72–74.
McFarland, M. W. Editor. *The Papers of Wilbur and Orville Wright*. New York: McGraw Hill, 1953, vol. 2.

[4] Wilm, A. *Metallurgie*, 1911, **8**, 225–227.

[5] Merica, P. D., Waltenberg, R. G. *and* Scott, H. *Trans. A.I.M.E.*, 1920, **64**, 41–79. Published also as *Bureau of Standards Scientific Paper No. 347*, 1919.
For an explanation of the phenomenon of *age-hardening*, see Chapter 14, Note 2.

[6] Rosenhain, W., Archbutt, S. L. *and* Hanson, D. 11*th Report to Alloys Research Cttee.* Instn. Mech. Engrs., 1921.

[7] Merica, P. D. *and* Pilling, N. B. U.S. Patent Application 356,870/1929 (U.S. Patent 2,048,163).

[8] S.A. Commentry Fourchambault et Decazeville. British Patents 371,334 (Convention (France)), 1929, and 404,876 (Convention (France)), 1932.

[9] Roxbee Cox, H. *Gas Turbine Principles and Practice*. London: George Newnes, 1955.

[10] Whittle, F. *Jet—The Story of a Pioneer*. London: Muller, 1953.

[11] Vicat, M. *Ann. des Ponts et Chaussées*, 1833, **6**, 201–268.
Howe, H. M. *Trans. Amer. Inst. Mining*, 1885, **13**, 646–656.

Notes

Dickenson, J. H. S. *Jnl. Iron and Steel Inst.*, 1922, **106**, 103–140.
Chevenard, P. *Procès Verbal Soc. Ing. Civils France*, 1927, No. 6, 134–140.

[12] Pfeil, L. B. British Patents 583,162, 1940; 583,212, 1940.

[13] After World War II the British authorities were anxious that there should be separate manufacturing facilities in the United Kingdom for production of the high-nickel alloys which are in growing demand in many branches of high-temperature engineering, particularly for gas turbines in aircraft. After consideration of several sites, a new plant was erected, for the U.K. Government, by Henry Wiggin and Company, at Hereford. Construction began in September 1951 and the first heat of metal was cast eighteen months later. The area of the factory amounted to nearly a quarter of a million square feet. In 1956 the Ministry of Supply sold the factory to Henry Wiggin, who extended the premises by purchase of additional land, enlarging the total area of the plant site to nearly a hundred acres. On completion, the Hereford works are scheduled to have an annual capacity of at least 50 million lbs. of processed nickel and nickel-alloy products, in the form of a wide range of bar, sheet, strip, tube and wire, various forms of forgings and pressings, and pig metal for re-melting.

[14] Whittle[10] records that 'by 1940 Mond Nickel were actively assisting on the material side and were working to develop improved materials for turbine blading and combustion-chamber parts'.

[15] Schlaifer, R. *and* Heron, S. D. *Development of Aircraft Engines and Fuels.* Boston: Harvard University, 1950.

[16] B.I.O.S. Final Report 396 (*Report on a Visit to Germany and Austria to Investigate Alloys for Use at High Temperature*), 1945.

Nickel: An Historical Review

[17] Betteridge, W. *The Nimonic Alloys*. London: Edward Arnold, 1959.

[18] A publication issued by the American Society for Testing Materials gives details of the nominal compositions and strength properties of some 280 high-temperature alloys which have been developed in the U.S.A., Great Britain and other countries. This compilation is the most comprehensive yet published, but the sponsoring committee emphasises that development in that field is now so rapid, and changes in practice are so frequent, that it is impossible to assemble, at any one time, exact data on composition, treatment and properties of the very large number of alloys used in high-temperature engineering.
A.S.T.M. Special Tech. Publn. No. 170B, 1961.
See also Appendix IV, pp. 310–314.

[19] Bergman, J. *Ninety Seconds to Space: the X-15 Story*. New York: Doubleday, 1960.

APPENDIX I

See opposite

Nickel: An Historical Review

APPENDIX II

Physical Properties of Nickel*

I. PHYSICAL PROPERTIES

(1) *Atomic Number and Weights: Isotopes*

Nickel is number 28 in the periodic tabulation of the elements. Its atomic weight is 58·69, representing a composite of the five stable isotopes: mass numbers 58, 60, 61, 62 and 64. The natural abundances of the stable isotopes are reported to be: 67·7% for Ni^{58}; 26·2% for Ni^{60}; 1·25% for Ni^{61}; 3·66% for Ni^{62}; 1·16% for Ni^{64}.

Seven radioactive isotopes of nickel have been identified: mass numbers 54, 56, 57, 59, 63, 65, 66.

(2) *Thermal Neutron Cross-Section*

The reaction of nickel to neutron bombardment has been recorded as (neutron velocity of 2,200 m/sec.): absorption, $4·5 \pm 0·2$ barns,† scattering cross-section average, $17·5 \pm 1·0$ barns.

---

* The summary is based on U.S. National Bureau of Standards Circular 592 (1958), which presents a review of available information on the occurrence, recovery and refining, properties and uses of high-purity and commercial forms of nickel, together with details of the properties and industrial applications of ferrous and non-ferrous nickel-containing materials. The text of the Circular is supported by a bibliography of 800 references to the relevant literature.

Unless otherwise stated, the data presented here are derived from reports relating to work on nickel of 99·95% purity.

(The publication is obtainable from the Superintendent of Documents, U.S. Government Printing Office, Washington 25, D.C., U.S.A.)

† 1 barn = 10^{-24} cm.²

Appendix II

(3) Crystal Form and Lattice Constant

The normal crystal form of nickel, at all temperatures, is face-centred cubic. The value 3·5168 Å at 24·8°C. has been generally accepted as the lattice constant.

(4) Density

The density of nickel has been computed, from atomic data, as 8·908 g./cm.³ at 20°C.

(Direct determinations of density are affected by the composition and physical condition of the metal and by prior treatment of the specimen.)

(5) Melting Point

The generally accepted value for the melting point of pure nickel is based on determinations made at the National Bureau of Standards, using 99·94% nickel. The value 1455° ± 1°C. was reported on the International Temperature Scale of 1927, but, because of slight changes in the constants of the radiation equations, the value of 1453°C. was assigned to the freezing point, as a secondary fixed point, on the 1948 and 1954 editions of the Scale.

The presence of impurities or alloying elements tends to lower the melting point and convert it to a melting range.

(6) Latent Heat of Fusion

The latent heat of fusion of nickel is 73·8 cal./g. A value of 1,756 d./cm. has been determined for the surface tension of the metal at the melting point.

(7) Boiling Point

The boiling point of nickel is too high to permit direct determination; it is therefore estimated by extrapolation of vapour-pressure data. A value of 2730°C. has been reported.

(8) Specific Heat

The specific heat of nickel at any temperature represents a combination of lattice vibration, a magnetic effect and a residual portion. Values established for temperatures in the range $-260°$ to $+1150°$C. are given below.

Nickel: An Historical Review

Temperature °C.	Specific Heat cal./g. °C.
− 260	0·00061
− 200	0·00355
0	0·1025
200	0·1225
357·5	0·1592
500	0·1260
700	0·1328
900	0·1397
1150	0·1525

(9) Thermal Expansion

Nickel expands with rising temperature, at a regular rate except for a sharp maximum at the Curie temperature. Numerical values for thermal expansion are affected by composition and by physical factors such as the presence of strains, etc.

(10) Thermal Conductivity

The thermal conductivity of nickel is lowered by the presence of impurities, and irregularities occur near the Curie temperature. The following values are reported for 99·94% nickel:

100°C.	0·198 cal. per cm. sec. °C.
200°C.	0·175 cal. per cm. sec. °C.
300°C.	0·152 cal. per cm. sec. °C.
400°C.	0·142 cal. per cm. sec. °C.
500°C.	0·148 cal. per cm. sec. °C.

(11) Electrical Resistivity

The resistivity of nickel, which is negligible at extremely low temperatures, increases with rise in temperature; a change in the slope of the curve occurs in the vicinity of the Curie temperature.

Resistivity varies also as a function of pressure and of the presence of impurities. A value of 6·844 microhm-cm. has been recorded at 20°C.

Values for temperature coefficient of electrical resistance of high-purity nickel, from 0° to 100°C., range from 0·00658 to 0·00692 per °C.

Appendix II

(12) *Magnetic Properties*

Nickel is ferromagnetic at ordinary temperatures, but at moderately elevated temperatures becomes paramagnetic. The magnetic properties of nickel, as of other ferromagnetic metals, are affected by atomic factors and by the chemical and physical condition of the metal. The Curie point for nickel (the temperature at which the change from ferromagnetism to paramagnetism occurs) is 350°–360°C., depending on the prior mechanical and thermal treatment of the specimen, and the nature and amount of the impurities present.

APPENDIX III

PUBLISHED PRICE OF NICKEL FROM 1840 TO 1961

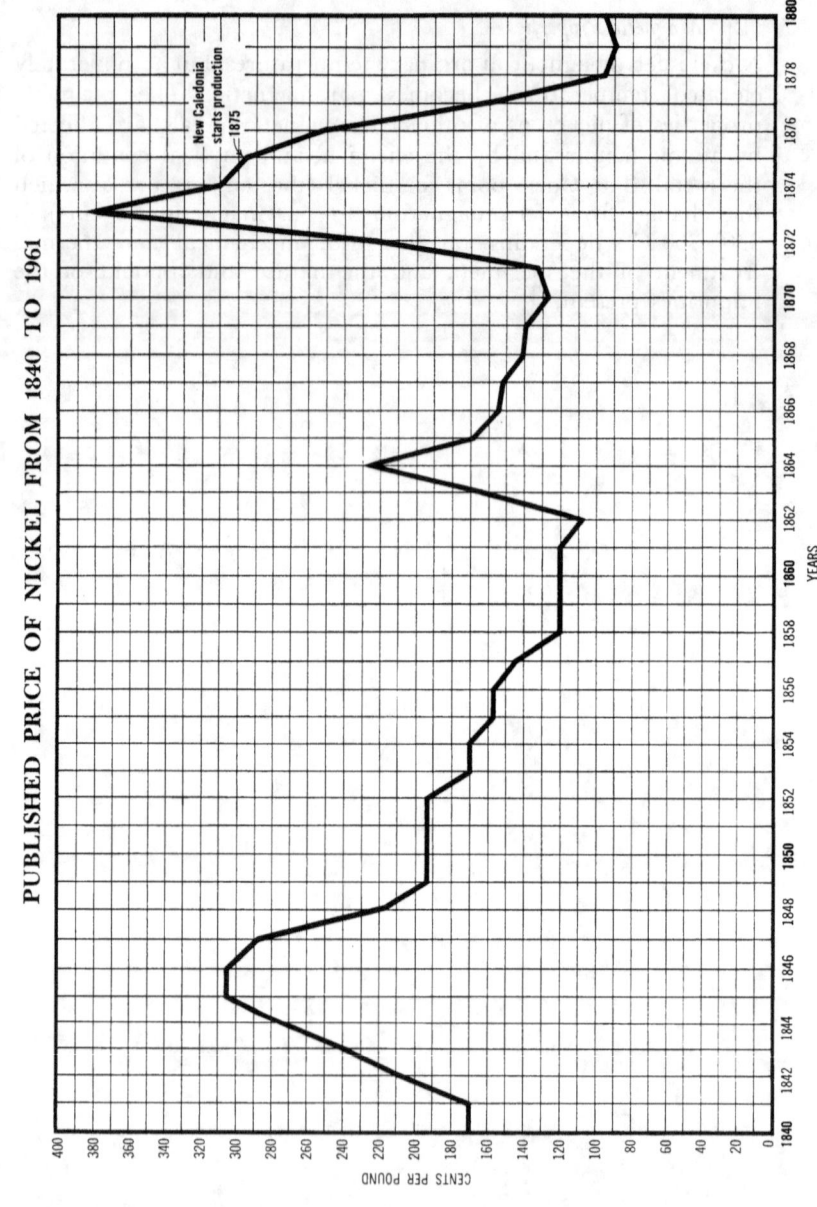

Appendix III

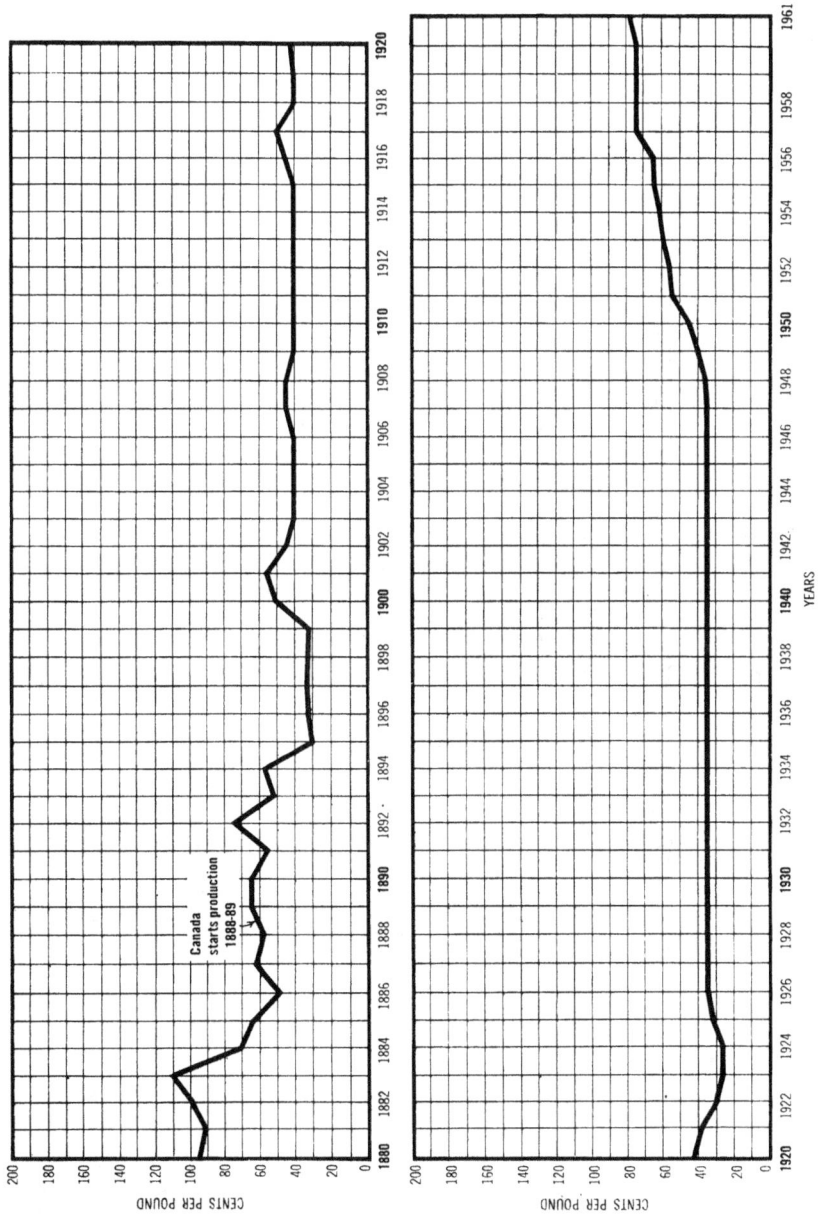

APPENDIX IV

Some High-Temperature, High-strength Nickel-containing Alloys for Aero Engines

NOMINAL COMPOSITIONS

1. IRON-NICKEL-CHROMIUM-BASE ALLOYS

	C %	Cr %	Ni %	Co %	Mo %	W %	Nb %	Ti %	Al %	Fe %	Other Elements† %
A-286	0·05	15	26	—	1·3	—	—	2	0·2	Bal.	V 0·3
Discaloy*	0·03	13·5	26	—	2·8	—	—	1·8	—	,,	—
G 18B	0·4	13	13	10	1·8	2·5	3	—	—	,,	—
Immaculate* 5	0·12	23·5	21·5	—	—	—	—	—	—	,,	—
Incoloy* alloy 800	0·1	20·5	32	—	—	—	—	—	—	,,	—
Incoloy* alloy 901	0·05	13·5	42·7	—	6·2	—	—	2·5	0·3	34	—
N 155	0·15	21	20	20	3	2·5	1	—	—	Bal.	—

Appendix IV

AM-350	0·1	16·5	4·3	—	2·8	—	—	—	—	″	—
Armco* PH 15-7Mo	0·1	15	7	—	2·2	—	—	—	1	″	—
Rex* 78	0·01	14	18	—	3·5	—	—	0·8	—	″	Cu 3·5
Staybrite* FDP	0·08	18	9	—	—	—	—	0·5	—	″	—
S-590	0·4	20·5	20	20	4	4	4	—	—	″	—
Tinidur*	0·08	15	30	—	—	—	—	1·8	0·4	″	—
Timken* 16-25-6	0·08	16	25	—	6	—	—	—	—	50	—
19-9 DL	0·3	19	9	—	1·3	1·2	0·4	0·3	—	Bal.	—
304 Stainless Steel	0·08 max.	19	10	—	—	—	—	—	—	″	—
321 ″ ″	0·08 max.	18	10·5	—	—	—	—	—	—	″	—
347 ″ ″	0·08 max.	18	11	—	—	—	—	—	—	″	—

* Trademark.

† All the alloys referred to in the above Tables contain incidental impurities and small amounts of elements added for purposes of deoxidation. In addition, it is common practice to take advantage of the relatively small but useful improvements of properties arising from very small additions of elements such as boron and zirconium.

II. NICKEL-CHROMIUM-BASE ALLOYS

	C %	Cr %	Ni %	Co %	Mo %	W %	Nb %	Ti %	Al %	Fe %	Other Elements† %
G 64	0·1	11	Bal.	—	3	4	2	—	6	—	—
GMR 235D	0·2	15·5	,,	—	5	—	—	2·5	3·5	4·5	—
Inconel* alloy 718	0·03	19	,,	—	3	—	5·5	0·6	0·6	—	—
Hastelloy* alloy X	0·1	22	,,	1·5	9	0·6	—	—	—	18·5	—
Inconel* alloy 600	0·04	15·8	,,	—	—	—	—	—	—	7·2	—
Inconel* alloy 700	0·1	15	,,	28·5	3·8	—	—	2·2	3	0·7	—
Inconel* alloy 713 (713C)	0·1	11·5	,,	—	4·5	—	2	0·5	6	1	—
Inconel* alloy X-750	0·04	15	,,	—	—	—	0·9	2·5	0·8	6·8	—
M-252	0·15	20	,,	10	10	—	—	3	1	—	—
Nimonic* alloy 75	0·12	20	,,	—	—	—	—	0·3	—	—	—
Nimonic* alloy 80A	0·08	20	,,	—	—	—	—	2·4	1·2	—	—

Appendix IV

Alloy	C	Cr	Ni	Co	Mo	W	Ti	Al	Fe	Other
Nimonic* alloy 90	0·1	20	,,	20	—	—	2·4	1·2	—	—
Nimonic* alloy 105	0·2 max.	15	,,	20	5	—	1·5	4·5	—	—
Nimonic* alloy 115	0·1	15	,,	14	3·5	—	4	5	—	—
IN 100	0·18	10	,,	15	3	—	5	5·5	1	V 1·0
René* 41	0·1	19	,,	11	10	—	3·1	1·5	—	—
Udimet* 500	0·08	19	,,	19·5	4	—	3	3	4·0 max.	—
Udimet* 700	0·15	15	,,	18·5	5·2	—	3·5	4·3	1·0 max.	—
Waspaloy*	0·07	19	,,	14	4·3	—	3	1·3	1	—
Nimocast* 258	0·2	10	,,	20	5	—	3·7	4·8	2·0 max.	—
Astroloy*	0·06	15	,,	15	5·3	—	3·5	4·4	—	—
S.M. 200	0·08	9	,,	10	—	12·5	2	5·3	—	—

* Trademark.

† All the alloys referred to in the above Tables contain incidental impurities and small amounts of elements added for purposes of deoxidation. In addition, it is common practice to take advantage of the relatively small but useful improvement of properties arising from very small additions of elements such as boron and zirconium.

III. COBALT-BASE ALLOYS

	C %	Cr %	Ni %	Co %	Mo %	W %	Nb %	Ti %	Al %	Fe %	Other Elements† %
G*34	0·8	19	12·0	45	2	—	1·3	—	—	Bal.	V 2·8
Haynes Stellite* alloy No. 21	0·3	27	3·0	Bal.	5	—	—	—	—	1	—
Haynes Stellite* alloy No. 31 (X-40 cast)	0·5	25	10	,,	—	7·5	—	—	—	1·5	—
S 816	0·4	20	20	,,	4	4	4	—	—	4	—
WI-52	0·5	21	1·0 max.	,,	—	11	2·0	—	—	2·0	—

* Trademark.

† All the alloys referred to in the above Tables contain incidental impurities and small amounts of elements added for purposes of deoxidation. In addition, it is common practice to take advantage of the relatively small but useful improvement of properties arising from very small additions of elements such as boron and zirconium.

The information given above is based mainly on *A.S.T.M. Special Technical Publication* No. 170 B, 1961. See Chapter 19, Note 18.

APPENDIX V

(Key to Frontispiece)

Annaberg Altar Piece
Hans Hesse, 1521

Top Left Sector

At the extreme left the Frohnau miner *Daniel Knappe* (*Knappius*),* in a brown cloak and carrying a hatchet over his right shoulder, is being guided by an angel to a high tree on Mount Schrecken. (The German word 'Grube' denotes not only a mine but a den, e.g. a lions' den, and because the prophet Daniel had interpreted King Nebuchadnezzar's dream about images of silver and other metals (*Daniel* II), the early Saxon miners had chosen him as their patron saint.) The legend is that, in a dream, Daniel Knappe had been promised by an angel he would find in the branches of a tree a nest containing silver eggs. Slightly to the right, Daniel Knappe is seen following the directions given him in the dream. Having embedded his hatchet in the tree and discarded his cloak, he had climbed a ladder into the tree, but is being told by another angel to prospect *under* the tree, where 'branches,' i.e. seams of ore containing silver, would be found. The miner digging at the foot of the tree is Daniel Knappe, obeying the angel's behest.

Bottom Left Sector

A miner, lamp in hand, is emerging from an adit. Lamps carried by miners in those days were called 'Froschlampen' or 'ladder-peg' lamps. The miner looks down into a brook carrying away the gangue which is being washed from the ore by another miner. Ore-bearing rock is being hand barrowed away for dressing. The saintly figure in the greenish-gold cloak symbolises Daniel, the patron saint. Wandering unseen among the miners, with outstretched hand, he blesses their work.

Top Right Sector

This sector includes a tall ventilating shaft and workings reached by a ladder. Each shaft was protected from the weather by a wooden hut or 'coe'; in the picture are several coes already in use and one is under construction. Inside one of them can be seen a 'whim', a machine used for raising ore from the mine. In the middle distance a miner with a 'ladder-peg' lamp on his head is emerging from a shaft. There is also a horse-drawn cart for transporting ore to the smelting furnace. On the far horizon a church spire is visible, and in front of it are gallows, as maintained in mediaeval times to mete out justice in urban communities.

Bottom Right Sector

A miner is entering an adit, hauling a 'pit-dog' or sled. A wooden winch is being operated by two miners. In the foreground a hammer is being used to break up the larger lumps of ore. Most of the miners have white hoods over their heads, leather aprons round their waists, and knee covers of leather, but apparently protective footwear had not yet been introduced, since the men are shod with a sort of slipper. Most of the faces are clean shaven, but two are adorned with 'handle-bar' moustaches.

* Frohnau is a place near Annaberg. '*Knappi*' is an abbreviation of '*knappius*', the Latin equivalent of the German '*Knappe*', a miner.

Index

NOTE *Names of authors quoted in bibliography are printed in capital letters*

A-286 alloy 310
Abbott, B., correspondence with Faraday 280-1
Abyssinia, coinage 202
Achondrites 265
Adams, I., develops nickel plating 109, 110
Aerial geophysical and other prospecting methods 141, 181, 222-3, 295, 299
Aero Engines. *See* Aircraft and Aero Engines
Aerojet Inc. 252
Aerolites 19
Aes album (white copper) 42
Africa
  bronzes from Transvaal 9
  meteorites in 20, 21, 264
  nickeliferous ores in 179-80, 295
Agathocles 9-12, 261-2
Age-Hardening (Precipitation-Hardening)
  aluminium as hardening agent 169-70, 174, 231, 232, 235, 239, 241, 244, 258, 294, 300
  mechanism of 231: *see also* 293, 300
  of aluminium-base alloys 231, 232, 258, 300
  of iron-base alloys 241
  of nickel-chromium-(iron) alloys 234-5, 239, 241, 244, 300

of nickel-copper alloys 174, 256, 294
  titanium as hardening agent 169-70, 174, 235, 238, 239, 241, 244
AGRICOLA, G. 23-5, 266
Ahnighito, Cape York meteorite 19
Aircraft and Aero Engines, including Rockets 230-58, 299-302
  aero-engine power (1915-1960) 236
  age-hardening alloys used in. *See* nickel-containing materials used in, *also* Age-hardening
  air-cooled radial types 233
  Air Ministry supports research on alloys for gas turbines 238-9
  airships 231
  Allis-Chalmers work on gas turbines 240
  aluminium alloys for components 231-2, 258, 300
  axial-flow types 239, 240, 244
  Bell X-1 and X-2 research aircraft 254, 257
  centrifugal-flow type 239
  'Conway' gas-turbine engine, *facing* 247, *see also* Rolls-Royce engines, 318
  creep, resistance to 238, 300
  Curtiss-Wright turbo-compound engine (schematic drawing) 243
  Douglas D-558-II aircraft 257

317

Index

Aircraft and Aero Engines (*cont.*)
  early types of aircraft 230-1
  fan-type (by-pass) engines 243, 247-8
  Firth-Vickers Stayblade and Rex 78 238
  gas-turbine (jet) engines 236 (power curve) 237, 239, 240, 241, 243, 244, 300
  General Electric Co. gas-turbine design 240
  German developments in gas turbines, and rocketry 241, 244, 251, 301
  Hawker v.t.o. (P.1127) aeroplane 249
  Hero of Alexandria conception of gas turbine 237, 300
  Inconel alloys in 241, 246, 312
  Italian developments in jet propulsion 241, 301
  K.E. 965 valve steel 234
  kinetic heating (thermal thicket) problem 254, 256
  Lindbergh aeroplane ('Spirit of St. Louis') 233
  liquid-cooled aero engines 233
  Mach number, definition and rating 230, 249, 257, 299
  Metropolitan-Vickers gas turbine 239
  Mond Nickel Co. research on Nimonic alloys 238-40, 245, 301
  nickel-containing materials used in 170-1, 231, 232, 233, 234, 238-40, 241, 244, 245, 246-7, *facing* 247, 249, 251-2, 256, 300, 302, 310-14
  Nimonic (nickel-chromium-base) alloys 238-40, 245, 302, 312-13
  North American Aviation 'X-15' research aircraft 249, 254, 255-6, 257
  piston types 235, 236 (power curve), 249
  Pratt and Whitney ('Wasp' and 'Turbofan') engines 233, 247-8
  rocket-propelled craft (solid- and liquid-propellant types) 249 ff., 254-8
  Rolls-Royce engines 233 ('Merlin'), 239 ('Welland'), 239 ('Derwent'), 243, *facing* 247 and 247 ('Conway'), 239 (turbo-jet), 252 (engine powering Blue Streak)
  rotating and reciprocating units 242 (schematic drawings), 243
  Schneider Trophy contests 233
  speed records 257-8
  superchargers, alloys used for 234-5, 240, 254
  'temperature capability' of materials 235, 244, 245, 246, 247, 302
  turbo-compound engines 235, 243
  turbo-jet engines 239
  turbo-prop engines 249-50
  U.S. Government Committee on jet propulsion 240
  valve materials 233-4, 254
  vertical-take-off aircraft 249
  Westinghouse engines 240 ('Yankee 19A', 'J30-WE20')
  Whittle gas turbine 237, 238, 239, 240, 300, 301
Alabama meteorite 20
Albania, coinage 202, 203, 205
Albata 71, 274
Alexander the Great, conquest of Bactria by 9
Alfenide 274
Alkaline sulphide extraction process. *See* Tops-and-bottoms
Allen. *See* Barker and Allen
Alloy steel. *See* individual types, e.g. Nickel steel, 346
Alnico magnet alloy 297
Alpaca 274
Alpakka 272, 274
Altar-piece of St. Anne's Church, Annaberg *Frontispiece*, 23, 315

318

Index

Aluminium in age precipitation-hardening alloys 169-170, 174, 231, 232, 235, 239, 241, 244, 258, 294, 300
Aluminium-base alloys
  age-hardening of 231, 232, 258, 300
  nickel in 232
  use in aircraft 231-2, 258, 300
AM-350 alloy 311
Ambrac 274
American Metal Company of Canada 296
American Museum, Hayden Planetarium, meteorite in 19
American Museum of Natural History
  coins lent by 11
  meteorites in 18
American Nickel Plating Company 109
American Nickel Works 76, 127, 128
American Numismatic Society, coins lent by 11
AMERICAN SOCIETY FOR TESTING MATERIALS 302, 310-14
Analysis of coins 9-12, 262
Angles, nickel deposits at 52
Anglo-French Nickel Co. 131, 144, 156, 290
Angola, coinage 202
Annaberg
  mining at *Frontispiece*, 23, 50, 315
  St. Anne's Church altarpiece, *Frontispiece*, 315
Annabergite 23
Annealing of coin blanks 200
Anodes, derivation of term 284
  See also Electrodeposition of nickel
Anti-knock fuels 187, 233
Antioch, bronze reamer 6
Arabia, meteors in 17, 21
ARCHBUTT, S. L. 300
Architecture, use of nickel-containing materials 137, 225, 227, 228, 291
Argent allemand 274

Argent neuf 274
Argentan 46, 105, 113, 198, 272, 274
Argentina, coinage 202
Argentine (nickel silver) 274
Argozie 274
Argozoil 274
Arguzoid 274
Argyrine 274
Argyrolith 274
Arizona, Barringer crater 21
Armaments, general 157, 216, 292
Armco PH 15-7Mo alloy 311
Armour plate
  trials and use 96-8, 99-102, 130-1, 290
  Washington and other disarmament treaties 161-2, 292
ARNOLD, H. D. 293
Arre, nickeliferous deposits at 52
Arrow-heads
  of meteoritic iron 17
  of nickel bronze 7, 9
Arsenical ores. *See* Nickel ores
ARVIDSSON, J. A. 38, 270
Askin, C. 46-8, 52, 71-2, 272-3
ASTON, J. 119, 289
Astroloy 313
Ataxites 18, 19, 20
Atlas missile 251
Atom, nature of 39, 260
Atomic numbers and structure of metals, *facing* 302, 304
Atomic Theory (Dalton) 39
Austin, H. 103
Australia
  coinage 208
  meteoric falls in 21, 264
  supplies fuel to New Caledonia 148, 178-9, 210, 295
Austria
  decree re use of nickel for cooking utensils 115
  plating developments in 112, 285
  token coins in cupro-nickel 113
Austria-Hungary
  coinage 201
  nickeliferous ores in 153

Index

Author's preface and acknowledgements ix-x
Automobiles, relation to nickel industry 102-3, 173
Axles and axle bearings 116, 172, 273
Aztecs, use meteoritic iron 17

Bactria
  bamboo articles in 12
  coinage 9-12, 261-2
Badische Anilin- und Soda-Fabrik 188
BAILEY, G. L. 297
Ballande, operations in New Caledonia, Europe, and U.S.A. 131, 134, 144, 147, 156, 179
Banco. *See* British America Nickel Corporation
Barker. *See* Webb and Barker
BARKER, S. 273
Barker and Allen 48
BARLOW, A. E. 275
Barringer crater 21
BARTLETT, C. C. 80, 279
Bartlett, C. C., 'tops-and-bottoms' process 79-81, 279
Basque Republic, coinage 202
Batteries, nickel in 120, 229
Bayonne. *See* International Nickel Company
Bazooka rocket 250
Beads, from Gerzah 15
Beardmore, W. 281
BEASLEY, N. 275, 279, 296
BECK, R. 275
BECQUEREL, A. C. 108-9, 285
Beggars Opera, The 36
Belgium
  coinage 198, 202, 203, 204, 206, 209
  Duffel refinery 131, 134, 145, 156
Bell X-1 and X-2 research aircraft 254, 257
Bells, of nickel silver 45

Benson, E. W.
  biographical note 278
  bleaching-powder separation of nickel salts and copper salts 72
Benz, K. 102
BEOWULF 268
Bergenport Chemical Works 79
BERGMAN, J. 302
BERGMAN, T. 37, 92, 270, 271
Bergmännischer Bericht oder Brennendes Grubenlicht, extract from v
Berndorfer Metallwarenfabrik, token coins in cupro-nickel 113
BERZELIUS, J. J. 284
Berzelius, J. J.
  electrochemical experiments 105
  finds nickel in Klefva ores 52
  symbols for elements 39
Bessemer, Sir Henry 96, 281
Bessemerising process for steel-making 96
Bethlehem Iron Company 97, 99
BETTERIDGE, W. 302
'Bewitched Burgrave' meteorite 16
Bicycle parts, nickel-plating of 112
Billion, definition of 259
BIRD, G. 107, 285
BIRINGUCCIO, A. 268
Birlec. *See* Birmingham Electric Furnaces Ltd.
Birmingham Electric Furnaces Ltd. 177, 295
Bismuth brass 274
Bismuth bronze 274
Black Prince 96
Black stone of Kaaba 16
Blake, J. B. 42
Blanca 274
Blasthole mining 220
Blaufarbenwerke (Saxony) 278
Bleaching powder, for separation of nickel salts from cobalt salts 72, 75
Blezard deposit 142
'Blue Streak' rocket 252
Blundevile's *Cosmographie* (1594) 4

Index

B.M.W. 003 jet engine 244
Boiler plate of nickel steel 172
BONNIN, A. 263, 271
Booster, 'Navaho,' use of nickel in 251
Booth-O'Brien Company 146
Boric acid in plating solutions 110, 183
BÖTTGER, R. 108, 285
Boulenger et Cie. 117
Bouse and Muncher 110
BOUSSINGAULT, J. B. J. 162, 292
Bouton, G. 103
Boyden, O. 95
Boyle, Robert 36
Braggite 295
BRAIDWOOD, R. J. 261
BRANDES. *See* Keferstein, C., *et al.*
BRANDT, G. 30, 269
Bratke, Fratelli 112
Braunhausen, nickel ores at 50
Brayton, G. 102
Brazil
  coinage 208
  meteorite found in 20
BREARLEY, H. 163, 293
BREDBERG, B. G. 271
BREWER, E. C. 268
Bridges 162, 163
Briquette nickel 217, 218
British America Nickel Corporation 146, 154, 156, 159
BRITISH ASSOCIATION 6, 261
British Broadcasting Corporation 106
British Museum
  coin assays 9, 10, 11
  Beowulf saga 267
  meteoritic iron objects from 18
British plate 274
British White Lead Company 72
Brittleness, elimination of, by magnesium 46, 115
Bronzes
  ancient, from various sources 6, 7, 9, 13

Brooklyn, Canadian Copper Co. plant 77
BROWN, H. 264
Brown, J. 281
BROWNE, D. H. 121, 289
Browne, D. H.
  electrolytic refining process developed by 121
  negotiations with Ludwig Mond 85
BRUGNATELLI, L. 105, 284
Brunner, Mond and Company 83, 126
BRUUN, A. F. 261
Bulgaria, coinage 208
BURGESS, C. F. 119, 289
BURKE, J. E. 261
Bushveld igneous complex 179

Cadmia (Kobelt), toxicity of 23
Calamine 14
Calédonia (formerly Hauts Fourneaux de Nouméa) 179, 295
Calédonickel (merger of S.A. Le Nickel and Calédonia) 179
Camden plant of Joseph Wharton 75-6, 121, 127-8
CAMMANN, S. V. R. 262
Cammell, C. 281
Canada
  see also companies operating in Canada, *and* Extraction and refining
  Canadian Pacific Railway, construction of 64
  coinage 202, 203, 204
  copper output (Ontario, 1914-1918) 154
  Garnier work on sulphide ores 68, 77
  International Nickel Co. mines in. *See* International Nickel Company
  Lynn Lake nickel deposits 217, 299
  Manitoba mines 223-4

321

Index

Canada (ctd.)
  meteoric falls in 21
  Mond deposits in. *See* Mond Nickel Company
  nickel and other mineral resources of 60, 66, 68, 145-6, 276, 291
  nickel industry of Ontario; Royal Commission reports 66, 145-6, 276, 291
  nickel production of 67, 90, 142, 145-6, 153-4, 156, 158, 160, 210-14, 280
  retrenchment in mining and refining after World Wars 158, 214
  Royal Ontario Nickel Commission report on mineral resources of Ontario 145-6
  Sudbury district, mines in 64, 121-2
  supply of nickel to Allied Forces (King George VI discussion with President Roosevelt) 298
  World War II, Canada's contribution in materials 210-14, 298
Canadian Copper Company
  Cleveland plant 77, 78, 121
  Copper Cliff mine and smelter 66, 68, 76-7; *see also* International Nickel Co.
  extraction experiments 77, 121
  financial difficulties 76
  first furnace started up 77
  formation of 65
  incorporation in International Nickel Co. 126
  matte production from Copper Cliff 66, 77
  Monell's report on 128
  negotiations with Ludwig Mond 85
  Sudbury deposits owned by 121, 122
  treatment of matte from 77, 78, 121, 135

Canadian Pacific Railway 64
Canadian Shield, exploration of 223
Candlesticks and snuffers, of nickel silver 45
Canning, W., and Co. 110, 111
Canyon Diablo (Barringer crater) 21
Cape York meteorite 17, 18, 19
Caproni-Campini aircraft 241
Cars. *See* Automobiles
Carbondale silver 274
Carbonyl process for extraction of nickel. *See* Mond carbonyl process, *also* I. G. Farbenindustrie A.G.
CARON, M. H. 298
Caron, M. H., ammoniacal-leaching process for treating lateritic ores 216
Carrier, M. 178
Casting alloys 45, 117, 246-7
Cast iron
  early history of 91-2
  nickel in 92, 94-5, 164, 171, 281, 294
  properties and uses of 92, 164, 171, 172, 294
Cathode
  derivation of term 284
Cathode nickel 147, 150, 180, 183
Centre d'Information du Nickel (Paris) 194-5
Chabanne en St. Romain, nickeliferous deposits at 52
Chalanches, silver ores containing nickel at 50
CHARLETON, A. G. 275, 285
Chemical plant, use of nickel-containing materials 115, 172, 225, 227
Chemical symbols for elements 39
CHENG, C. F. 261, 262
Cherwell, Lord 40
CHEVENARD, P. 301
Chikashige, M. 7, 261
Children, Mr., supplies meteoritic iron to Faraday 93

Index

China
  bronze articles from   7, 9, 12, 13, 262
  coinage   7, 202
  history of   13, 42, 263
  nickeliferous ores in   12, 262
  pai-thung (white copper) from   12-14, 42-4, 262-3
  rocketry in   250
China silver   274
Chiodoni, Fratelli   112
Chiu Thang Shu (History of Thang Dynasty)   13
Chondrites and *chondrules*   265
Chromax bronze   274
Chromite, in New Caledonia   178
Chromium-nickel alloys. *See* Nickel-chromium alloys
Chromium steel and chromium-nickel steels. *See* Nickel-chromium steels   346
Chronometers, nickel-iron alloys in   119
Churchill, Sir Winston, on 'condenseritis'   194; on Petsamo   299
CHURCHILL, W. S.   299
'Chymists'   36
Cladding. *See* Coating and Cladding
Close plating. *See* Coating and Cladding
Clydach refinery. *See* Mond Nickel Company
Coating and Cladding of metals
  See also Electrodeposition
  cladding with foil   105
  close-plating process   104-5
  fire gilding   105
  Fleitmann process for cladding   115-16
  wiping process   104
Cobalt
  See also Kobelt, Kobold, Kobolt
  classified as semi-metal   30
  derivation of name   267-8
  extraction of   71-2, 150
  in magnetic alloys   194
  in nickel-chromium-base alloys   244, 245
  Los cobalt mines   30, 31
  mined in Erzgebirge   23, 26, 270
  mined in France   52
  mined in U.S.A.   60
  nickel considered impure regulus of   37
  separation of cobalt salts from nickel salts   71-2
Cobalt-base alloys, in aero engines   234, 240, 241, 246, 312, 314
Cobalt blue pigment   23, 70, 278
Cobaltiferous 'mud' found in refinery   47-8
Cobalt oxide   72
Cockburn, A. J.   65
COHEN, J. M.   279
Coinage
  for coinage of individual countries. *See* names of countries
  advantages of nickel-containing coinage   197-209, 298
  aluminium bronze   209
  Bactrian coins   9-12
  composite materials   202
  copper-nickel alloys   9-12, 113, 114, 116, 151, 165, 197, 198, 199, 206-7, 208, 209, 285, 292
  copper-nickel-silver-zinc alloys   198, 207-8
  copper-nickel-zinc (nickel silver)   113, 198, 209
  early history   113, 197
  Feuchtwanger's composition   113
  German coins used as nickel reserve, World War I   151, 292
  knife coins in China   7
  nickel brass   208-9
  nickel consumption for   197
  numismatic treatises   261
  powder-metallurgical production of coins   209

Index

Coinage (ctd.)
  production methods 198, 200, 201, 202
  production of German coins by Fleitmann and others 114
  pure nickel 57, 151, 198, 200-5, 292
  Wharton memorandum on coinage 116, 285
Coke. *See* Fuel
Colby, Mr., letter from Wharton 287, 288
Colcothar 31, 269
COLEMAN, A. P. 292
COLEMAN, E. E. 299
Colombia, coinage 208
Colorado silver 274
Columbium (niobium) 244
Compagnie des Forges de la Marine 100
Condenser tubes 193-4, 229, 297
Coniston smelter. *See* International Nickel Company and Mond Nickel Company
Consolidated Mining and Smelting Company of Canada 296
Constable Hook (Bayonne). *See* International Nickel Company
Constantan 119, 120
Constructional nickel steels. *See* Nickel steels and Nickel-chromium (low-alloy) steels 346
Controlled (slow) cooling process. *See* International Nickel Company
'Conway' aero-engine (schematic drawing) 243, *facing* 247, 247
Cook, Capt. J. 54
Cooking utensils, of nickel 115
Cooperite 295
Copper
  extraction and refining of 50, 60, 63-4, 65, 66, 76, 181, 185, 187, 296. *See also* Extraction and refining of nickel
  output of Ontario in World War I 154

International Nickel Co. production, World War II 214
Copper Cliff mine and smelter
  See Canadian Copper Company, *also* International Nickel Company
Copper-manganese-nickel alloy (Manganin) 119
Copper-nickel alloys
  50-50 alloy produced from matte 78, 279
  condenser tubes 193, 229, 297
  in coinage. *See* Coinage
  in thermocouples 119-20
Copper-nickel steels. *See* Nickel-copper steels 346
Copper-nickel-zinc alloys. *See also* Nickel silver 13, 45, 46, 48, 119, 209
Copper sulphate, Mond production of 124, 187
Copper sulphide, formed in extraction processes 79, 219
  See also 'Tops-and-bottoms' process
Corrosion-resistant materials containing nickel
  cast irons 171
  copper-nickel alloys 193-4, 199, 229, 294
  general 170, 192, 252
  Monel 136, 174
  nickel 41, 115, 199, 229, 252
  nickel and nickel-copper steels 99, 173
  stainless steels 164, 225, 252
Corrosion test station (Kure Beach) 192
Cosmographie (Blundevile) 4
Cox, H. ROXBEE 300
Craig gold 274
Crankshafts 231, 232
Crean, F. C. 65
Crean Hill deposit 65
Creep-resistance 238, 300

324

Index

Creighton mine, discovery of 65
  For activities at Creighton mine
    See International Nickel
    Company
Crete, meteorites in 16
Cromadur alloy 244
CRONSTEDT, A. F. 30, 31, 33, 36, 269, 270
Cronstedt, A. F.
  biographical notes 29-30
  classification of minerals 33, 270
  death of 34
  discovery and naming of nickel 29-34, 269-70
  examination of Kupfer Nickel ore from Kuhschacht mine 32
  examination of Los cobalt ores 30, 31
Crown mine 63
Crushing and grinding equipment, Ni-Hard for 171
Cryogenic engineering, nickel steels for 227
Cuba, nickel deposits and nickel production 67, 216-17
Cube nickel *facing* 75, 132, 134, 222
Cupro-nickel alloys. *See* Copper-nickel alloys
Curtain-wall construction 225, 228
Curtiss-Wright, turbo-compound engine 235, 243
Cutler, Job 279
Cutlery. *See* Tableware
Cylinder heads 232
Czechoslovakia, coinage 202, 203, 204, 207

19-9 DL alloy 311
D-558-II research aircraft 257
Daimler, G. 103
Dalton, John 39
Damascened swords 94
Damascus, magic sword blades from 16
Daniel Knappe *Frontispiece*, 315
Daniell, J. F. 284

Danzig, coinage 202, 203, 205
Davy, Humphry 92, 284
DAWSON, S. E. 294
Decomposer, Mond carbonyl process (sketch) 88
de Dion, A. 103
Delphi, holy stone at 16
Denison (later Victoria) mine 122
De Re Metallica 25, 26
'Derwent' aero engine 239
DESCH, C. H. 6, 9, 261
Deschênes (Banco) 146, 154, 156
Deutsche Edelstahl Werke 228
DHAVERNAS, J. 295
Dhavernas, J., President, Centre d'Information du Nickel 195
DICKENSON, J. H. S. 301
Dillenburg, nickeliferous ores at 50
Dion, A. de 103
Dip-needle surveying 181, 295
Disarmament treaties 161-2, 292
Discaloy 310
Disk nickel *facing* 75
Dobsina (Dobschau) 50
Dominion Mineral Company 122
Dominion Nickel-Copper Company 146, 291
Doniambo plant of S.A. Le Nickel 223
DONNAN, F. G. 279, 291
Douglas D-558-II research aircraft 257
Downwind Expedition 260
Drury Nickel Company 122
Duffel (Ballande) refinery 131, 134, 145, 156
Duralumin 231, 258
Durant, W. 103
Duryea, C. E. 103

Earth
  age and structure of 1, *facing* 2
  gravitational effect of 258
  Mohorovicic discontinuity. *See* sketch *facing* 2

325

Index

Earth (ctd.)
  nickel in core, crust and mantle of 1-2
Ecuador, coinage 202
Eddystone Supercritical Unit 227
EDISON, THOMAS 120, 289
Edison, Thomas
  dip-needle survey technique 295
  nickel in batteries 120
Egypt, iron beads found in Gerzah 15
Elbogen meteorite 16, 263
Electric irons 120
Electric shunts 119
Electrical-resistance materials 119, 165, 170, 175, 177, 239, 295
Electricity generators, nickel-containing materials in 227
Electrodeposition of nickel and other metals
  Adams and other plating solutions 108, 109-12
  anodes for 109, 110, 112, 165, 175, 192-3
  boric acid in plating solutions 110, 183
  Bouse and Muncher plating plant 110
  Canning and Co. catalogues and plant 110-11
  cathode nickel produced in refining 147, 150, 180, 183
  commercial development in 19th century 108, 112, 285
  dynamos introduced by Weston 109-10, 285
  early history of 105, 284
  electrolytic nickel-refining processes and products 112, 121, 139, 141, 146, 147, 149-50, 180, 183, 189, 212, 291
  electroplated nickel silver (EPNS) 49
  European process for treating silicate ores *facing* 75
  Faraday formulates laws of electrolysis 105, 284-5
  flake nickel produced by electrodeposition 120, 289
  Hybinette electrolytic refining process 139, 141, 149-50, 291
  Langbein-Pfanhauser founded 112, 285
  technical progress in 19th century 107-12, 285
  Whewell/Faraday correspondence on terminology 284-6
Electrolysis. *See* Electrodeposition
Electrum 274
Elements, Periodic Table *facing* 302
Elements of Natural History and Chemistry (Fourcroy) 38
Elinvar 164
Elsie deposit 65
ELMEN, G. W. 293
EMMENS, S. H. 280
ENGESTRÖM, G. VON 33, 43, 270, 271, 279
Engeström, G. von
  hepar sulphuris for separation of copper from nickel 80
  on *pai-thung* 263
  translation of Cronstedt's work 33
  treatise on nickel 36, 43, 80
Ensisheim meteorite 16, 263
Ephesians, worship of meteorite 16
E.P.N.S. 49
ERCKER, L. 268
Erdington refinery 75, 148, 149, 156
ERDMANN, O. L. 272
Erteli mine 52
Erzgebirge
  Kupfer Nickel from 24, 270
  minerals found in 274-5
  mining practice in *Frontispiece*, 23, 315
  nickel deposits in 50, 270, 274
  silver deposits in 23, 50
  visit by P. N. Johnson 45
Eschel (blue pigment) 278
Eskimos, knives of meteoritic iron 17

Index

Espedalen mines 52, 53
Estonia
 coinage 207
 meteoric falls in 21
Eustis Mining Company 276
Eustis, W. E. C. 62, 63, 275
Euthydemus II 9-12, 261-2
Evans, B. 46-8, 52, 71-2
Evans deposit 66
Evans, D. Owen 211, 296
Evans, R. D. 97
Evje mine and smelter 53, 149
Exploitation of the Works of Nature 14
Extraction and refining of nickel
 1914, 1918 output of refineries
  156
 Caron process for lateritic ores
  216
 Cronstedt's experiments 30-4,
  269, 270
 early processes, review 39
 electrolytic refining processes
  121, 139, 141, 146, 147, 149-50,
  154, 156, 180, 181-3, 186, 189,
  212, 296
 Falconbridge Nickel Mines
  process 188-9
 I.G. Farbenindustrie carbonyl
  process 187-8, 298
 Fleitmann refinery at Iserlohn
  75, 113
 Forward pressure-leaching
  process 217-18, 299
 Freeport Nickel Co. process 217
 Geitner process 69-70
 Hoepfner electrolytic process 121
 Hybinette electrolytic process
  139, 141, 146, 149-50, 154, 181,
  189, 291
 International Nickel slow-cooling
  process (Sproule *et al.*) 218-19
 mining and refining development
  in 1920's 178-87

 Mond carbonyl process 83-90,
  124, 154, 187, 279-80
 Perrin pyrometallurgical process
  (ferro-nickel) 217-18
 processes in use in 1918 154
 recent developments in extraction
  and refining 216-24
 refining, in Canada, from New
  Caledonia matte 213
 refining, in Europe, from New
  Caledonia matte, 75, *facing* 75
 separation of nickel salts from
  cobalt salts; bleaching powder
  71-2, 73, 278
 tops-and-bottoms (Orford)
  process 78-82, 121, 154-5, 218,
  279
 treatment of arsenical ores 30, 57,
  69-70, 73, 275
 treatment of lateritic (oxide) ores
  216-18
 treatment of silicate ores 57,
  facing 75
 treatment of sulphide ores 78-82,
  83-90, 155, 180-3, 186-7, 188-9,
  189-91, 211-13, 217, 296
 Wharton process 75-6, 279
Extrusion of high-temperature alloys
 247

Fairbairn, W. 95
Fairchild Aerial Surveys 21
Falconbridge Nickel Mines
 extraction and refining process of
  181, 188-9
 incorporation and expansion
  181, 188-9
 Kristiansand refinery of 181,
  189, 210, 213, 297. *See also
  earlier references under* Kristiansand
 matte from, processed by International Nickel 213
 post-war development and
  current production 220-1

327

Index

Falconbridge Nikkelverk Aktieselskap 181
FARADAY 281
Faraday, Michael
  birth and early life of 92, 280-1
  correspondence with Whewell 284-6
  formulates laws of electrolysis 105, 284-5
  interest in nickel 92-93
  portrait of 106
Farbenindustrie, I. G. 187-8, 298
FEDDEN, R. 300
Feely, E. F. 298
Ferro-nickel 74, 130, 153, 178, 179, 218, 221, 222
  See also Fonte
Feuchtwanger, L. 113
Fiji, coinage 207
Finland
  coinage 209
  nickeliferous deposits 189-91, 210, 213, 222, 299
  supply of nickel to Germany 213
Fire gilding 105
Firth-Vickers
  Stayblade and Rex 78 238
Fischer, J. C. 94
Flaad mine (Norway) 53
Flanagan, T. 64
FLEITMANN, T. 115, 287
Fleitmann, T.
  cladding of metals 115-16
  Iserlohn works 75
  malleablises nickel 113-16, 287
  production of cupro-nickel coins 114
  Schwerte mill 114
FLIGHT, W. 9, 11, 261
Fonderies de Nouméa 57
Fonte (ferro-nickel) 74, 130, 178, 179. See also 221
Food-handling equipment and processing 172, 225
Ford, Henry 103
Foreword vii

Forks. See Tableware
Fort Saskatchewan refinery 217
FORWARD, F. A. 217, 299
Forward extraction process 217, 299
FOURCROY, A. F. DE 38, 39, 271
France
  coinage 201-4
  French operations in New Caledonia. See New Caledonia
  nickel-bearing silver deposits in 50, 52
  plating developments in 107 ff.
Frankenstein, nickeliferous ores at 50, 121, 153
Fredericktown (Mo.) 60, 141
FREDRIKSSON, K. 261
Freeport Nickel Company 217
Freiberg Bergakademie, archives in 24-7, 268
Frick, H. C. 45, 281
Fritz, J. 281
Frohnau, near Annaberg 315
Frood mine and Frood extension 65, 66, 141, 142, 183, 185, 186
  See also International Nickel Company; Mond Nickel Company
Frood-Stobie mine
  See International Nickel Company
Frood, T. 64
Froschlampen (ladder-peg lamps) 315
Frose-bei-Nachterstedt 188
Fuel, supplies for New Caledonia 148, 178-9, 210, 295
Furnaces, nickel-chromium heating elements in 120
FYFE, A. 44, 272

G 18B alloy 310
G 34 alloy 314
G 64 alloy 312
Gap mine 60, 75, 76
Gardner, H. 89-90, 127, 280
Gardner, Henry, and Co. 127

Index

GARDNER, P. 261
GARLAND, J. 58, 275
GARNIER, J. 55, 275
Garnier, J.
  work on Canadian ores 68, 77
  work on New Caledonian ores 54-8, 74
Garnierite 55, 68, 74
Garson mine 122, 211
Gas turbines
  See Aircraft and Aero Engines
GAUTIER, F. 117, 289
Gay, J., *The Beggars Opera* 36
Gears, of nickel-alloy steel 232
Geitner, E. A. 69, 272
Geitner extraction process 69-70
General Electric Co.
  'I' series gas turbines 240
  magnet development 297
  René 41 alloy 256
Generator shafts of nickel steel 172
George VI, King, discussion with President Roosevelt 298
  visit to Clydach refinery 211
German silver 14, 274
Germany
  coinage 114, 151, 198, 201, 203, 204, 292
  I.G. Farbenindustrie carbonyl extraction process 187-8
  gas-turbine development in 241, 244
  nickel from Finland (World War II) 213; from Norway (World War I) 150, 153
  nickel-bearing ores in 50, 153
  nickel production and imports 67, 90, 142, 150-3, 188, 213, 297, 298
  nickel silver trade in 45
  plating developments in 108, 112, 285
  restrictions on nickel 150-3, 292 (World War I); 213, 241, 244, 298 (World War II)
  silver deposits in 45

German silver 14, 274
GERSDORFF, J. R. VON 45, 272
Gersdorff, J. R. von 69, 80, 272
Gersdorffite 30
Gerzah, iron beads found at 15
Gilchrist, P. 96
Gladenbach 50
GLASSER, E. 72, 74, 278
Globe Works of Mond Nickel Company 175
Gloire 96
G.M.R. 235 and 235D alloys 246, 312
Goddard, R. H. 250
Goranssön, F. 281
Goranssön, G. 281
Gossan (iron oxide capping on pyrites) 64
GOUGH, H. J. 300
GRAHAM, R. P. 264
Grain nickel *facing* 75, 110
Greco, S. *facing* 142
Greek coinage
  contemporary 202, 203, 205
  in Bactria 8-11
GREEN, J. 261
Greenland, meteoritic iron knives in 17, 18
GRIFFITHS, W. T. 294
GRIMM, J. 268
GRIMM, W. 268
GRONNINGSATER, A. 297
Grotthus 284
Guatemala, coinage 208
GUILLAUME, C. E. 118, 164, 289
GUILLET, L. 163, 293
Guns, of nickel-containing steel 99, 130

HADFIELD, R. A. 118, 162, 289, 293
Hadfield, R. A. 281
Hafod Isha refinery 131, 148, 156
Hägg, Prof., search of Cronstedt archives 269,
HALDE, J. B. DU 42, 263, 271

329

Index

Hallett, G. 71
HAMPTON, T. 285
Han dynasty, records of 12
Hanna Mining Co., process and product 218-19, 299
HANSON, D. 300
Hardening. *See* Age-hardening
Hardware, nickel stainless steel for 225
Hardy mine 189
Harshaw Chemical Company 192
Harvey, H. A. 99
Harvey surface-hardening process 99-100
Hastelloy alloys.
 See Haynes Stellite
Hauts Fourneaux de Nouméa 179
Hawker P.1127 vertical-take-off aircraft 249
HAYNES, E. 163, 293
Haynes Stellite alloys
 Nos. 21 and 31 246, 314
 Hastelloy B 240, 241, 246
 Hastelloy X 312
Heap-roasting process 77
Heating elements 119-20, 165, 170, 175, 177
'Heaven-sent' metal 15, 263
Hébert, C. 58
Hébert, P. 58
HEIDE, F. 264
Heinkel, jet-plane flight 241
Henne mine (Saxony) 45
Hepar sulphuris 43, 80, 271, 279
Hereford plant. *See* Wiggin, Henry and Company
Hermannshütte smelter 153
Hero of Alexandria, conception of gas turbine 237, 300
HERON, S. D. 301
Hesse, Hans *Frontispiece*, 23, 315
HEURTEAU, E. 57, 275
Hexahedrites 18
Hickling, S. S. 92
Higginson, J. 58
Higginson, John, and Co. 57

High Duty Alloys Ltd. 232
High-temperature materials 41, 119, 170, 192, 233-4, 235, 244, 301, 302, 310-14
HISINGER, W. 105, 284
History of China 42
HJÄRNE, U. 27, 269
Hoba meteorite 20
Hochheim, J. C. 272
Hoepfner electrolytic refining process 121
Holley, A. 281
Holtzer, J. 281
Holy stone at Delphi 16
Hong Kong, coinage 202
Hoover, H. C. 266
Hoover, L. H. 266
Horse harness, of nickel silver 45
HOWE, H. M. 300
Hsü, Liu 13
Hungary, nickel ores in 50
Huntington plant. *See* International Nickel Company
'Hurricane' aircraft 233
Hutton, W. C., close plating of cutlery 105
HYBINETTE, N. V. 141, 291
Hybinette electrolytic refining process 139, 141, 149-50, 154, 181, 189, 291
Hygiene, International Conference for 115

Iceland, coinage 209
Iliffe Books Ltd. 242
Immaculate 5 alloy 310
Imperial Chemical Industries Ltd. 138
IN 100 alloy 245, 246, 313
Inco. *See* International Nickel Company
Incoloy alloys Nos. 800 and 901 310
Inconel alloys, general 170, 239
Inconel alloys Nos. 600, 700, 713, 713C, 718, 722, 751 192, 241, 256, 312

330

Index

Inconel alloys X and X-750 241, 246, 254, 256, 312
India, coinage 202, 203, 204, 208
Indo-China, coinage 202
Indonesia, coinage 207
Induced-caving mining method 219
Information bureaux, Inco/Mond 194-5, 214
Instrumentation, alloys for use in 164, 229
International Conference for Hygiene 115
International Geophysical Year 260
International Nickel Company
  aerial geophysical prospecting developed by 222-3
  Bayonne refinery 63, 66, 77, 79, 121, 128, 135, 141, 145, 146, 156, 158
  Bayonne research laboratory 192
  Chairmen of 127, 167, 275
  Coniston smelter 141 (Mond); 186 (Inco)
  Constable Hook. See Bayonne, above
  controlled (slow) cooling process (Sproule et al.) replaces tops-and-bottoms method 218-19
  copper supplied to Allies during World War II 214
  Copper Cliff mine, smelter and copper refinery 66, 68, 76, 77, 129, 141, 142, 185, 186, 296
  Creighton mine 65, 139, 141, 158-9, 183, 185, 186, 211, 219
  development and research department formed 169
  expansion after post-war and financial depressions 154-6, 183-7, 189-91
  finances of 159, 161
  Frood mine 65, 66, 141, 142, 185, 186
  Frood-Stobie open pit 211-12, 220
  Garson mine 211
  Huntington plant (semi-fabricated products) 174, 213, 294

  Hybinette, N. V., association with 139, 141
  Inconel alloys developed 170. For later references to these alloys see Inconel alloys
  incorporation of 126
  information services 194, 214
  Kure Beach corrosion-test station 192
  labour conditions 129
  Manitoba project; Thompson mine 222-4
  Merica, P. D. leads research team 169
  mining methods used; expansion of ore production 214-20
  Monel 400 and Monel K 500 developed 135-6, 174. For later references to these materials, see Monel 400, Monel K 500
  Monell's comments on plants forming part of International Nickel Company 127-8
  nickel production and potential 141 (Bayonne); 146, 186 (Port Colborne); 156 (Bayonne 1914, 1918); 159 (1921); 186 (1933); 214 (World War II); 224 (current capacity)
  Ontario Refining Company, subsidiary of 296
  Orford process. See tops-and-bottoms process, 332
  Petsamo deposit developed 189-91
  physical laboratory at Orford works 136
  Port Colborne refinery 146, 154, 156, 158, 159, 181-3, 186, 212
  precious metals supplied to Allies, World War II 214
  refineries of 128, 146, 154, 156, 158, 159, 181, 182, 186, 212

Index

International Nickel Company (ctd.)
  research and market development by 136, 161 ff., 168-70, 171-4, 191-6, 214, 224-5, 294
  retrenchment after wartime expansion 158-9, 214
  semi-fabricated products (Huntington plant) 174, 294
  Stanley, R. C. 141 (Superintendent, Bayonne); 167 (Chairman)
  'tops-and-bottoms' process 79 (discovery), 81, 82, 121, 146, 154, 155, 183, 186-7, 218 (replaced)
  Thompson, J. F., association with 136, 168 (Chairman), 275
  Thompson, R. M., association with 126, 127, 138 (Chairman), 275
  unites with Mond Nickel Co. 185, 296
  Wadhams, A. J., directs market development project 168
  wartime treatment of matte from Falconbridge Nickel Mines and from New Caledonia 213
  World War I problems 144 ff.
  World War II achievement 214
Invar 118, 164
Inveraray, nickel deposit at 281
Invocation on mining v
Ionization of atoms 261
Iraq, coinage 202, 203, 205
Iridium argyroide 274
Irish Free State, coinage 202, 203, 204
Iron
  cast. *See* Cast iron
  meteoritic. *See* Meteors; Meteoritic iron
  nickel in 93, 281
Iron carbonyl as anti-knock ingredient 187
Iron-nickel alloys. *See* Nickel-iron alloys
Iron-nickel-aluminium alloys. *See* Nickel-aluminium-iron alloys

Iron-nickel-chromium alloys, compositions of 310
  See also Nickel-chromium-(iron) alloys and Nickel-chromium (stainless) high-alloy steels
Iserlohn refinery 75, 113
Isotopes of nickel 304
Italy
  Caproni-Campini aero engines 241
  coinage 201

J30-WE20 axial-flow gas turbine 240
JAEGER, K. 292
Jalandhar, meteorite at 16
Janikoski, hydro-electric power plant at 190, 191
Japan
  coinage 202, 203, 205
  nickel industry in 222
  Russo-Japanese war 130
Jessop, W. 281
Jet engines. *See* Aircraft and Aero Engines
Johnson, Matthey and Co. 45, 180
Johnson, P. N. 45, 70-71, 278
Junkers 004 aero engine 244
'Jupiter' missile 251

Kaaba, black stone of 16
Kamacite, in meteorites 18, 265
K.E. 965 steel 234, 246
Keates, H. W. 272
Keene's alloy 274
KEFERSTEIN, C. *et al.*, 45, 272
Kelly, W. 95
Kelvin, Lord 87
Khorassan, magic sword blades from 17
Kinetic heating problem in spacecraft 254
Kirkintilloch intermediate treatment plant 75, 148, 149
Kirkwood nickel deposit 142
Kish, bronze articles from 6, 7

Index

Kitty Hawk, Wright Brothers' flights at 231
Klaustal, arsenical nickel ores in 50
Klefva, nickeliferous ores at 39, 52
Knife coin of China 7, 9
Knife-handles, of nickel silver 45
Kobelt *or* Cobelt (*cadmia*), toxicity of 23
Kobold, Kobolt 26, 267
Kolojoski 189, 190
Korea, war in, effect on nickel industry 214-16
KRAINER, H. 163, 293
Kriegsmetall A.G. 151, 153
KRINOV, E. L. 265
Krisses, of meteoritic iron 16, 18, 264
Kristiansand, nickel refinery 141, 149-50, 153, 156, 181, 189, 210, 213, 297. *See also* Falconbridge Nickel Mines
Kristiansand Nikkelraffineringsverk Aktieselskap 149, 156, 181
Krupp, F. 281
Krupp, Fried., A.G.
  Cromadur alloy 244
  smelting of low-nickel ores 153
  Tinidur alloy 241
  V 2A steel 163
Kuhschacht mine 32
Kupfer Nickel (and variant forms) v, 25-32, 34, 269, 270
Kupfernicklicht 26
Kure Beach corrosion-research station
  See International Nickel Company

La Motte mine 60
LACROIX, A. 275
LAEVASTU, T. 2, 259
Lake Inari hydroelectric plant 191
Lamps, miners' ladder-peg type 315
Lancaster County (Penn.), pyrrhotite-chalcopyrite deposit 60
Lanchester, F. W. 103

LANGBEIN, G. E. L. 285
Langbein-Pfanhauser plating plant established 112, 285
Langer, C. 83, 124, 290
LANGER, E. 261
Langley, S. P. 230
Lateritic ores
  See Nickel ores
LATHROP, W. G. 274
Latvia, coinage 202
Laundry machinery, nickel-containing materials in 225
Lavoisier, A. L. 36, 38
Leaching of nickel ores 150, 216-17
Lead ores containing nickel 60
Le Chêsne 58, 98
Le Ferro-Nickel. *See* Société le Ferro-Nickel
Le Havre, refinery of S.A. Le Nickel 75, 144, 149, 156, 210, 213
Le Nickel. *See* Société Anonyme Le Nickel
Lenoir, J. 102
Levack deposit 122, 142
Levassor, E. 103
LIBAVIUS, A. 42, 271
Light, speed of 258
Liinahamari 189, 190
Lime Creek meteorite 20
Lindbergh, C. 233
LINDECK, S. 289
Liquid-propellant engines. *See* Aircraft and Aero Engines, including Rockets
Litchfield, (Conn.), nickel deposit at 59
Livy, report of meteoric fall 15
Lizy-sur-Ourcq, plant of Le Ferro-Nickel 58
Locomotive frames, nickel steel for 172
London (Disarmament) Treaty (1930) 161
Longyear, E. J., Company 181

Index

Los cobalt mines 30, 31, 52
Lost-wax casting process 247
Low-temperature applications of nickel-containing steels 173, 227
Lu kan shih 14
Lutecin 274
Luxembourg, coinage 202
Lynn Lake nickel deposits 217, 299

M-252 alloy 246, 312
McConnell, R. 64, 122
McDonald, D. 278
McFarland, M. W. 300
Mach
  definition of 230, 299-300
  speeds in excess of Mach 1 249, 256, 257
McKinley, President 230
Madison County (Mo.), La Motte mine 60
Magnesium as malleablising agent 115, 199
Magnesium silicates. *See* Nickel ores
Magnets, permanent 194, 293
Maillechort 274
Manganese, substituted for nickel in high-temperature alloys 199, 244
Manganese nodules 3, 260
Manganin 119, 289
Manitoba
  Lynn Lake deposit 217, 299
  International Nickel development in 223-4
Maraging steels 227, 299
Marbeau, H. 57, 58, 98
Marine organisms, nickel in 259
Markus alloy 274
Markus, S. 102
Marsh, A. L. 119, 289
Marshall, J. H. 261
Martin, E. 281
Martin, P. 281
Martineau, J. 94
Mason, B. 259, 264
Mathesius 267-8

Mathias, R. 290
Matte. *See* Extraction and Refining
Maurer, E. 163, 292
Maximilian I 16, 263
Mecca, black stone of the Kaaba 16
Melchett, Baron, of Landford. *See* Mond, A
Menard, H. W. 260
Merica, P. D. 169, 231, 291, 292, 293, 294, 300
Merica, P. D.
  at National Bureau of Standards 169, 293
  leads International Nickel research 169
  researches on age-hardening 169-70, 231, 294, 300
'Merlin' aero-engine 233
Merry, H. 46
Merry's metal blanc 274
Merry's plate 274
Merton, Henry R., and Company 89, 127
Metabolites (octahedrites) 19-20
'Metallists' 36
Metals, devices and symbols for 4, 37
Metals Reserve Co. 213
Meteorites 15-22, 263-5
  behaviour of 20-22
  classification and nature of 18-19, 265
  geographical distribution 15 ff., 264
  nickel content of individual specimens 15 ff., 265
Meteoritic iron, use of 15, 16, 17, 18, 20, 93, 94
Metric ton, definition 259
Metropolitan Museum of Art, New York 17
Metropolitan Vickers, axial-flow turbine 239
Mexico
  coinage 208
  use of meteoritic iron in 17

Index

Michaud, assistant to Garnier 68
Middle East countries, nickel ores in 12, 262
Mine, typical model *facing* 142
Minerals, classification of 33
Mineralogical Society 265
Mining methods
  developments in 1920's 178-85, 295-7
  invocation on mining v
  mining in Saxony *Frontispiece*, 23, 315
  open-cast mining in New Caledonia 72
  open-pit mining at Frood-Stobie 211-12
  recent developments (blast-hole, induced-caving and undercut-and-fill) 219-22
Mining Review or Lighted Pit Candle, extract from v
Ministry of Munitions, control of nickel, World War I 148
Minuteman Intercontinental Ballistic Missile 250
MISHIMA, T. 297
Missiles 250-2
Mississippi (Oktibbeha) meteorite 20
Mitterberg, nickeliferous ores at 50
MK magnet alloy 194, 297
Moa Bay, Freeport Nickel Co. 217
Mohenjo-Daro, bronze articles from 6, 7, 261
Mohorovicic discontinuity, *see* sketch *facing* 2
Mohr, B., surveys deposits for Mond 121-2
Monaco, coinage 201
Monchegorsk, nickel-sulphide ores at 222
Mond, Alfred (later Lord Melchett)
  biographical notes 137, 139
  Mond Nickel Co. 124 (Director); 170 (Chairman)
  portrait 138

Mond carbonyl process
  See also Mond Nickel Company, Clydach refinery, 336
  discovery of formation of nickel carbonyl 83-4
  flow sheet of process 86, 87, 280; *see also* 88 (decomposer)
  Langer's contribution to 83, 124, 290
  negotiations with Canadian Copper Company re purchase of process 85
  pellets produced by 133, 142, 187
  pilot-scale development 84-9, 124
  position in 1918 154
  powder produced by 134
  problems in early stages of development 124-6
  reaction of industry to carbonyl process 84-5, 87-8
  types of matte processed by 186-7
MOND, L 279
Mond, Ludwig
  biographical notes on 82 ff., 126, 137, 279, 291
  carbonyl extraction process invented by. *See* Mond carbonyl process
  commissions survey of nickel deposits 121, 122
  discussions with R. McConnell re deposits in Canada 122
  founds Brunner Mond and Co. 83
  founds Mond Nickel Company and becomes Chairman 124, 126, 290
  honours accorded to 291
  letters from H. H. Vivian and Co. and Henry Merton and Co., re carbonyl nickel 87, 89-90
  memorial lecture by F. G. Donnan 291
  negotiations with Canadian Copper Co. 85

335

Index

Mond, Ludwig (ctd.)
  options on Canadian deposits;
    starts operation 122, 124,
  portrait 123
Mond Nickel Company
  Clydach refinery 124, 137, 142,
    147, 156, 159, 180-1, 186-7,
    191, 211, 290
  Coniston smelter (Mond) 141;
    (Inco) 186
  copper sulphate production by
    124, 187
  finances of 126, 147-8, 159, 161,
    290
  formation of 124
  Frood mine, and Frood extension
    65, 66, 85, 141, 142, 183.
    See also later entries under
    International Nickel Company
  Globe Works 175
  information service 195, 214
  mines owned by, and mining
    activities in Canada 65, 122,
    124, 141, 142, 183. *See also*
    Frood mine
  nickel production by 141, 142,
    147, 156, 157, 180, 187.
    See also Clydach refinery (above)
  nickel salts produced by 137
  Nimonic alloys developed by
    238-40
  research and market development
    by 168, 170, 195
  semi-fabricated products made by
    175, 294
  unites with International Nickel
    Co. 185, 296
  Wiggin, Henry and Co. becomes
    subsidiary of 175, 295
  World War I, effect on activities
    144, 158-9, 161
Mond, R. 292
Mond, Robert
  biographical notes 139
  contribution to scientific research
    139

Mond Nickel Co., Director of
  124
  portrait 140
Monel
  composition 135, 173-4
  origin and early development of
    135, 136, 164-5, 290
Monel alloy-400 135-6, 159, 165,
  168, 173-4, 192, 194, 294
Monel alloy K-500 174, 256
Monell, A.
  Monel alloys named after 135
  President, International Nickel
    Co. 127
  reorganisation of Company's
    plants 127-8
Montenegro, coinage 201
Moon, nickel in lunar dust 3
MOORE, C. 264
Morocco, coinage 202
MORRAL, F. R. 268
Moss, S. A. 234
Motor cars. *See* Automobiles
Mount Alban meteor 15
Mount Nickel mine 189
MUDGE, W. A. 294
Mühlhofener Hütte, treatment of
  low-grade nickel ores 153
MÜLLER. *See* Keferstein, C. *et al.*
Müller, F. 112
Muncher. *See* Bouse and Muncher
Munitions, Ministry of 148
Murray, A. 62, 64
MURRAY, J. 268
Murray mine 64
Murray, T. 64
Murray, W. 64
Mushet, R. 96

N 155 alloy 310
NACHTRIEB, N. H. 261
NARAIN, A. K. 262
National Institute of Oceanography,
  nickel in sea water 3
National Lead Company 60
Nature, Works of 14

336

Index

Navaho booster 251
Naval Disarmament Treaties 161, 292
Naval Ordnance Proving Ground, Annapolis, armour tests 99, 101
NEEDHAM, J. 262
Needham, J., on *pai-thung* 13, 14, 262
Neogen 274
Nepal, coinage 209
Netherlands, coinage 201, 203, 205
NEUMANN, B. 272
Neusilber 274
Neuville, A. de 56
Nevada, nickeliferous ores in 122
Nevada silver 274
New Brunswick refinery, U.S. Nickel Co. 134, 147, 156, 179
New Caledonia
  Ballande starts operation in 131, 144, 147
  chromite deposits developed 178
  companies operating in 57-8, 74, 130, 178, 295 (*see also* under names of companies)
  discovered by Cook, but claimed for France 54
  Doniambo plant 223
  extraction process used on silicate ores *facing* 75
  ferro-nickel (fonte) production in 74, *facing* 74, 178-9, 221-2, 295
  Fonderies de Nouméa 57, 74
  fuel supplies to 148, 178-9, 210, 295
  grade of ore mined 59, 74, 179
  improvements in plant and operations in 178-9, 221-2, 223, 295
  labour conditions in 58, 74, 129, 275, 278
  mineral resources of, reports on 54-57, 275 (Garnier); 72, 278 (Glasser); 57, 275 (Heurteau)
  mining methods and developments 72, 178-9, 221, 223

  nickel and nickel-ore production 58, 59, 67, 72, 90, 142, 159, 160, 179, 222, 280
  Pointe Chaleix plant 58
  purity of nickel and nickel oxide produced from ores in 74
  supply of nickel to Steel Manufacturers' Nickel Syndicate 131, 290
  Thio, smelter at 59, 130, 179
  treatment, in France, Great Britain and Canada, of matte and ore from 57, 75, 134, 148, 213
  World Wars I and II, effect on nickel industry of 144, 159, 210
New silver 274
Newton, Keates and Company 272
New York, Chicago and St. Louis Railroad (Nickel Plate Road) 112
New Zealand, coinage 208
Ni, chemical symbol 39. *See also* 37
Nicaro, lateritic ores at 216, 217
Niccolite 14, 24
Nichols Copper Company 66
Nick (and variants), derivation of 266-8
Nickel
  devices and symbols for 37, 39
  extraction and refining of. *See* Extraction and refining of nickel
  isolation, classification and naming of (semi-metal) 31-3, 36, 38, 269, (pure and noble metal) 37-41
  price of (1840-1961) 308-9
  production and consumption statistics
    consumption
      (19th century) 72 (1931-1938) 195, 196
    production
      (1751-1961) 67
      (1775-1900) 90
      (1900-1914) 142-3

337

Index

Nickel (ctd.)
    (1901-1922) 160
    (1914, 1918) 156, 195
    (1922-1929) 177, 184, 195
    (1929-1945) 214-16
    (1945-1961) 226
  for production by individual countries and firms, *see* names of countries and firms
  properties. *See* Summary of physical properties 304-7
    atomic number, and weight; isotopes *facing* 302, 304
    boiling point 305
    colour 33, 38, 40
    corrosion-resistance 40, 115, 229
    density 33, 40, 305
    electrical resistivity 306
    hygienic characteristics 115
    latent heat of fusion 305
    magnetic 41, 307
    malleability 36, 40, 114-15, 199-200
    mechanical 40
    melting point 41, 199, 305
    oxidation-resistance 33, 36, 40, 41, 169
    specific heat 305-6
    structure 38, 305
    thermal conductivity 306
    thermal expansion 306
  purity of specific forms of 74-5, 81, 181
  stockpiling of 216
  ubiquity of 1-5, 259-61
  uses
    civilian uses in relation to wartime restrictions 144-54, 157-65, 195, 210-16
    in aircraft and Aero Engines. *See* Aircraft and aero engines
    in anodes. *See* Electrodeposition
    in armaments. *See* Wars; effect on nickel industry
    in batteries 120, 229
    in coinage. *See* Coinage
    in food-handling equipment 115
    in telecommunication engineering 229
    in thermionic valves 165, 229
    in water meters
    prehistoric uses 6-22, 261-66
    present-day uses 225-9
Nickel alloys. *See also* individual types, e.g. Nickel-iron alloys
  high-temperature alloys, typical compositions 310-14
  production of, by Mond and Wiggin 175, 177, 295, 301
  typical current uses 225-9
Nickel-aluminium alloys 120
Nickel-aluminium-iron-base magnet alloys 194, 293
Nickel anodes. *See* Electrodeposition of nickel
Nickel arsenide. *See* Nickel ores
Nickel bloom 23
Nickel bottoms 187
Nickel briquettes 217, 218
Nickel bronze 6-9, 193, 274
Nickel carbonyl. *See* Mond carbonyl process, *also* I. G. Farbenindustrie A.G.
Nickel cathodes produced in electrolytic refining 147, 150, 180, 183
Nickel chloride in plating solutions 107, 108, 212
Nickel-chloride/nickel-sulphate electrolyte used in refining 212
Nickel-chromium and nickel-chromium-iron alloys
  See also Inconel alloys, *and* Nimonic alloys
  age-hardening of 234-5, 239, 241, 244, 300
  compositions, typical 312-13

Index

Nickel chromium alloys (ctd.)
　in aero engines　170-1, 233, 234, 238-40, 241, 244, 245, 246, *facing* 247, 247, 256, 300-2, 312-13
　in electrical-resistance materials 119, 165, 170, 175, 177, 239
　in thermocouples　120
　production by Henry Wiggin and Co.　175, 177, 295, 301
　protective coatings on exhaust valves　233
　temperature capability of　245, 246
Nickel-chromium-cobalt alloys　245
Nickel-copper alloys. *See* Monel
See also Copper-Nickel alloys
Nickel cubes　*facing* 75, 132, 134, 222
Nickel disks　*facing* 75
Nickel grain　*facing* 75, 110
Nickel industry
　for developments in individual countries. *See* names of countries
　foundation and development 121-143
　recent expansion and future potential　210-29
　war and post-war effects on 144-54, 157-62, 210-14, 214-16
Nickeline　274
Nickel-iron alloys
　See also Meteorites
　early development of　116-17, 164
　Faraday's experiments　93
　for components used in telecommunication engineering 164, 293
　for springs of watches and clocks 118-19, 164, 289
　for standards of weight and length　118, 289
　in earth's core and mantle　1-2
　production by Le Ferro-Nickel and others　117
　properties, physical　117, 118, 119, 164, 289, 293
　research on　93, 116-18, 289
　statuette of Venus de Milo　117
Nickelising　108
Nickel ochre　23
Nickel ores
　A. Locations where found
　Oman　7
　Canada　60 ff., 121-2, 145, 189, 217
　China, India and Middle East 7, 12, 262
　Cuba　67, 216-17
　Finland　189-91, 213
　France　50, 52
　Germany　23, 50, 121, 153
　Hungary　50
　New Caledonia　54-7, 72, 275, 277
　Norway　52-4
　Ontario; *see* Canada
　Russia (U.S.S.R.)　54, 222
　Sudbury; *see* Canada
　Sweden　52
　United States　59-60, 62, 75, 122, 218-19, 299
　B. Types of deposit in which nickel has occurred
　arsenical (silver) ores　23, 24, 30, 50, 52, 62, 69-70, 153
　lateritic (oxide) ores　54, 216, 217-18, 222
　lead ores　60
　silicate ores　50, 54-7, 59, 121
　sulphide ores　50, 53, 60, 66, 68, 122, 145, 179-80, 187, 189-91, 222, 276
　unspecified types　7, 12, 50, 52, 59, 75, 122, 141, 153
　C. Mode of formation and weathering of ores
　(lateritic and sulphide types) 276-7
　D. Types known in 18th century; review　39, 271
Nickel ore body, model *facing* 142

Index

Nickel oreide 274
Nickel oxide
  intermediate in production of nickel and nickel silver 69, 70-1, 74, *facing* 75, 77, 78, 149, 183
  intermediate in Orford Copper Co. extraction process 78
  powder used for cementing out copper from nickel 183
  production by Port Colborne refinery 186
Nickel pellets 88, 133, 142, 187
Nickel Plate, significance of term 112-13
Nickel plating. *See* Electrodeposition, *also* Coating of Metals
Nickel powder 134, 188, 209, 217, 297
Nickel rondelles *facing* 75, 132, 134, 148, 222, 292
Nickel salts, purity of, for plating 110
  See also Electrodeposition
Nickel shot 133, 134
Nickel silicates. *See* Nickel ores
Nickel silver (Copper-nickel-zinc alloys). *See also* Pai-thung
  coinage. *See* Coinage
  commercial development in Europe and Great Britain 14, 44-6, 47, 48, 50, 69, 70-1, 96, 134, 165, 193, 273-4
  compositions, typical 43, 45, 48, 71
  fabrication of 46, 48
  for cutlery and tableware (including E.P.N.S.) 45, 48-9, 105
  in architecture 193, 227
  in springs, telecommunications equipment and zip fasteners 193
  properties 42, 44, 45, 46, 209
  trade names of 113, 272, 274 (consolidated list)

  treatise on (von Engeström) 43, 271
  uses, miscellaneous 44-6, 48-9, 105, 113, 193, 227
Nickel speiss (pottery nickel) 70; *see also* 73
Nickel sulphate and nickel-ammonium sulphate
  in plating solutions, *see* Electrodeposition
  production at Clydach refinery 137
Nickel sulphide, formed in 'tops-and-bottoms' process
  See 'Tops-and-bottoms' process, *also* 80, 187
Nickelton (Banco) 146
Ni-Hard abrasion-resisting cast iron 171, 294
Nimocast alloys 245, 246, 313
Nimonic alloys (Nos. 75, 80, 80A, 90, 100, 105, 115) 239, 246, 312-13
NININGER, H. H. 263
Niobium (columbium) 244
Ni-Resist non-magnetic cast irons 171, 294
Nitre cake (in 'tops-and-bottoms' process) 79
Nivala, nickel deposit at 213
Norilsk, nickel deposits at 222
North American Aviation, Rocketdyne Division 251, 252, 253, 254, 255
North American Lead Company 141, 291
North Carolina, nickel deposits in 122
North Star Mine 142
Norway
  coinage 208
  nickel ore deposits in 52-4
  nickel production 54, 67, 90, 141, 142, 149, 156, 181, 221, 280, 299

Index

Norway (ctd.)
  See also Kristiansand Nickel Refinery, Falconbridge Nickel Mines, *and* Kristiansand Nikkelraffineringsverk Aktieselskap
  supply of nickel to Allies and to Germany in World War II 150
Nouméa. *See* New Caledonia
Nuclear power plant, nickel in 229
Numa Pompilius, iron shield of 16

Octahedrites (metabolites) 18-20
Oelsner, O. 269
Ohain, P. von 241
Oil industry, nickel-alloy steels for 172, 227
'Old Nick' 24, 266-7
Olds, R. E. 102, 103
Oman, nickel ores of 7
Ontario. *Included under* Canada
Ontario Refining Company 296
Open-cast mining 72
Open-hearth process, invention and use of 96, 98
Open-pit mining 211-12, 219
Oppau plant of I.G. Farbenindustrie A.G. 188
Oregon, nickel ores in 122
Orel 130
Orford, naming of 62
Orford Copper Company
  Bayonne plant 77, 78, 121, 141, 146
  becomes part of International Nickel Co. 126
  incorporation of 65, 275
  Monell's report on 128
  Orford mine 63
  research laboratory built 136
  Stanley, R. C. at 135, 139, 167
  Thomson, J. L., superintendent at 79
  'tops-and-bottoms' process, development and use 79-80, 81, 82, 121, 154, 155, 183, 187 (replaced) 218
  treatment of matte from Canadian Copper Co. 77, 78, 121
  Wadhams, A. J., association with 168
Orford Copper and Sulphur Company 275, 276
Orford Nickel and Copper Company 63, 275
Orford process. *See* 'Tops-and-bottoms' process
Otto, N. A. 102
Oxidation-resistant materials 119, 171, 175, 239
Oxide ores. *See* Nickel ores

Pai-thung and variant romanised forms 13-14, 42, 45, 46, 60, 69, 271-2
  see also White copper
Pakistan, coinage 208
Pamir, meteoritic iron 16
Paneth, F. A. 16, 263
Pantaleon 9-12, 261-2
Paraguay, coinage 208
Parkes, A. 117
Parkes, O. 292
Pauly, H. 261
Peary, R. E. 17
Peek, R. L. 296
Pellet nickel 88, 133, 142, 187
Pên Tshao Kang Mu 14
Pennsylvania Railroad Station, Monel roof 137
Percy, J. 117, 287
Peridotite 2
Periodic Table *facing* 302
Perrin, R., process for treating lateritic ores 217
Pertile Cesare e C. 112
Peru, coinage 208
Petrochemical industry, nickel in 227

Index

Petrovsk mine, oxide nickel ores   54
Petsamo nickel deposit   189-91, 210, 213, 222, 299
Pfanhauser, W.   112
PFEIL, L. B.   301
Pharmacopoeia, Great (of China)   14
Phi-shih, meaning of   14
Philippines, coinage   208
PHILLIPS, W. M.   284
Phipps, H.   281
Phipson, Mr.   46
Phlogiston theory   33, 36, 38
PILLING, N. B.   300
Pistons, of light alloys containing nickel   232
Planets, association of metals with   4
Plankton   259-60
Plating. *See* Electrodeposition, *also* Coating and Cladding
Platinoid   274
Platinum metals
  in Canadian nickel ores   137, 150
  in South African ores   179, 180, 295
  supplied to the Allies in World War II   214
Pliny reports meteoric fall   15
Pointe Chaleix (Nouméa)   58
Poland, coinage   203, 204
Polaris missile   250
Poole, M.   94
Pope's Island metal   274
Porsche, F.   103
Port Colborne. *See* International Nickel Company
Portugal, coinage   208, 209
Potosi silver   274
Pottery and glass, colouring of   23
Pottery nickel   70
Powder metallurgy for production of coins   209
Powder nickel   134, 188, 209, 217, 297
Power plant. *See* individual types, e.g. Electricity generators; Nuclear power plant
Prata teutonica   274

Pratt and Witney aero engines   233, 247
Precious metals in nickel ores   137, 150, 179-80, 214, 295
Precipitation-hardening. *See* Age-hardening, *also* 258
Press-forging of high-temperature alloys   247
Pressure-leaching, Forward extraction process   217
Pressure vessels, maraging steels for   227
Prices
  of nickel   48, 308-9
  of nickel silver   45
Priestley, Joseph   38
PRIOR, G. T.   264
Prospecting, aerial geophysical and other methods   141, 181, 222-3, 295, 299
PROUST, J. L.   40, 271
Punjab, meteorite in   16
Pyrenees, nickel deposits in   52

Quebec Bridge   163
Queen Elizabeth   193-4
Queen Mary   193-4
Queen's metal   274
Quincke, F., associated with L. Mond   85

Radio Equipment   229
RANDALL, W. F.   293
Ranger, H.   65
Rateau invents supercharger   234
Reaction Motors. *See* Thiokol Chemical Corporation
Reamer, bronze   6
Reciprocating and rotating power units (schematic diagrams)   242
'Redstone' missile   251
Refining. *See* Extraction and Refining
René 41 alloy   256, 313
Revdin mine   54
Rex 78 alloy   238, 311

Index

Richardson, nickel-iron alloys made by 117
Richelsdorf, nickeliferous ores at 50
RICHTER, J. B. 40, 41, 271
RICKARD, T. A. 263
Riddle deposit; ferro-nickel production 218, 299
RILEY, J. 98, 282
Riley, J., properties of nickel steels 98, 282-3
Ringerike mines 52, 53
Rio Tinto Copper Company 63
Ritchie, S. J. 65
Rive, Professor de la (Faraday correspondence) 93
Roasting practice at Orford Copper Company 77
Roberts, S. 104
ROBERTS-AUSTEN, W. C. 87, 275, 278, 280
Roberts-Austen, W. C. 281
Rockets. *See* Aircraft and Aero Engines, including Rockets
Rocketdyne. *See* North American Aviation, Rocketdyne Division
Rolls, nickel cast iron for 171
Rolling
  of nickel, for coinage 200
  of nickel silver 46
Rolls-Royce
  'Blue Streak' rocket engine 252
  'Conway' aero-engine (schematic drawing) 243, *facing* 247, 247
  'Derwent' aero engine 239
  'Merlin' aero engine 233
  R.R. alloys 232
  'Welland' aero engine 239
Rome, meteoric fall near 15
Rondelles *facing* 75, 132, 134, 148, 222, 292
Roos, P. F. VAN 115, 287
Rose, Sir Thomas Kirke 199
Roseleur, A. 108
ROSENHAIN, W. 300
Ross, Sir John 17

Rotating and reciprocating power units (schematic diagrams) 242
Rotor shafts 227
Rouquayrol, Directeur, Mines de Decazeville 57
Rovaniemi 189, 190
Rover Co., W. and B. turbo-jet 239
ROXBEE COX, H. 300
ROYAL COMMISSION ON MINERAL RESOURCES OF ONTARIO (1890) 276
ROYAL ONTARIO NICKEL COMMISSION 278, 290, 291, 296
Royal Ontario Nickel Commission on resources of Ontario and refining facilities 145-6, 291
R.R. alloys 232
Ruda, nickel deposit at 52
RUDELOFF, M. 117, 289
Ruder, W. E. 194
Rumania, coinage 202, 208
Ruolz alloy 274
RUOLZ-MONTCHAL, H. C. de 107, 285
Russia. *See also* U.S.S.R.
  armoured vessels at battle of Tsushima 130, 290
  armour plate trials 102
  coinage 116
  nickel industry of 222
  nickel ore deposits 54, 222
Rustenburg, nickel in platiniferous ores at 179, 180, 295

S-590 alloy 311
S-816 alloy 246, 314
Safflor 278
Sagmyra nickel works 52
St. Anne's Church, Annaberg *Frontispiece*, 23, 315
St. Chamond steelworks 100
St. Dunstan 266-7
Ste. Marie aux Mines, nickeliferous ores at 52
Sal enixum ('Sally Nixon') 79, 279

343

Index

Salter, A. P. 62, 64
Salvador, coinage 209
Santa Catharina meteorite 20
'Saturn' rocket 252
Saxony, Blaufarbenwerke and other pigment producers 153, 278
  See also Germany
Scheerer 52
SCHEFFER, H. T. 270
Scheffer, H. T. 37
Schellhas, W. 269
SCHLAIFER, R. 301
Schneeberg
  Agricola lived there 23-4
  Bergamt, archives in 24-7, 268
  Blaufarbenwerke and other pigment producers 69, 153, 278
  mining of cobalt in 270
  mining of nickel in 50, 69
  mining of silver in 23, 50
Schneider, J. 97, 98, 281
Schneider Trophy contests 233
Schwab, C. M. 126, 281
SCHWITTER, C. M. 261, 262
Scientific and technical progress (1751-1851) 35
SCOTT, H. 300
Sea water, nickel in 2, 259, 261
Selden, G. B. 102
Semi-argent 274
Semi-fabricated products in nickel and nickel alloys
  Globe Works 175
  Hereford 301
  Huntingdon 174, 294
  Schwerte 114
Septèmes, 58
Sherritt Gordon Mines, process and products 217, 218, 299
Shih-Chen, Li 14
Shingles, of space capsules 256
SHIPEK, C. J. 260
Ships, steel 97-102
SHORE, J. 107, 285
Shortt, H. de S., coins from 11

Shot nickel 133, 134
Siam, coinage 202
Siberia, Tunguska River meteorite 20
Siderites 18
Siderolites 19
Siemens Brothers invent open-hearth process 96
Silesia, nickeliferous ores in 50
Silicate rocks and ores. *See* Nickel ores
Silver bronze 281
Silver deposits
  in Canada 62
  in France, 50, 52
  in Germany 23, 24, 28, 50
Silver Islet mine 62
Silver close-plating process 104
Silverine 274
Silverite 274
Slattberg, nickeliferous deposit at 52
SM 200 alloy 246, 313
Smalt 24, 70, 278
Smelters and smelting practice 52, 53, 58, 59, 63, 74, 76, 124, 130, 141, 158, 179
Smith, H. W. 94
Société Anonyme de Commentry Fourchambault et Decazeville 118, 164, 235, 293, 300
Société Anonyme d'Exploitation des Mines de Nickel 74
Société Anonyme Le Nickel (système Garnier)
  association with Steel Manufacturers' Nickel Syndicate Ltd. 131
  M. Carrier, President of 178
  early mining in New Caledonia 74
  ferro-nickel ('fonte') production 74, 130, 178, 221
  finances of 161
  formation of 58

Index

Société Anonyme Le Nickel (ctd.)
  Le Havre refinery 75, 144, 149, 156, 210, 213
  merger, with Calédonia, into Calédonickel 179
  nickel production 74, 156, 222
  post-World War I position 161
  recent improvements in plant 221-3
  smelters at Nouméa and at Thio 59, 74, 130, 179
  World Wars I and II, effects of 144, 148-9, 161, 210, 213
  Yaté hydroelectric plant 178
Société d'Electro-Chimie, d'Electro-Métallurgie et des Aciéries Electriques d'Ugine 217
Société des Etudes Coloniales et Maritimes 57
Société Hauts-Fourneaux de Nouméa 131
Société Le Chrome 178
Société Le Ferro-Nickel 58, 117
Société Métallurgique d'Imphy 293
Société Minière Calédonienne 295
Société pour la Fonderie de Nickel et Métaux Blancs 58
Société pour le Traitement de Minérais de Nickel, Cobalt, Cuivre et Autres (système Jules Garnier) 57-9
Sodium sulphate. *See* 'Tops-and-bottoms' process
Sons of Vulcan 16
Sorby, H. C. 281
Sound, speed of 258, 299
Space capsules, speeds attained in 258
Space travel, nickel as an aid to 249-58
Sparking plugs, alloys for 170
Special Metals, producer of Udimet 700 alloy 245; of alloy SM 200 313
Specific impulse, definition 251
Spectrographic analysis 3, 5, 260

Speculum metal 13
Speed, progress in 257-8
  records, 1906-1939, 1945 to date *facing* 256, 258
Speiss. *See* Nickel speiss, *and* Pottery nickel
Spencer, L. J. 20
Sperrylite 295
'Spirit of St. Louis' aircraft 233
'Spitfire' aeroplane 233
Spoon metal 274
Spoons. *See* Tableware
Springs, of nickel alloys 118-19, 164, 193, 289
SPROULE, K. 299
Spurs, of nickel silver 45
Stainless steel. *See* Nickel-chromium and chromium high-alloy steels
Standard Oil Company 63
STANLEY, R. C. 291
Stanley, R. C.
  biographical note and character 128, 141, 167
  Chairman, International Nickel Co. 167
  portrait 166
  work on Orford process 135
Stars, nickel in 3-5
Stayblade steel 238
Staybrite FDP 311
Steam plant, nickel alloys in 193, 227
Steel. *See also* various alloy steels referred to immediately below
  armour plate 97-102
  for ships 97
  early development of the industry 95 ff., 281
  Nickel steel
    See also other nickel-containing steels, below
    aircraft components of 162, 173, 231, 232

345

Index

Steel (ctd.)
    armour plate 98, 99-102, 281
    boiler plate and frames in locomotives 172
    bridges 162, 163, 292
    competitive alloy elements 172
    crankshafts 231
    Faraday's experiments 93
    Harveyising of 99-100
    heat treatment of 98, 172, 282-3
    in constructional and structural engineering 162, 172
    in oil-well equipment 172, 227
    low-temperature applications 227
    maraging steels 227, 299
    Mond Nickel Co. research on constitution and properties 170, 294
    pressure vessels of 227
    properties 98-9, 170, 172, 173, 192, 227, 281-3, 294
    Riley's experiments 98-9, 282, 283
    U.S. Navy armour-plate trials, Annapolis 99, 101
Nickel-chromium low-alloy steels
    aircraft components 173, 232
    armour and ordnance 100, 130, 290
    crankshafts and gears 232
    for highly stressed parts 162, 173, 192, 232
    low-temperature applications 173
    properties and constitution of 170, 172, 192, 294
Nickel-chromium and chromium (stainless) high-alloy steels
    current uses 225, 229
    in aircraft and aero engines 233-4, 238, 241, 246, 252, 256, 310-11
    in architecture 225, 227, 228
    early development of 162-3, 164, 173, 192, 292-3
    in chemical plant 164
    in nuclear power plant 229
    valves of aero engines 233-4
Nickel-copper steels
    corrosion-resistance, and toughness at low temperatures 173
Steel Manufacturers' Nickel Syndicate 131
Stephenson's Rocket engine 35
Sterlin 274
Sterline 274
Stobie mine 65. *See also* International Nickel Company, Frood-Stobie pit
Stobie, J. 65
Stockpiling of nickel 216
STONE, G. C. 264
Storage batteries. *See* Batteries
STRAUSS, B. 163, 293
Stuffing-box alloy 274
Sub-zero temperatures. *See* Low-temperature applications
Sudbury. *Included under* Canada
Suhl white copper 274
Sulphide ores. *See* Nickel ores
Sun
    constituents of 260
    nickel in 5, 261
Superchargers for aero engines 234, 235, 240, 254
Sweden, nickel-ore deposits 30, 31, 39, 52-3
    production of nickel 67, 90, 280
Swedish nickel 274
Swiss Telephone Company 112
Switzerland
    coinage 113, 198, 201, 203, 205
    plating development in 112
Swords 7, 9, 16, 94, 263, 264
Symbols and devices for metals 4, 37, 39
Syria, bronze reamer from 6

Tableware 45, 46, 48-9, 105, 108, 112, 115, 163

Index

Taenite 266
TARN, W. W. 262
Technical information services 194-5, 214,
Telecommunications engineering 35, 164, 165, 193, 229
Television tubes, nickel in 229
'Telstar' communications satellite 229
Temperature capability. *See* Aircraft and Aero Engines
Tennant, C., Sons and Company 63, 77, 98
Texas, meteoric falls in 21
Textile machinery 225
Thang dynasty, old history of 13
THÉNARD, L. J. 40, 271
Thermal thicket problem 254, 256
Thermionic valves, nickel for 165, 229
Thermocouples, nickel alloys for 120
Thien Kung Khai Wu 14
Thio (New Caledonia) 59, 130, 179
Thiokol Chemical Corporation, Reaction Motors Division 256
Thomas, S. 96
THOMASON, E. 44, 272
THOMPSON, J. F. 275, 279, 296
Thompson, J. F. *Foreword* vii, 290
  association with R. C. Stanley 168
  Chairman of International Nickel 275
  directs research laboratory at Orford Works 136
Thompson mine, Manitoba 223
THOMPSON, R. M. 279, 289
Thompson, R. M.
  association with N. V. Hybinette 138
  biographical note on 62-3, 275, 290
  Chairman of International Nickel Co. 271

extraction of sulphur from copper ores 63
incorporation of International Nickel Co. 126
nickel-containing matte treated for U.S. Navy 78
Orford Copper Co. 66, 275
'tops-and-bottoms' process, statement on 79, 81
THOMPSON, T. G. 2, 259
THOMSON, J. L. 80, 279
Thor missile 252
Thornton, J. 110
Thrust chambers of rockets 251, 252, 256
Thurber, P. 117
Thyssen Haus, use of stainless steel 228
Timken 16-25-6 alloy 241, 311
Tinidur 241, 311
Titanium, as hardener in nickel and iron alloys 169-70, 174, 235, 238, 239, 241, 244
'Titan' missile 252
Topping, F. and S. R. 46
'Tops-and-bottoms' process 79-80 (discovery), 81, 82, 121, 154, 155 183, 186-7, 218 (replaced by controlled (slow)cooling process)
Toucas metal 274
Tracy, B. F. 99
Transvaal, bronzes of 9
Trinity College, Cambridge 286
Troilite 19
Tsushima, battle of 130
TUCEK, K. 263
Tuc tur 274
Tungsten brass 274
Tunguska River meteorite 20
Turbines
  gas. *See* Aircraft and Aero Engines
  steam. *See* Steam plant
'Turbofan' aero engines 247-8
Turkey, coinage 201, 203, 205, 207

Index

Udimet No. 500 and No. 700 alloys 245, 246, 313
ULKE, T. 279
Undercut-and-fill mining 220
United Kingdom coinage 207-9
United Nickel Company 109
United States
  builds Nicaro plant 216
  Bureau of Mines Surveys 222, 280
  coinage 113, 197, 198, 206
  Government Committee on jet propulsion 240
  nickel-ore deposits in 59-60, 122, 218-19, 299
  nickel production by 67, 75-6, 90, 218
  stockpiling of metals by 216
United States National Archives 101
United States National Bureau of Standards
  Circular on nickel and nickel alloys 169, 293, 304-7
  Merica's work at 231
United States Navy, armour-plate trials 99-102
United States Nickel Company
  formation 134
  output (1914, 1918) 156
  owned by Calédonia 179
  refinery at New Brunswick 147, 156
Universal Cyclops Company 234
Ur
  bronze articles from 6, 7
  dagger of meteoritic iron from 15, 263
U.S.S.R. *See also* Russia
  nickel ores in 54, 222
  nickel production capacity 67, 222
  working of Petsamo mines by 222

V-2 rocket missile 251
V 2A steel 163

Valve materials for aero engines 164, 233, 234
VANICK, J. S. 294
Vatican State, coinage 202, 203, 204
VEAL, C. B. 300
VEDENSKY, D. N. 299
Ventures Ltd. 296
Venus de Milo, statuette in nickel-iron alloy 117
Vereinigte Deutsche Nickelwerke 287
Verein zur Beförderung des Gewerbefleisses 45
Vertical-take-off aircraft 249
Vespucci, A. 17
VICAT, M. 300
Vickers, E. 281
Victor metal 274
Victoria mine 65, 122, 124, 141, 142
Vienna Museum 16
VINOGRADOV, A. G. 265
Virginia silver 274
Vivian, H. H., and Co. 52, 66, 77, 89, 122
Volatilisers (Mond carbonyl process) 142
Volta, A. 35, 284

17 W alloy 246
Wadhams, A. J. 168
Wages of miners in New Caledonia 278
WAGNER, P. A. 295
Wallace mine 60
Wallace, R. 48
WALLERIUS, J. G. 29, 269
WALTENBERG, R. G. 300
War, effect on nickel industry
  World War I 144-54, 157
  World War II 210-14
  War in Korea 202, 214-16
Warrior 96
Warships scrapped or cancelled under disarmament treaties 161-2, 292

Index

Wash-basins of nickel silver 44-5
Washington Disarmament Treaty 161
'Wasp' aero engine 233
Waspaloy 246, 313
Watches, nickel-iron alloys in
Water meters, nickel in 165
WATSON, R. 272
Weathering of rocks; ore formation 276-7
Webb and Barker 48
Weiss Kupfer 274
'Welland' aero engine 239
Werner collection of minerals 274
Werra, nickel ores at 50
Wessels silver 274
West Indies, coinage 201
Westinghouse aero engines 240
Weston, E. 109-10, 285
WHARTON, J. 116, 121, 279, 285, 287, 288, 289
Wharton, J.
  association with T. Fleitmann 114
  association with A. J. Wadhams 77
  Camden plant 75-8, 121, 127, 128
  malleablises nickel 116, 287-8
  memorandum on cupro-nickel coinage 116, 285
  pure nickel products made by 75, 116
WHEELER-BENNETT, J. W. 298
Whewell, W., assists Faraday on terminology of electrolysis 284-5, 286
'Whirlwind' aero engine 233
White Argentan 274
White copper 12-14, 42, 44, 45, 274
  See also Pai-thung
White metal 274
White S. S., Dental Company 129, 167
White solder 274
WHITTLE, F. 300

Whittle gas turbine. *See* Aircraft and Aero Engines
Whitworth and Company 97
Whitworth, J. 281
WI-52 alloy 314
WICKENDEN, T. H. 294
Widmanstätten figures in meteorites 265-6
WIGGIN, H. A. 281
Wiggin, H. A.
  assistant to C. Askin 47
  formation of Henry Wiggin and Co. 48
  partnership with Evans 48
  portrait 176
  source of Askin biography 272
Wiggin, Henry, and Company
  (formerly Evans and Askin)
  association of L. Mond with 87
  centenary of 295
  cupro-nickel coin blanks produced for Germany 114
  formation of 48
  Hereford plant 301
  subsidiary of Mond Nickel Co. 175, 295
  Nimonic alloys produced by 239
  products of 175
  Smethwick works 279
  Wiggin Street, Birmingham plant 175
Wiggin, Sir Henry; portrait 176
WILM, A. 300
Wilm, A., discovers age-hardening phenomenon 231, 300
Winkler, K. A. 70
Wiping (coating) process 104
Wolfram brass 274
Wollaston, W. H. 284
WOODBURY, D. O. 285
Worthington deposit 65, 142
WOTHERSPOON, W. L. 294
Wright engines ('Cyclone' and 'Whirlwind') 233
Wright, Orville and Wilbur 230-1

Index

Wu, meaning of 13
WÜNSCH, H. 292
Wyandotte (Mich.), nickeliferous ores at 62
X-1 and X-2 research aircraft 254, 257
X-15 research aircraft 249, 254, 255, 256, 257
X-40 alloy 314
X-ray fluorescence analysis 11, 12, 262

'Y' alloy 232, 300
'Yankee 19A' gas turbine 240

Yaté, hydroelectric plant 178
Ying-Hsing Sung 14
Yunnan, Province of 14

Zaffer (Zaffre) pigment 70, 278
Zanzibar, coins struck for 201
Zeppelin airship 231
ZIMMER, G. F. 263
ZIMMERMANN, C. F. 270
Zinc oxide 14
Zip fasteners 193
Zodiacal signs for metals 4
Zolliker, J. 112

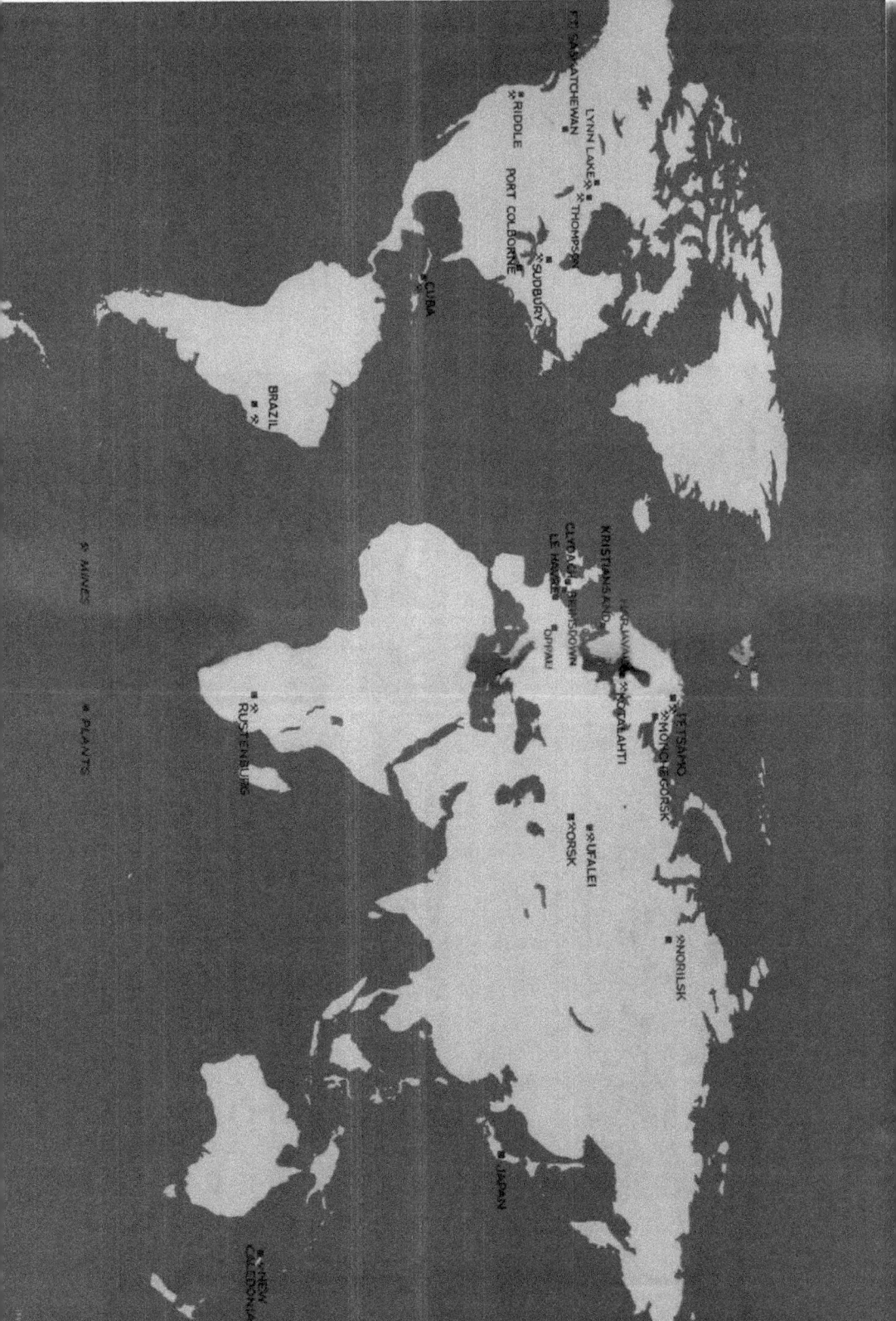

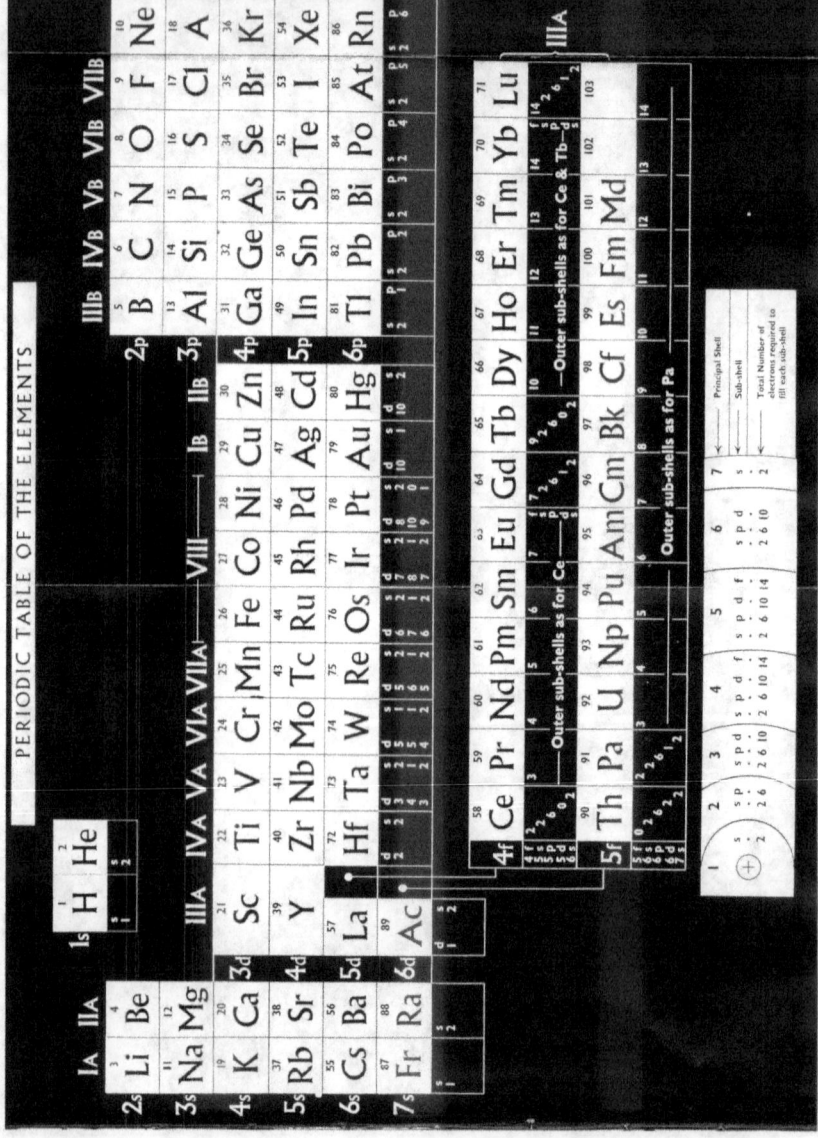

Notes on Atomic Structure

1. The atomic number indicates the number of protons in the nucleus of an atom. In the neutral atom these protons are electrically balanced by an equal number of electrons outside the nucleus. Only neutral atoms are considered in the Periodic Classification.

2. Electrons travel far from the nucleus but if those regions where they spend most of their time are considered, a well-defined pattern of layers or 'Principal Shells' appears. Each shell is known by a Principal Quantum Number, 1, 2, 3 . . . 7 or sometimes by the letters K, L, M . . . etc.

3. In each shell the electrons move around the nucleus in complicated, three-dimensional patterns called Orbitals. The laws of Quantum Mechanics permit only certain types of orbital. An electron following one of these paths possesses an amount of energy (Energy Level) characteristic of that orbital.

4. Four types of orbital are encountered; they are identified by the letters s p d and f. s is the simplest whilst p, d and f are progressively more complex.

5. The number of orbitals per shell increases with shell number. (See the lower diagram overleaf.) The first contains only an s orbital, the second an s and three p's, the third adds five d orbitals and the fourth seven f's. These groups of like orbitals in any Principal Shell are called s p d or f sub-shells.

6. Each sub-shell, depending on its principal quantum number and type, has a characteristic energy the order of which is generally proportional to the distance of the sub-shell from the nucleus.

7. Each orbital accepts either one or two electrons and the maximum number of electrons per sub-shell is shown on the diagram.

8. Electrons take positions in orbitals where the energy level is lowest. Up to element 18 (Argon) sub-shells and shells are built in an orderly pattern of maximum capacity. But in the next group the order changes because it happens that the energy level of the 4 s state is a little lower than that of the 3 d state.

9. The first transition series begins with Scandium (element 21) where the energy levels of the 4 s and 3 d orbitals are so nearly equal that there is a tendency for electrons to move from one orbital to another, causing variable valency. The same happens in the fifth period with 5 s and 4 d orbitals and in the sixth period with the 6 s and 5 d orbitals.

10. In the Lanthanide and Actinide series of elements, the 4 f and 5 f orbitals are occupied only after the s p d and s orbitals outside them have filled or begun to fill. The effect upon the chemistry of the elements is very small because the f orbitals are deep in the core of the atom. For this reason there is little difference between one element and its immediate neighbours.

11. In any element, the so called Valency Electrons are those moving in orbitals of the highest energy levels. In this Wall Chart of the Periodic Classification, the number and position of the valency electrons is indicated in the boxes underneath the various columns e.g. Rhodium—element 45—has nine valency electrons; 8 in the 4 d sub-shell and 1 in the 5 s.

The particular sub-shell being filled with electrons is shown by the figures 4 s, 3 d, 4 p etc. in front of the rows of elements e.g. the 3 d in front of elements 21—30.

For Product Safety Concerns and Information please contact our EU
representative GPSR@taylorandfrancis.com
Taylor & Francis Verlag GmbH, Kaufingerstraße 24, 80331 München, Germany

www.ingramcontent.com/pod-product-compliance
Lightning Source LLC
Chambersburg PA
CBHW071144300426
44113CB00009B/1083